LAKE FISHING
WITH A FLY

By Ron Cordes
and
Randall Kaufmann

Foreword by Gary LaFontaine

Illustrations by Mike Stidham

Frank Amato Publications

Box 82112, Portland, Oregon 97282

Dedication

To my brother Lance, who unselfishly attended to all the chores of our business during the countless times I was away with camera, pen and fly rod.

Randall Kaufmann

To Hal Janssen, Percy Banks, Jay Rowland, Gordon Sherman, and those other profound anglers whose friendships have made fly fishing more rewarding than the big ones that didn't get away.

Ron Cordes

Acknowledgements

Special thanks go to my wonderful mother, Oda Moore, for all the wisdom and understanding over the years and who always seems to encourage me at just the right time. Thanks to Joyce Findley, publication manager of *Fly Fishing* magazine, for giving me the "final push" and for typing the final manuscript. Thanks to all the friends, too numerous to mention, who read and reread the rough drafts, offering valuable help, encouragement and advice. Thanks also to the many enthusiastic fly fishing school visitors whose endless questions about lake fishing helped me put this manuscript into its proper perspective. And as always, thanks to my stepfather, Jack Moore, for introducing me to the intricate fascinations and magical beauty of lake fishing.

Randall Kaufmann

I would like to extend my thanks to those individuals who encouraged and in some cases contributed in different ways to this book: John Goddard, Jay Rowland, Harley Reno, Charles Brooks, and Gary LaFontaine, who reviewed the manuscript and made valuable suggestions, Frank Mikesh, whose love of angling literature yielded fascinating quotations, Matt Koller — a young angler of great promise who broke in his father's home computer in the preparation of the index, and those persons too numerous to mention individually who knew of our project and nurtured it along with us.

Ron Cordes

Contents

About the Authors

Randall Kaufmann developed an early addiction to remote alpine trout waters of the West. This addiction continues today and has led him to several hundred pristine waters where new ideas and techniques are constantly being refined. He has published articles in outdoor magazines and is the author of *The American Nymph Fly Tying Manual*. He is widely recognized for his versatile fly tying skills and diverse fly fishing experience. In conjunction with Kaufmann's Fly Fishing Expeditions, Inc., Randall leads exotic adventures to remote corners of the fishing world and has fished such fabled meccas as Chile, Argentina, Mexico, Costa Rica, Canada, Alaska, Iceland, Australia, Tasmania and New Zealand. Closer to home in Oregon, Randall conducts three day fishing schools which he likes to describe as "an intensive, yet easy going, on-the-water crash course in fly fishing." Randall is co-owner of Kaufmann's Streamborn, a mail order fly fishing supply house with retail outlets in Bellevue, Washington and Tigard, Oregon. The Kaufmann catalog is free for the asking. Randall can be reached at P.O. Box 23032, Portland, Oregon 97223 (503-639-6400).

The angling adventures of Ron Cordes have taken him to the wilds of Alaska and Africa, to the jungles of Nepal, to Lapland in the far northern hemisphere, and to the rain forests of New Zealand in the southern hemisphere. He has a Ph.D in chemical engineering and a J.D. in law, both from the University of California at Berkeley. He has worked in research and development for Exxon as a scientific advisor to the government of Iran's Department of Environmental Conservation, and most recently as an attorney for the high technology firm of EG&G Idaho, Inc.

Ron now resides outside of Idaho Falls in southeast Idaho where his home looks out over a small lake where the lake studies continue.

About the Illustrator

Angler/artist Mike Stidham is uniquely qualified to portray in watercolors and etchings the art of the angler. His years spent as a guide in the Yellowstone country have given him a sound understanding of the subject he most enjoys to render: the world of trout and fly fishing. In 1978, with a growing demand for his paintings, Mike began a full time art career. Since then his work has appeared on the covers of *Outdoor Life* and in publications such as *Fly Fisherman* and *Trout*. His pen and ink illustrations appear in *The Western Fly Tying Manual*, Volume 2, by Jack Dennis. Mike's watercolors have been juried into numerous exhibitions and in 1984 his painting, "Springcreek Rainbows" was awarded "Best of Show/Fishing" at the Ducks Unlimited National Wildlife Art Show in Kansas City. A member of Trout Unlimited, The Federation of Fly Fishers, and Ducks Unlimited, Mike is a frequent contributor to these fine organizations with his work commanding strong prices at fund raising events.

Foreword

Ponds and lakes are frequently called "stillwater fisheries." There's nothing wrong with the name. It's a good way to distinguish them from "running-water fisheries." But every careful writer on the subject quickly points out that there's nothing still about ponds and lakes. A basin of water, large or small, has a fascinating array of currents, moving from side to side and top to bottom, that orient both fish and forage as completely as the flow of a stream.

And that's the game for the dedicated lake angler — understanding the internal intricacies of his favorite haunts. It has to be that way. Who would enjoy flogging a faceless and formless puddle? That would be nothing but casting exercise. Fly fishing is a thinking game, and for us the key to enjoying lake fishing is an appreciation for the rules imposed by the environment.

Fly fishermen as a group vary greatly in their attitudes towards lakes. A small number, which seems to be steadily decreasing, don't like stillwater fishing and rarely do it. There are reasons they feel this way; some are so overwhelmed by the difficulty of finding trout or fooling trout in lakes that they refuse to even try it. The majority of fly fishermen fall into a middle category — their first love is stream fishing, but they also enjoy lake fishing. Given a free choice of opportunities, they might decide to fish a lake once or twice out of every ten trips. For them lakes provide a change; it is still fly fishing but different, so like a freshwater devotee who occasionally visits saltwater, they do it because it's there.

A final group, not as rare as one might think, prefers lake fishing over stream fishing. They become so expert at reading the water and mimicking the food that they consistently fool trout in stillwaters. For them, familiarity breeds not contempt but intimacy.

One of my fly fishing surveys focused on attitudes towards lake fishing:

Dislike lake fishing — rarely do it:	18%
Primarily a stream fisherman, but enjoy lake fishing — do it 10% to 40% of the time:	63%
Concentrate on lake fishing — do it more than 50% of the time:	19%

This new book, *Lake Fishing With a Fly* by Randall Kaufmann and Ron Cordes, serves all three groups admirably. In that respect, it is a rarity among angling works. How many books can appeal to beginner, intermediate and advanced fly fishermen? It makes lakes less intimidating for novices and more interesting for experts. It does this by explaining how the lake environment controls trout.

Lake Fishing is the most coherent and comprehensive book ever written in this country about lake fishing. But there is a bonus — what makes it such fascinating reading is some of the finest science writing ever done in our field. The authors took the great body of technical literature on the biology and limnology of lakes and molded it lovingly into a fly fishing blueprint. All of the suggested methods and fly patterns flow naturally and easily from this lattice of information.

Here is an example of a gem:

> "In August, predation on shiners (was) greatest on hot days when the lake was calm and exceptionally clear. During this time the sun's reflection off the silvery scales of shiners was clearly visible at 25 feet and perhaps even further. Visibility seemed to be a strong reason for such predation."

How much does this tell us about using shiner imitations? It's so easy to apply such information to our fishing. It tells us for one thing that reflective flies, with a lot of mylar or tinsel, should work best in clear water on calm, bright days.

Five years ago, when I read a rough, typewritten draft of this work, sections like this impressed me so much that I recommended the book without hesitation in *Caddisflies*. It was listed there under the title, *The Art and Science of Lake Fishing with a Fly*, the working name at that time — of course, such a pre-publication endorsement represented a lot of faith. But the fine marriage of fly fishing and scientific information had such an impact on me — and ultimately even on the final form of *Caddisflies* — that I felt as if I owed the authors all possible support.

Now in the finished book Ron Cordes and Randall Kaufmann fulfill that promise. They combine not only their talents but also their strengths. Every word shines with the years of actual lake fishing experience; every fact rings with the years of solid biological research. *Lake Fishing With a Fly* is an angling text that will quickly become the standard work on stillwaters.

Gary LaFontaine

Introduction

The late summer sun had long since erased its warming rays from the surrounding Cascade volcanic summits. A lighter sky to the west faded to blue, purple and finally to black in the east, signaling that the onset of the most productive fishing time for big, wary trout was upon us. We slowly eased ourselves between floating weedbeds, carefully stalking an oversize rainbow which was repeatedly feeding in the shallows along the fringe of the ghostly aquatic forest. By now darkness had nearly engulfed us, and nighttime began to play its shadowy tunes. Crickets, frogs, the whistle of late flying ducks, a shattered twig in the forest and the penetrating call of an osprey all vied for our attention. The scents of the watery twilight, first cool, then warm, entranced us, but this deep, tasteful drink of the hypnotic air was rudely interrupted as a huge rainbow suddenly struck our leech pattern and exploded head high not more than 15 feet away! Its awesome impact splashed water droplets in our wide-eyed faces. But in that same motion this somewhat perplexed and bewildered rainbow began its return to its normal daytime refuge of drowned lodgepole pine, complete with all the expected underwater entanglements.

Our terminal tackle was finely tuned and steady pressure turned the big trout short of its underwater refuge. Panic slowly overtook its calm composure, and a series of surface lunges and half jumps revealed a deep-bodied rainbow the size of which is all too often reserved for steelhead. As the fish came close we could see the barbless leech tucked securely into the corner of its jaw. The rainbow was eased in quickly, revived and carefully released to thrill others who would come after us and, hopefully, to spawn another generation of that same hearty stock.

This incredible fish was not the result of "blind luck." There were no "series of accidents" which led to its capture, but rather a series of steps based upon highly calculated research expected to pay high dividends. We had spent the previous day-and-a-half chatting with other anglers and

Lakes are generous with big fish, like this gorgeous rainbow which Randall Kaufmann gently eased onto soft shoreline weeds for a quick photo prior to release. R.K.

Golden trout this size are a possible reward for adventerous alpine anglers who travel western mountain trails. R.K.

carefully studying the lake. We became familiar with both its physical characteristics and its currently available food sources. Such information told us where, when and how such big rainbows would be feeding.

Our tackle was carefully prepared and the fly was selected for its realistic, lifelike portrayal of the specific food source we knew would be sought. We were at our fishing station long before any fish began feeding and it was not until we located a consistent feeder that we began our stalk. We were careful not to announce our coming and once in position our cast was accurate and flawless. The fly landed without commotion a few seconds ahead of where the fish was calculated to resume its feeding. The take was not merely hoped for, but expected, and when the tiny surface disturbance signaled a tightening of the fly line we knew the deception was complete. The six-pound rainbow was a bit heavier than expected, more handsome than most fish and certainly the thrill of a lifetime for any angler.

This was fly fishing at its best yet there were no other anglers around. Many anglers shy away from fishing lakes and their reasons are as numerous as summer insect hatches. We suspect the comparative lack of fly fishermen on lakes can be attributed mainly to a lack of knowledge or understanding of lake waters. Lakes, just like rivers, have a character all their own and once understood offer an entirely new, fascinating and challenging frontier.

Lakes are certainly more generous with their fish and frequently they produce on the average bigger fish than many streams. In addition, lakes offer a solitude seldom encountered on today's over-crowded rivers. Unknown to most anglers, however, is the fact that a productive lake is usually within a reasonable distance.

Surprising to many is that lake fishing is not extraordinarily difficult. Some lakes provide such fast action that neophytes can hook a fish on nearly every cast. But other lakes will demand every skill and trick at your command, and yet the fish may still outwit you.

When first confronted with a lake the uninitiated stream angler will be perplexed beyond belief. Water stretches far beyond his casting range and little is revealed to him other than his puzzled reflection on the lake's undisturbed surface. In lakes fish move — water doesn't. This characteristic is the single biggest difference between stream and lake fishing. Gone are the changing currents which can impart lifelike qualities to your fly, hide your sloppy casts, betraying shadows, noisy approaches and unlifelike imitations. Gone are your pet trout which you have caught from a favorite lie more than once, and gone are the familiar visual clues which lead you to the fish . . . or are they?

The lake angler must rely on a different set of clues to determine where and how to fish. Despite the broad physical differences between lake and stream environments, the same fundamentals of fly fishing prevail. The successful lake angler must totally immerse himself in the world of fish. The angler's senses must begin ingesting, sorting, filing and correlating every possible bit of information that the angling environment makes available.

Generally speaking, the most important aspects of lake fishing fall under the following trilogy:

1. HABITAT: The location of fish and the location of their food sources.

2. AVAILABILITY — FOOD PREFERENCE: What food sources are currently making themselves available, as well as how, when and where these food sources are making themselves available to fish; and, in the case of multiple possibilities, what the food preferences of the fish are likely to be.

3. FISHING STRATEGY: How to best present a believable imitation of the available food sources.

Fly fishing is an individual sport which in many respects is a thinking man's game. Perhaps no other sport allows such a full use of all of a man's faculties. Yet, at the same time, the sport can demand little while giving so much in return. Fly fishing is a well-defined sport, a one-on-one proposition, man's intellect versus the fish's instincts. There need be no killing to meet the challenge and complete the pursuit. To kill such a wild creature which provides man with so much pleasure and enjoyment is self defeating. Satisfaction comes not from the killing but from the preparation, the deception, the gentle release, the pursuit itself. Perhaps both man and fish learn from the encounter and perhaps both become wiser adversaries in the future.

There are no big mysteries to successful fly fishing, and there is no *one* magical fly pattern or technique which guarantees perennial success. Fly fishing is, to a great degree, common sense. There is a reason for everything, little happens by chance. We like to think of fly fishing as a complex, probably unsolvable, jigsaw puzzle. No one person has all the pieces but the more pieces you have the clearer the picture becomes and the more fish you are able to consistently deceive. There are no absolutes in fly fishing other than the fact that you will not always catch fish. It was a wise man who said, "If there is not a little challenge, there is more than a little boredom."

The state of the art of fly fishing is continually changing. New pieces to the puzzle are constantly being set in place, and old pieces are being found to have been incorrectly placed. The enlightened follower of the sport contemplates, then challenges all information, taking little as absolute fact, always seeking better answers and raising new questions. Hopefully the following pages will help you recognize and sort out some of the available pieces of that fascinating puzzle called *LAKE FISHING . . . WITH A FLY.*

To assist you this book has been divided into two parts. Part I represents a general overview of the sort of basic information that will quickly get you started toward successful lake fishing. This is the very sort of information that you might receive during a day with a lake fishing instructor who wants to impart the greatest benefit that he can in the short period of time that he has available with you.

Part II, on the other hand, is a far more comprehensive investigation of all aspects of lake fishing with a fly. In many instances information presented in Part I is developed in much greater detail in Part II. Together, however, Part I and Part II will provide you with what you need to know to develop your skills as a successful lake fisherman.

Solitude and larger than average fish characterize lake fishing. R.K.

Chapter One

Reading Lakes

Indeed, my friend, you will find angling to be like the virtue of Humility, which has a calmness of spirit, and a world of other blessings attending upon it. Isaac Walton, *The Compleat Angler*

Reading a lake should be the first cast, so to speak, toward successful fishing. Determine all you can about the physical characteristics of a lake. Such habitat information will ultimately lead you to the fish and reveal their current food source(s). Such a general understanding can even dictate your basic strategy.

Lakes, just like rivers, have a character of their own. Once a few basic principles are understood the phobia of "reading" stillwaters is forgotten. Remember the first time you fished a river? You probably recognized a few possible holding areas but for the most part you were confused and perhaps even disenchanted. Effectively fishing such big water was only a matter of intimacy, discovering its character and learning to "see" small waters within the whole. When approaching any strange water attempt to take advantage of all available information in order to begin defining that character. If there is a book available on the area read it. If there is a resort on the lake perhaps they will have a general map of the lake. Talk to other anglers at the boat dock, the local sport shop and the campground.

Begin constructing your own map of the lake. When water conditions are calm frequently you can see many of the important underwater physical characteristics which will reveal where fish and their foods are likely to be found. Note the locations of shallows, drop-offs, weedbeds, old stream channels, cliffs, shoals, springs, inlet and outlet areas. Note which part of the lake stays in shadow the longest, observe the wind direction and the location of the vegetation. Don't rely on your memory — make explicit notes. Once you are *in* the water, distances become difficult to judge and landmarks take on different perspectives. Triangulate areas of importance.

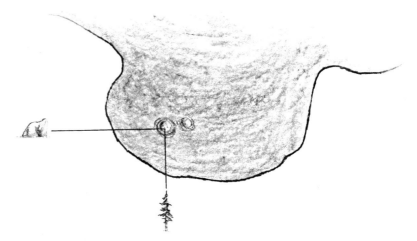

While you are in the process of preparing your map you should always be scanning the water watching for feeding fish. To a degree every foot of elevation above the lake level increases your chances of spotting fish. Binoculars are a great aid and polarized glasses are a must. Always make

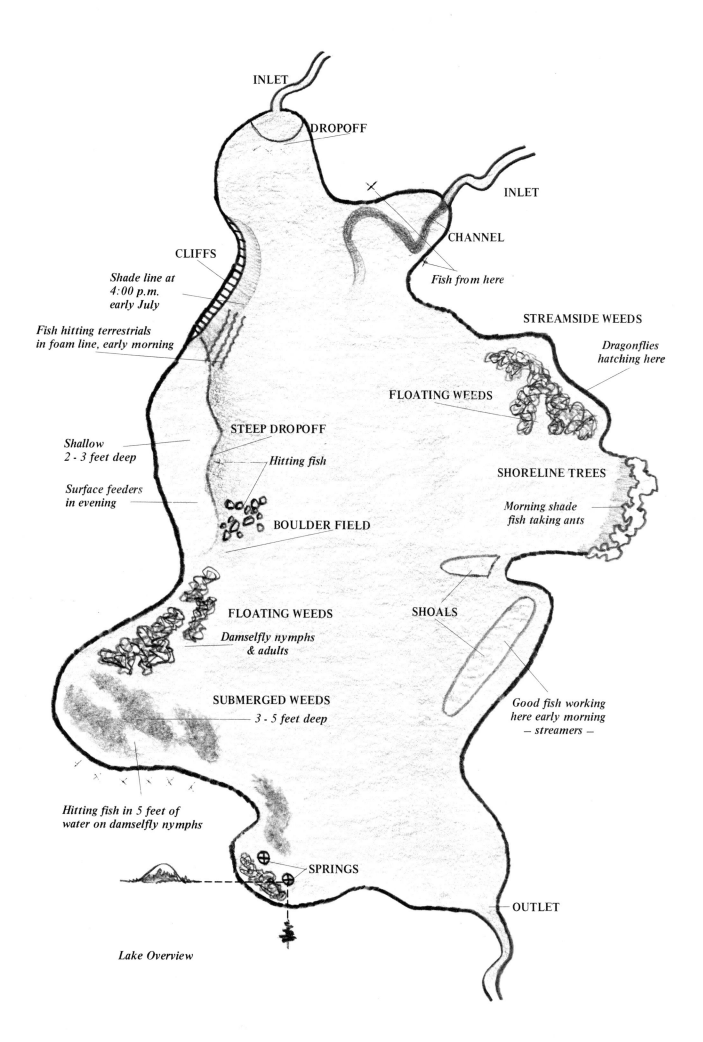

INLET

DROPOFF

INLET

CHANNEL

Fish from here

CLIFFS

*Shade line at
4:00 p.m.
early July*

STREAMSIDE WEEDS

*Dragonflies
hatching here*

*Fish hitting terrestrials
in foam line, early morning*

FLOATING WEEDS

STEEP DROPOFF

SHORELINE TREES

*Shallow
2 - 3 feet deep*

Hitting fish

*Surface feeders
in evening*

*Morning shade
fish taking ants*

BOULDER FIELD

FLOATING WEEDS

SHOALS

*Damselfly nymphs
& adults*

SUBMERGED WEEDS

3 - 5 feet deep

*Good fish working
here early morning
— streamers —*

*Hitting fish in 5 feet of
water on damselfly nymphs*

SPRINGS

OUTLET

Lake Overview

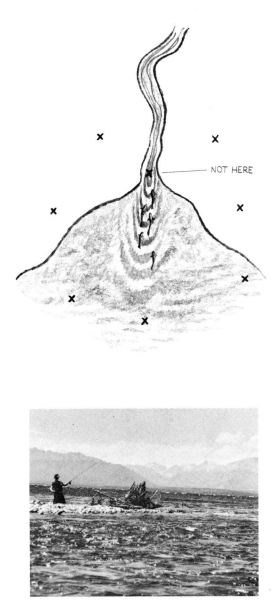

NOT HERE

note of the location of any observed insect activity. Plot or mark the location of any visible fish always making mention of time of day.

This chapter will help you to better understand shoreline and subsurface structure and give you some insight into how to approach them.

INLET WATERS

Inlet areas will usually hold fish which are often difficult to spot and easily spooked. The stream entering a lake generally provides trout with cooler, well oxygenated water and with it drifts a multitude of the very food sources the fish are anticipating. In particular fish will concentrate in such areas during spawning time and when good flows are present it is common to observe fish spawning in the alluvial gravel fan in the lake itself. Fish will often hold right in the strongest current, strung out like emeralds in a long line from the point where the current first meets the lake until it dissipates into the stillwater. In large lakes fish may travel some distance to reach inlet spawning areas and they will often school up just off the stream's mouth. Rainbow and salmon are noted for such behavior, usually waiting for proper conditions before moving upstream. Once such a school is located some exceptional fishing is to be had. Such fish often hold in relatively shallow water and are easily spooked. Sloppy casts, approaching too closely and constant harassment are certain to scatter or drive them into deeper water.

Along small inlet areas never walk close to the running water and always stay well back from the shore. Keep a low silhouette away from the "window" of the fish, taking advantage of any lakeside cover such as trees or rocks. When no cover is available stay low and well back from the water's edge. When a fish is hooked pull it away from other fish immediately, fighting and releasing it well away from the fishing area.

In many New Zealand lakes anglers expertly position their boats or wade in line with the strongest current, called the "rip." Most fish will line up facing into the rip and an angler positioned a few feet to either side will have less success than the angler who can keep his presentation in the main current.

Inlets are best fished like a stream. Allow your imitation to drift and tumble with the current. If you are using a floating line allow for a long and sufficiently limp leader so the current can easily pull it toward the bottom where the fish are holding. Anglers will encounter all the drag problems associated with stream angling, plus the added dilemma of calm water to either side of the current.

Often smaller baitfish will also be available to the larger predators cruising in the inlet areas, especially during their spawning season. When such is the case a proper streamer imitation can be deadly, especially during late evening hours. If at all possible spot and cast to specific fish. By selecting fish closest to you it is less likely that other fish will be spooked by the fly line or, hopefully, by the ensuing battle.

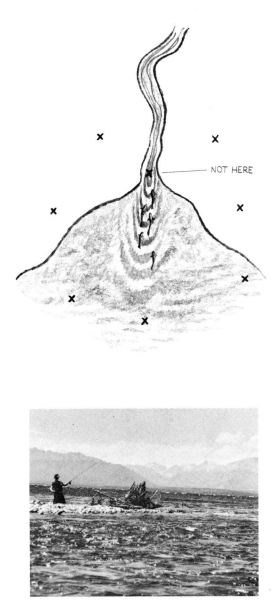

Don McCollum angling for rainbow at inlet of New Zealand Lake. Note how Don is taking advantage of streamside cover, staying low and well away from the water's edge. R.K.

OUTLETS

Outlets can act as a magnet for the entire lake. The resulting water currents slowly draw both surface and subsurface insects toward the outlet. Unlike inlet areas, which can offer the cover of moving water and the proximity of deeper water, outlet areas are usually somewhat more exposed. Where human visitation occurs fish are usually reluctant to feed in such areas except under the cover of darkness. But outlets which offer deep water just off shore are reasonably sheltered and provide trout with a good selection of protective cover and food and thus such areas harbor numerous fish.

Fish in outlets will be wary, selective and often exasperating beyond the normal level of tolerance. We once sneaked up on a dozen or more golden trout strung out in the narrow neck of an unnamed lake high in the Wyoming Rockies. The fish seemed to be the size of steelhead and equally demanding. Hours of fishing yielded nothing, but just the privileged glimpse into their almost inaccessible environment was worth the 20-mile hike.

Anglers fishing small outlet areas should consider fishing as a team. One spots and the other fishes. The spotter positions himself with a clear view of the fish and advises on the proper line length, on the presentation, and on the response of the fish. Ultimately, when a fish is deceived, both anglers share the rewards, but it is the spotter who catches the lion's share of the excitement. Never forget that many valuable insights are gained through such observations.

CHANNELS

For two days we had fished Oregon's Davis Lake intently with only little success. Other anglers seemed to be experiencing the same frustrations except for one gentlemanly type who had been releasing three to seven fish in the three- to six-pound category every day. He was obviously doing something right and though we had our binoculars trained on him, and edged a bit closer each time he hooked a fish, we were unable to discover his secret. That afternoon we changed campgrounds and placed ourselves across from his camp. Conversations come easily in the woods and we were soon tying "killer" nymphs at the picnic table, drinking beer and adding fuel to the lantern.

As with most successful fishermen there were many reasons for his success but the master key was his location. He explained that as the lake warmed fish congregated in the old stream channel which provided food, shade, protection and much needed cooler water temperatures. The fly was cast beyond the channel then retrieved to a point where it would sink into the channel. Finally it was slowly drawn across the channel and eventually inched up and out. Strikes occurred as the fly was crawling up and out, usually just at the lip of the channel.

Natural lakes with fluctuating water levels and dammed natural lakes will usually have a channel winding partway into the lake. Reservoirs will commonly have an old channel winding through their entire length with feeder channels funneling in from side canyons. On a sunny day when the wind is calm look for a winding ribbon of darker colored water which will denote the channel. Low water seasons and late fall are especially good times to map lake bottoms but remember to be as accurate and complete as possible. Pay particular attention to depressions in the channel and if a large rock or other underwater structure exists mark its position as well.

Fishing information is gathered from many sources and local anglers can offer some of the best. Don't be afraid to query them in a casual manner. If they feel you are genuinely interested and are not the catch and kill type they will usually be very helpful. If the channels exist the locals will know about them!

A deserted lake in Argentina. Salty Saltzman photo.

Note how this Alaskan angler is holding his rod high, thus lifting as much fly line off the water as possible, eliminating line drag. R.K.

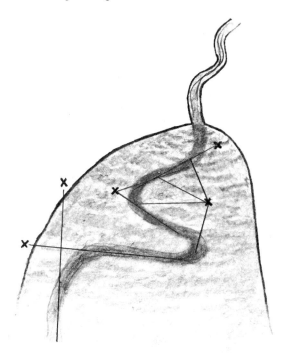

John Goddard hooked this fish in knee deep water. When hooked in shallow water fish usually panic and jump several times. R.K.

Lakes with erratic shorelines offer many productive shallow areas. R.K.

SHALLOWS

Most species of lake fish seldom spend any time swimming at great depths. The most significant reason is that such areas offer little food. Both lake and stream anglers are guilty of believing that farther and deeper are better. Anglers can always be observed wading as deep as possible and trying to cast out of sight. Odds are, fish were lying or cruising where the same unthinking angler was standing, and his long, uncontrolled casts were probably spooking even more fish!

By now every reader should be "thinking shallow." We consider water ten feet or less as shallow, though limnologically speaking, productive, littoral (shallow) zones often extend to about 30 feet in depth depending on the clarity of the water.

The shape of the shoreline of a lake, in particular the nature and extent of irregularities, can influence the character of the shallows and can be of critical importance in determining the potential productivity of both plants and animals. An irregular shoreline can result in more protected bays free from the destructive effects of intense wave action. Consequently, more shallow-water areas may contain good growths of rooted aquatic plants. The richer growth of aquatic plants leads to the accumulation of important organic bottom materials and a more diverse population of aquatic insects and the fish that seek them out. The bottom materials, upon decomposing, return important nutrients to the surviving plant life as well as to the aquatic insects. If the shoreline were significantly steeper, and the area less protected from winds, the water movement could slowly remove the bottom deposits and transport them to deeper regions of the lake where they would be essentially lost. And as a result far fewer rooted aquatic plants would be found.

Gentle slopes allow for the accumulation of organic matter; steep slopes generally do not. It is this difference that results in some lakes being classified as eutrophic (rich in nutrients) while others are classified as oligotrophic (poor in nutrients). While not all oligotrophic lakes have steep sides and great depths, as a general rule these facts are characteristic of such waters.

Bear in mind that it is the shallow areas which provide fish with most of their food. Learn to "read" the shallows and mentally construct an image of the physical characteristics of the lake bottom, visualizing areas of rock, sand, mud, weeds, depressions, bottom debris, shoals, etc. Every type of bottom will attract specific aquatic organisms, but it is over the weedy shallows that you will generally encounter the greatest angling success.

Lake fish are not nearly as territorial as their stream counterparts, but the biggest and strongest fish will frequent the choice feeding locations. Fishing shallow areas for big fish demands confidence, patience and the ability to stalk wary fish. If you have ever watched a heron fish you will understand what we mean when we say stealth. Many successful big fish anglers are very familiar with the areas they fish. They have located the largest fish and have been unsuccessful in the past at capturing them, but they know where they are. We have stalked and observed big fish for incredible lengths of time before ever making a cast!

It is advisable to scout the area you intend to fish beforehand. Locate the best feeders and determine what they are likely to be feeding on. If possible, wade the water, getting a general feel for any possible snags, pitfalls and other possible concerns. You should arrive in position before fish begin feeding, thus alleviating any risk of spooking them during your approach. If you can position yourself behind a rock, stump or weedbed, so much the better.

Remember, fish are particularly wary and on guard in shallow water. If you remain still and look like part of the surroundings, there should be no problem "short lining" them! We have hooked many good-sized fish with no more than 20 feet of line out in shallow water when it was too dark to change flies. Generally speaking the largest trout rarely expose themselves to bright sunlight, preferring to feed during periods of darkness. We, as anglers, often only get in on the fringe of the primary feeding activity of the biggest fish . . . dusk and perhaps dawn.

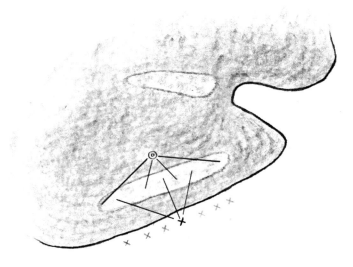

SHOALS

Islands peek above the surface, shoals do not. There is no mystery why fish hang around such areas. In an otherwise deep lake, a shoal can provide a littoral zone which attracts many aquatic creatures, including fish and their food sources. When hanging around the edge of a shoal fish have access to both deep and moderately shallow water. Such extremes can provide a variety of temperature zones, offer security, plus the obvious attraction of a nearby source of food. Often missing, of course, are shoreline areas which provide various insects with hatching platforms and much needed shoreline vegetation. An ideal shoal is one that is located just off shore.

Productive shallow shoal areas are relatively easy to spot during early morning calm. Look for lighter-colored water surrounded by darker water or reasonably level areas tucked between shore and drop-offs or level extensions of a land point.

SPRINGS

Underwater springs frequently provide the best fishing areas in lakes. Water seeping from the ground is usually at a constant temperature, and fish congregate in such areas throughout the year. Springs often provide fish with much needed oxygen throughout lean winter months and can even be a determining factor in preventing winter kill in shallow lakes. During early spring such seepage areas are usually warmer than surrounding waters. As lake waters warm, fish eventually seek out springs for the cooler, oxygenated water rising from the ground. Springs also provide excellent habitat for underwater vegetation which, in turn, is inhabited by numerous aquatic animals which are preyed upon by fish. Springs, in conjunction with weedbeds, will usually provide trout with everything they need — food, cover (shelter and shade), and ample oxygen.

Early in our fishing adventures we spent an entire October day prospecting three miles of an irregular timberline lake shoreline, casting into every shallow bay and drop-off in an attempt to locate brook trout which we knew inhabited the waters . . . and we finally did, only a hundred yards short of camp! A well-placed cast brought an anxious brookie measuring 12 to 14 inches twisting and flopping at our feet. If one fish was missed or soon lost, another one seemed to be waiting in line. We enjoyed our magical place until darkness and hunger forced us back into camp. That evening we mused over how we could fish so much water without success and then locate hundreds of fish in one spot. There had to be an obvious explanation.

Early the next morning the tundra-fringed waters were slick as glass and a dark cloud of fish was easily spotted where we had been so successful the night before. The brookies were milling around an open sandy area in about eight feet of water. Periodic bubbles, which we mistook for feeding fish in the dim light of the previous evening, made their appearance on the lake's surface, tipping us off as to the underwater attraction. The lake had only very tiny inlet areas, and a good percentage of the fish population had assembled here, hoping to spawn. Since that enlightening day we have always made it a point to include the search for springs in our examination of any lake — especially when fishing brook trout lakes in the fall.

Springs have been discovered by anglers in many of the more popular lakes. Resorts will often advise you to "fish over the springs along the far shore," and while such information will not direct you to the exact spot, it will certainly get you into the right vicinity. Keep moving until you are over the "hot spot," and once you have found it, be certain you can easily find it again.

If you are exploring a less populated lake look for air bubbles dissipating on the surface. Lakes may have secondary springs but try to locate the strongest ones. If the lake bottom is reasonably visible, look for mounded sandy areas, or barren areas among the weeds. If you notice fish spooking away from your boat, pay particular attention to the bottom — perhaps a spring has attracted them.

WEEDS

If you locate a weedy lake capable of supporting fish you have probably found some potentially exciting angling. There are few lakes which offer outstanding angling which do not have extensive weedbeds. Nearly every type of aquatic food source is attracted to one or more of the various species of aquatic weeds, hence fish find not only shelter but a major concentration of food which is usually rich in caloric value.

There are two types of weedbeds: floating and submerged. While it is often very productive to fish around floating weedbeds, it is the submerged weedbeds which offer the most outstanding and consistent action.

Weeds can also offer anglers unlimited frustrations in the way of snags and weeds hanging onto flies. This is reason enough for not fishing in dense weedbeds, but rather around and over them. Best results will be had when fishing just above, to either side and in between weeds. In many respects the aquatic insects, crustaceans and the small forage fish are very similar to the larger predatory fish. They seek out food and shelter, both of which many types of weeds offer in abundance.

Each weedbed can require a different tackle combination in order to present your fly in the most effective manner. For instance, if you are fishing damselfly nymphs over a bed that is submerged two feet, a floating line, 12-foot leader and slightly weighted fly would probably be perfect. Should you change location and be fishing over a weedy carpet along the lake bottom in eight feet of water, perhaps an unweighted fly in conjunction with a medium sinking line would be best. In such a case you would want to select a somewhat shorter leader which would keep your fly above the weeds, invariably the prime location.

The countdown technique is invaluable in determining how deep you can fish, which in turn influences the selection of your line and leader. Let your line sink as you count off the seconds. With each cast let your line sink further until you have determined how long it takes to position your fly right above the weeds.

Submerged weedbeds are easily spotted from a boat in clearer lakes. Often small lakes and shoreline areas can be checked out directly from shore or from a high vantage point. In murky lakes let your line sink until you can snag weeds, then back off several seconds in your countdown.

Neil Heiman gently handling a rainbow hooked in a weed-infested Colorado pond. R.K.

Weeds may protrude onto the water's surface or be submerged at varying depths.

SHORELINE VEGETATION

Densely vegetated shorelines are probably the most difficult to fish. If the shoreline is too deep to wade, a boat or preferably a float tube is a must. Besides providing shade and cover such areas are often key sources of food for fish. Not only do most adult aquatic insects seek vegetation for shelter, but so do terrestrials — ants, hoppers, leaf worms, leaf hoppers, beetles, etc. From time to time these insects lose their grasp or, more often than not, gusty winds will blow them onto the water. Such instances provide easy feeding for trout and fast action for anglers if their approach is right.

Casting along the bank will usually spook more fish than you realize. The best approach is to get out into the lake and cast back toward shoreline vegetation. Attempt to duplicate the presentation of the natural. In the case of hoppers you want to cast onto shoreline vegetation, pulling your fly off and making it land on the water with a resounding "splat!" Fish easily hear such sounds and such a presentation is like ringing the dinner bell. Play fish out into the lake away from the main feeding area to minimize disturbing other nearby fish.

Betty Cordes casts to fish cruising dropoff along lily pad contour. R.C.

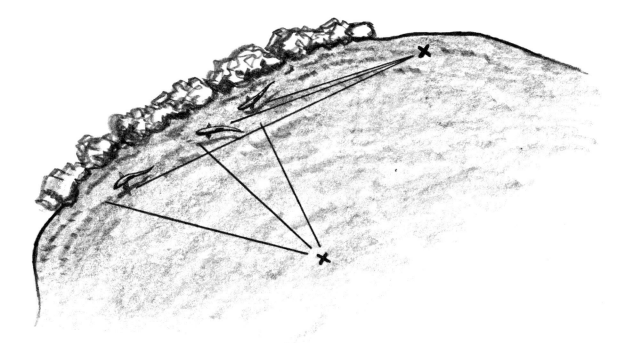

FOAM LINES

Foam lines are formed by wind and water currents. When insects come in contact with foam they become helplessly stuck. As a result foam lines act like an aquatic fly paper. As wind carries hapless insects on the current they pile up or "catch" in the foam. Fish are often observed feeding around and through foam, but when the foam lines are particularly dense and the insects abundant, fish will feed from the underside of the foam.

Often fish feel secure under foam lines and thus can be relatively easy to approach. On occasion we have stood on shore and cast blind into and around nearby foam lines and hooked unseen fish until our arms ached. When terrestrials are present foam lines can be particularly productive.

If a lake has experienced a period of wind check windward shores and bays. Sometimes shorelines act as a type of buffer and foam lines will form off shore. Also, look for foam lines where winds meet or merge from side canyons or from slightly different directions.

George Hunker fishing foam line. R.K.

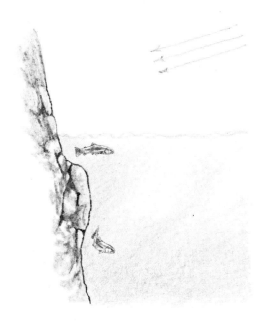

CLIFFS

Cliffs are usually good observation points from which to survey lakes and many times you will see fish directly below you. Cliffs can provide constant shade, slightly cooler surface temperatures and more consistent insect action. Lakes of volcanic and glacial origin are noted for their erratic vertical structure lines and lend themselves to such circumstances. Some cliffs are sources of cool seepage water while other cliffs may bracket a small rivulet flowing into a small bay.

Cliffs can also be terrestrial traps into which insects inadvertently fly or against which they are blown. Cliff fish will often school or mill about lazily with their attention tuned toward the surface. Anytime you hook a fish in the middle of a school it is advisable to immediately pull it away from the others, thereby not spooking them.

Avoid advertising the fact that you are in the area. Keep a low profile, do not make any sloppy casts and fish the area methodically. Start with short casts and slowly increase their length. Such strategy may allow you to hook more fish since you have been careful to minimize spooking others in that same general area.

Cliffs need not be large to be productive areas. We have hooked many trout by fishing over snowbanks which extend into the water forming overhanging cornices. Such fish feel very secure and are usually ready takers.

Anglers can easily conceal themselves among rocks from fish cruising steep shoreline areas. R.K.

DROP-OFFS

Crane Prairie Reservoir in Central Oregon is home to dozens of osprey and quite a few cormorants drop in for an occasional meal. The birds, coupled with all the boat traffic, pretty well keep fish in deeper water until shadows are long. We have witnessed strong damselfly hatching activity during midday, yet have seen virtually no fish exposing themselves. This is not to say fish are not feeding. They are just not cruising the flats or exposing themselves at the surface.

Under more typical circumstances the areas in close proximity to drop-offs are actually a good bet both early and late in the day as fish are often reluctant to forage far from the protective cover of the nearby depths. Such feeders will often stake out a "beat" or feeding path which closely parallels the drop-off contour. When these fish are hooked you can expect them to zoom non-stop in that direction, resting only when they have reached deeper water.

Occasionally, drop-offs can be amazingly productive during midday, especially if they are in close proximity to a key concentration of food sources. The most productive midday methods will entail a retrieve that allows your imitation to sink into deeper water and then crawl up toward the edge of the drop-off. Fish will often follow the imitation, not grabbing it until it reaches the lip of the drop-off, so pay particular attention during this phase of your retrieve.

A floating-sinking combination line is a must in situations like these. The idea is to get your fly to the bottom quickly and keep it near bottom during the retrieve.

Drop-off areas are very easy to locate. Look for areas of darker water. Often you can see the abrupt slope disappearing from view and even see fish scattered about under extremely clear conditions. If you spot fish cruising along the drop-off randomly searching for food, cast well ahead of these cruisers so your fly has a chance to sink below their feeding level. As fish cruise into view of your offering, retrieve it back toward the surface.

Chapter Two

Retrieves and Presentation Techniques

The trout is no single, common, identical, definite, determined and measurable fish, but rather ten thousand tantalizing, distinct and different devils.
Sir Charles J. Holmes, *The Tarn and the Lake*

There are little or no currents in lakes to give life to your imitation so it is of paramount importance that you have a broad range of retrieves at your command. A thorough understanding of how each retrieve affects the motion of various styles of flies in your attempt to imitate the motion of the naturals is also of the utmost importance. An excellent way to develop a good understanding of how the retrieve truly affects your fly is to get out into the water with a friend and take turns casting, experimenting and observing the various possibilities. Always relate this knowledge to the locomotion of the natural food sources that you intend to imitate. Such knowledge will invariably lead you to drastically improved angling success.

Depending upon the food source being represented one or a combination of two or more retrieves will be necessary to impart the necessary action to your imitation.

1. Strip Retrieve: Grasp the fly line between your thumb and first finger and strip line down or back. Loosen your grasp and slide your fingers back up the line and repeat. The strip in various lengths and speeds is used to simulate the movements of many underwater creatures. For example, a series of very short, quick pulls characteristic of darting baitfish would bring a marabou-type fly to optimum liveliness.

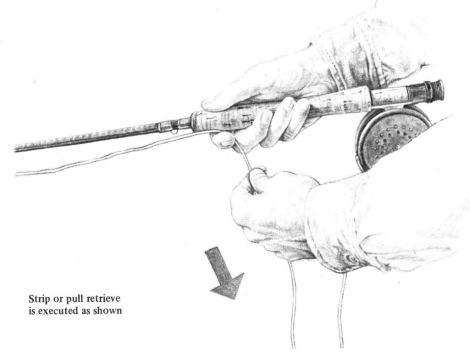

Strip or pull retrieve is executed as shown

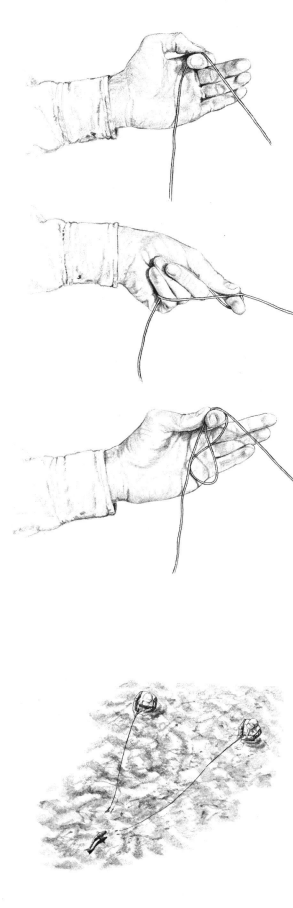

2. Pull Retrieve: As with the strip, hold the line between your thumb and first finger and steadily pull down or back. The pull differs from the strip in that it is slower and more steady.

3. Hand Twist Retrieve: A popular and useful retrieve popularized by the late Ray Bergman. Grasp the fly line between the thumb and first finger or first two fingers of your retrieving hand. Pull an inch or two of fly line toward your palm. Now, rotate your wrist and recover more line with the other three fingers. The hand twist can be used to create action from a dead crawl to a quick-paced, erratic retrieve.

Each of these three basic retrieves can be carried out at various speeds, referred to by some anglers as the crawl, creep, stop and wait, steady, quick, erratic and twitch. Use whatever speed is appropriate for the food source you are attempting to imitate.

Furthermore, as with all retrieves, the speeds can be mixed. Just the few mentioned here in conjunction with the following presentation techniques create nearly unlimited possibilities.

SINK AND DRAW

Sink and draw is the basic presentation technique employed most frequently by lake anglers. It is simple, straightforward and productive, both when imitating a specific insect emergence or when casting to specific feeders, sporadic cruisers or when simply "covering the water." As the name implies your fly is allowed to sink to the desired depth and then it is slowly, but steadily, drawn or pulled toward the surface.

A floating line is appropriate for this technique with leaders varying in length from four to 20 feet depending on the depth of water and its clarity. Full sinking lines will not allow you to swim your fly steadily toward the surface and are seldom used with this technique.

The sink and draw when initiated from the lake bottom is frequently productive because fish often seem to focus intently upon a steadily rising insect. This motion is characteristic, for example, of some emerging mayfly nymphs. Strikes will often be quick and forceful; fish seem to realize that an ascending pupa or nymph can easily escape. Frequently the strike will occur the instant the fly is lifted off the lake bottom, while at other times fish will attack as the fly sinks or just as it arrives below the surface film. Bear in mind that depending upon the speed of the retrieve a strike can be very delicate.

When employing this technique a weighted fly might be needed to reach bottom quickly. Unweighted imitations sink slowly and sometimes precious fishing time is lost while waiting for the fly to reach the bottom.

A variation of this technique, which is extremely effective for presenting an emerging pupa or ascending nymph in shallow water just under the surface, is to grease all but the tippet section of leader. This will keep the bulk of the leader floating while allowing the fly to sink to the depth of the ungreased leader section. With this technique you can imitate a rising nymph or pupa several times during the same cast by simply retrieving the fly a short distance, thereby swimming it to the surface, then halting the retrieve and allowing it to sink again before repeating the process. Retrieves should be varied in speed until the most productive retrieve is determined.

LURE AND WAIT

Everyone has experienced fish following an attractor fly or lure toward shore only to have it melt back into the water as quickly as it appeared, without hitting the offering. We observed this frustrating occurrence for years before we recognized how to capitalize upon it. We call the technique "lure and wait" and find it to be effective during times when fish appear to be off the feed and lazing in the depths. It is especially productive

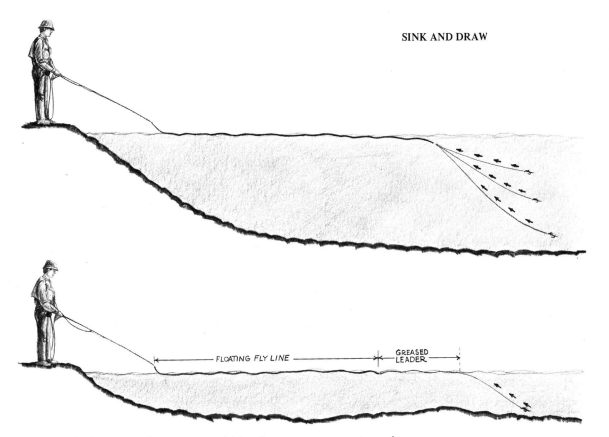

in lakes which contain large trout which often act more curious than hungry.

The lure and wait technique should be employed whenever you notice fish following your imitations. Two anglers must work as a team. One person casts an attractor fly (streamers are best), hoping to tease a fish into following it into view, while the other person waits with a lifelike nymph already positioned and waiting on the lake bottom. Once the fish is in view, begin to swim the nymph toward the surface, using the sink and draw technique. Lure and wait definitely preys on curiosity and on conditioned hunger of fish. More often than not fish will grab the nymph as they turn back and away from your "lure."

When you are casting to a specific subsurface position remember that as your line sinks it will not sink straight down but rather back toward you. To reach a particular spot you will have to cast beyond it. Also, remember that trout are conditioned to seeing most of their subsurface food rising from bottom to top, not falling from the sky and sinking, so make your presentation accordingly.

LIFT OFF AND SETTLE

Fish are known to grab many food sources as they "browse" along the lake bottom. It is important to remember that most aquatic insects are not resting along the bottom with no thought of protection from other predators. Fish key into such food sources when they make themselves available, which is usually as they leave their resting place to begin their perilous journey toward shore, or, depending on the insect, toward the surface, where they may transform into winged adults. It is during that initial bottom "lift off" that insects betray their presence and subsequently make themselves available. Often these surface-bound insects repeat their lift off before they finally get under way toward the surface. The lift off and

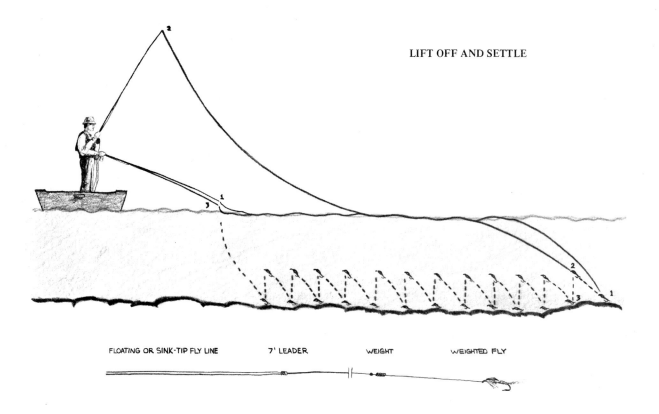

FLOATING OR SINK-TIP FLY LINE   7' LEADER   WEIGHT   WEIGHTED FLY

settle technique used to imitate this migration is a variation of the "rising to the surface" method described in Charles Brooks' book, *Nymph Fishing for Larger Trout.*

While the lift off and settle technique can be executed from shore with a certain degree of effectiveness, it is best practiced from a boat or a float tube. A combination floating-extra fast sinking line is generally used with this technique. Leaders will usually be about seven feet and your fly should be weighted. Occasionally a split shot 15 inches or so above the fly can greatly increase the effectiveness of this ploy. The fly should be cast long over a reasonably clean bottom and allowed to sink. After it has reached the bottom pull in any slack then smoothly and evenly lift the rod tip from the water's surface to the 1 o'clock position. Immediately drop the rod tip and quickly recover the slack.

Strikes will occur at any time so pay close attention and keep the line tight. When the fly settles repeat the process until the fly is below you. This retrieve allows you to effectively cover a wide area of bottom territory.

RISE AND FALL

Once nymphs lift off the bottom and head toward the surface they are vulnerable to predation at any time. Some insects make their way to the surface fairly quickly, while others rise and swim more slowly, settling from time to time. Sometimes what is known as a "false start" occurs, when nymphs rise toward the surface and, for whatever reason, do not emerge or hatch, returning to their subsurface hideaway.

The rise and fall technique is perfect for imitating emerging, or ascending and settling nymphs, cruising scuds and other underwater organisms that display the tendency to rise and fall as they move through the water. A floating or a ten- or 20-foot sinking-tip line is used with a weighted fly. The idea is to sink the nymph down and retrieve it up toward the surface, allowing it to settle and then retrieving it once again, duplicating the actions of the food source you are imitating. Attractor and probing flies can be fished this way also.

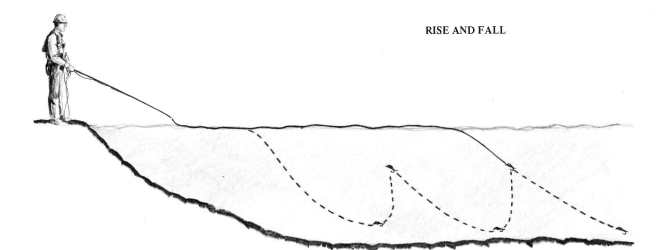

Leader length will be determined somewhat by water conditions and fly size but when using a floating line you will want a leader long enough to just reach the bottom.

Pay close attention for strikes, both when retrieving the fly toward the surface and when allowing it to settle.

WIND DRIFT

A boat and slight breeze are needed to utilize this method. The boat is positioned into the wind and drifted over either side of the desired water. The boat must be pointed into the wind — if allowed to become broadside to the wind it will travel faster than your fly.

Cast your line, either floating or sinking, at a right angle to the boat imparting occasional twitches to enhance the natural drift and simulate struggling actions. Watch the line for any indication of unnecessary drag, possible weak hang-ups and takes.

We use the wind drift technique to probe likely water during midday. If two anglers are fishing it is a good idea to fish two different patterns at different depths. When a fish is hooked mark the location carefully and drift over the area again. Float tubers can also use this method; an occasional kick of the fins will correct for any inconsistent speeds. Many fish have been hooked and new "hot spots" located while lazily wind drifting back to camp.

WIND DIRECTION

DEAD DRIFT

Dead drifting is suitable for imitating a multitude of food sources swimming slowly toward the surface, for imitating behavior just under the surface, or for imitating organisms generally browsing, such as leeches.

Dead drifting can best be practiced during a slight-to-moderate breeze and is most easily executed from an anchored boat though shore anglers can easily employ the technique if the wind direction is right. Casts are quartered upwind and the fly is allowed to drift naturally downwind toward the boat without any particular retrieve, other than to gather in the slack in the line. Waves will provide the necessary action.

This is much like fishing a slow-moving river but in this instance the wind moves the line and the fly instead of the water. In either case line drag can develop causing the fly line to belly and as a consequence the fly can rise and drag cross wind at the surface. To impede drag you should quarter into the wind with a slack line cast and as the belly forms mend your line. When you mend the line be careful not to move the fly. This is easily avoided by mending only a portion of the line — part of the line length is lifted up and set down upwind. When it is no longer feasible to counter the line drift you should let the belly form and allow the fly to rise and come around. Strikes can occur at this time also.

Dead drifting usually requires a minimum cast of 40 feet, patience and a highly trained eye. Intense concentration is required if you are to be successful; fish often will accept and reject the fly before you can tighten up any slack line. You must keep a reasonably tight line and pay very close attention for any line movement indicating a possible strike. Under ideal conditions you may be able to detect the underwater "flash" of a fish as it turns to take the fly. You should, of course, tighten up when such a flash is observed in the vicinity of your fly, regardless of whether or not the take actually was felt. If there was no take drop the rod tip and continue the drift.

Polaroid glasses are helpful in detecting such subtle movement. Nine- to 12-foot leaders are about right and your fly may or may not be weighted.

DROPPER TECHNIQUE

When multiple hatches are occurring many anglers use the dropper technique to assist them in determining what food source the fish are eating. Other anglers use it to cover the varying interests of foraging fish, while still others use it to fish both surface and subsurface flies simultaneously.

The technique involves attaching two, three, or even four flies to your leader. One fly is attached to the end, or "point" of the leader, while the other flies (droppers), are attached up the leader at two-foot intervals. There are two styles of droppers: the right angle dropper and the slider.

While there are several knots to attach the right angle dropper, the blood knot is perhaps the simplest. As you tippet out your leader leave an extra few inches on the heavier of the two ends. Tie the fly as short as possible thus minimizing entanglements.

The sliding dropper is rigged up by sliding the first fly onto the leader and blood knotting a two foot section in place. The fly is allowed to slide freely between the two confining blood knots. Additional flies may be attached in the same manner, with the point fly completing the team. Blood knots must be large enough in diameter to prevent the sliding flies from slipping over them.

Droppers may be fished at any depth. Grease the leader to within an inch of the fly and you have a surface clinger. When all flies are to be fished subsurface the point fly should be the largest or heaviest. A weighted fly will sink faster pulling down the other droppers at an angle and allowing you more vertical coverage. If you are using the dropper technique only to determine the depth, size and color of the preferred insect you should vary

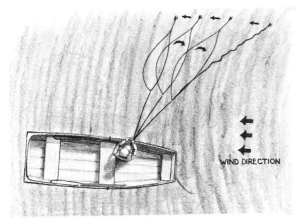

WIND DIRECTION

your imitations accordingly. When such information is determined the other flies may be removed allowing you to concentrate your efforts in one particular location and with one imitation.

However, when fishing is exceptionally fast it is not uncommon to hook two fish at once, both rushing off in different directions. We have heard stories where anglers have assembled a "school" of minnow imitations on multiple droppers and presented these to fish which, seemingly, would not move for just one or two imitations, but which went berserk when confronted with many possibilities.

When using the sliding dropper ring-eye hooks will hang in a vertical position, while up-eye and down-eye hooks will stand out at an angle. We have found the ring-eye hooks perfect for imitating chironomid pupa hanging in the surface film prior to hatching.

One interesting and productive variation of this technique is to attach a dry fly on the point and a nymph, emerger or pupa on the dropper(s). The dry fly on the point will keep the nymphs close to the surface.

Another variation is to attach the dry fly as the top dropper thus allowing the point fly to sink as deep as desired. The team of three flies is cast as far as possible and allowed to drift naturally with prevailing winds. A twitch or two may be imparted if desired. The high floating dry fly acts as a bobber, and, when the subsurface imitations sink directly below the dry fly, which is the case with the latter method, the bouncing of the dry fly on the windy waves imparts a very convincing movement to the nymphs below. The floating dry fly also acts as a perfect strike indicator and at the slightest sign of unusual movement you should tighten up in case a fish is responsible for the disturbance. Even when using a dry fly as an indicator close concentration is the key to detecting the often light pick-up of the artificial fly by the fish. Occasionally fish will take the floating imitation so you should also be prepared for subtle rises and splashy surface takes.

The selection of fly patterns, leader length, the dropper array and the retrieve will all be dictated by the prevailing circumstances. We have only presented a few of the more widely-used ideas here, but the possibilities are legion. No doubt you will eventually come up with a few ideas of your own.

COUNT DOWN

This very valuable technique will allow you to consistently present your fly just over the top of submerged weeds or just over the bottom without becoming snagged. Cast your fly to the desired area and allow it to sink for 15 seconds. If, during the retrieve, no snags or weeds are encountered, the prime bottom habitat is not being reached. If a count of 20 is allowed on the next cast and snags and debris are encountered you know you are too deep. Back off the count until no problems are encountered.

When you are presenting an imitation on or near the lake bottom or over submerged weedbeds, water depth, weight of fly and speed of the retrieve will determine what fly line should be used and what leader length is best. Once the ideal combination has been obtained make detailed notes so experimentation will not be necessary next time.

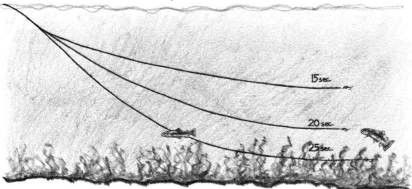

SKATING

Skating a fly across the surface is relatively easy to accomplish. The fly is usually visible and so are the strikes. Besides bringing the fly to life, the hops, skips, skates and skittering motions attract fish from a larger than normal area.

This technique is especially effective when imitating adult caddis, some terrestrials and, to a lesser degree, chironomids. Under specific circumstances it can be used to represent the feeble struggles of cripples and the more obvious actions of injured or dying damselflies and dragonflies.

We often fish unweighted minnows with this technique. The extra flash of light striking the sides of the imitation, coupled with the surface disturbance and associated noise, is often enough to entice a smashing strike. Minnow imitations are not skated for long distances, just for a foot or two.

A fly is best skated by retrieving the line in one hand with a long, fast pull and simultaneously accelerating by lifting the rod from the horizontal to the vertical position. By varying the line speed on acceleration you can make the fly hop, skip or skitter across the surface. The imitation can be made to move so fast that on a rough-water day the fly actually will skip along the tops of the waves.

Fish will often strike and miss the fly several times before they are successful, perhaps finally striking with full vengeance. Sometimes fish will literally jump out of the water to grab an imitation fished in this manner, usually hooking themselves in the process. For this reason it is a good idea to use a strong leader tippet. We suggest a leader length of 12- to 15-feet which will enable you to get much of your fly line off the water's surface, thereby lessening the drag, commotion and resistance of the fly line. A nine-foot rod is also a great aid allowing you a higher lift and longer reach.

To achieve maximum animation a heavily hackled, palmer-style fly with a hair wing is necessary. Such flies will also remain afloat far longer than flies dressed in a sparse, low profile manner.

CLASSIC DRY FLY

Except for specific times and specific hatches fish will seldom be observed sipping surface insects on lakes. The surface of the lake may be disturbed by dimpling fish, but the odds are no better than one in ten that fish are feeding on adult insects. Once an emerging insect breaks through the surface film it is nearly ready to take flight and fish usually pay little attention to such insects, preferring instead to capitalize on the aquatic stage. But, when surface activity demands the attention of fish the resulting fishing can be spectacular. Everything from beetles to delicate mayfly spinners can entice fish to the surface.

Dry fly fishing can occur when adults are resting on or trapped in the surface film. Such occurrences usually happen in the early morning before the wind makes it difficult for insects to fly and during late evening when calm conditions again prevail. During such periods visibility can be quite good and if the lighting is right you can often observe fish cruising toward your fly, only to tip their jaw and sip a natural inches from your imitation, the widening rise ring bouncing your fly like a lost bottle at sea. Dry fly fishing lakes can be very frustrating for there is seldom success without perfection.

More often than not lake dry fly conditions require that your stalk, presentation and leader and fly be highly refined; during dead calm conditions every detail is highly magnified. Fish have a clear, unobstructed view of your offering and they are seldom in a hurry. The more realistic your fly appears the greater your chances of success. This type of fishing can be compared to the most demanding spring creeks — but, then again, there *are* those times when *any* and *everything* works!

Classic dry fly fishing is, of course, executed with a floating line and leaders 10- to 20-feet long. Refrain from sloppy casts and retrieve your fly *slowly* from the feeding area before casting again. After casting all slack should be immediately taken out of the line. The fly is allowed to rest quietly and drift naturally with perhaps an occasional slight twitch imparted to give the illusion of life. Close attention must be paid to the high-riding bogus fly, as hits can be extremely subtle, with fish sometimes sucking the fly through the surface film. Remember, there is seldom a need to strike fish. If the barb is smashed flat, the hook point sharp and the fish there, just a slight tightening of the line is all that is needed to hook them.

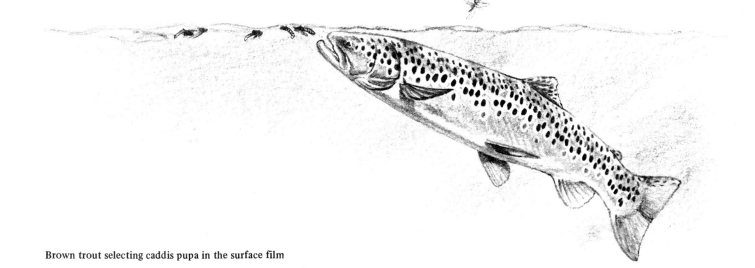

Brown trout selecting caddis pupa in the surface film

Chapter Three

Special Fishing Considerations

Certainly there is nothing simple about Dame Juliana's treatise, the first book on fly fishing. Deception is her keynote and deception is not simplicity. Imitation is her constant theme and that requires considerable skill, artfulness, and good craftsmanship. V. Marinaro, *A Modern Dry-Fly Code* (1950)

DRAG

Drag is usually associated with moving water but drag is also a problem lake fishermen must contend with, especially near inlet and outlet areas and during windy periods. In lakes there is no fast current to sweep away a potential food source and fish seldom need to make a split second decision to accept or reject an offering. Such a situation allows fish a long, clear look and drag is easily noticed. Why is it a problem? Because you lose control over the motion you wish to impart to the fly! And it no longer looks natural.

An overly large diameter tippet may hinder a fly as it drifts with the surface breeze, or the same breeze may create a belly in your fly line, dragging your fly. An intermediate line will alleviate much of this problem; it will sink just slightly subsurface where wind cannot play its whimsical games as easily.

Your boat might get turned sideways to the wind, or you might kick your float tube fins in error. Whatever the reasons, drag is always a potential problem.

Many anglers, lake and stream alike, watch their fly floating nicely on the surface from 30 or 40 feet and assume the presentation was "drag free." Unfortunately, fish do not inspect flies from 30 feet but from a foot or less. To more fully understand the potential complications of drag move in for a close-up view of your own.

VISUALS

Fly fishing is a visual sport. The more often you can see the fish, your fly, your leader where it enters the water or your fly line, the better your chances for success.

When surface fishing it is of paramount importance that you follow your fly at *all* times. The moment a fish hits your fly you will be able to tighten up and hook the fish before the fly is rejected. If you notice your surface fly has sunk or is dragging, chances are you will not hook any fish and the situation should be corrected immediately.

Because you can seldom see your fly subsurface fishing demands even more attention. While your fly is usually invisible your fly line is not. That point where the leader or fly line disappears below the water's surface is your focal point. Watch this point closely because the slightest movement or hesitation denotes either a snag or a strike. The strike is seldom an arm-jolting experience, but rather a slight "pick-up" by the fish.

When retrieving your imitation you must have a direct line of contact between your rod tip and your fly. If you do not chances are good you will not hook the fish or even know you had a take. The shortest line of contact between rod tip and fly occurs when you are retrieving your fly and the rod tip is *on*, or slightly *in*, the water. To properly tighten up on a strike

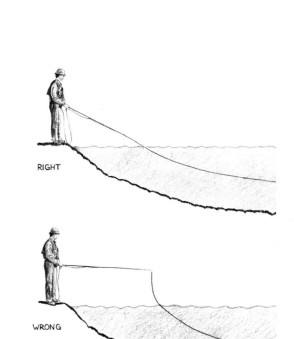

FLOATING FLY LINE

INTERMEDIATE FLY LINE

RIGHT

WRONG

the rod tip is raised slightly. If no fish is there drop the rod tip and continue the retrieve.

If you can see both your fly and the fish so much the better. Such visual contact gives you a decided advantage in that you can see the response of fish and be ready for any ensuing strike. Often underwater strikes will be very subtle and fish will only move slightly or perhaps merely open and close their mouths. Watch for fin movements, the reaction of your line and the disappearance of the fly. All movement or lack of movement will suggest what is likely to happen next.

Like all wild animals fish are alerted by quick movements. Any moving shadow such as your own, or those of your fly line or leader as you false cast can alarm fish.

Consequently, some general rules are to *stay low, move cautiously* and *blend in* with your surroundings. Most anglers want to at least get their toes into the water before fishing. A lesson was learned by accident many years ago when after fishing without success some small outlet ponds where fish were clearly visible we sat down behind a lakeside willow for lunch. Upon completing lunch we decided to make a half-hearted sit-down cast from behind the willows and a 14-inch brookie immediately grabbed the fly. The remaining day was spent crouching behind vegetation, releasing numerous brook trout up to two pounds.

Some thought should be given to clothing. A light or bright hat or shirt is not going to help you approach fish. Knowledgeable anglers will often have two fishing vests — a dark green one for timbered areas and a tan one for drier areas to match their background surroundings.

The vision of trout is a highly complex and many-faceted phenomenon. Their sight adjusts to any level of light from bright daylight to darkness. Did you know that trout can "see" around and above a bank or rock, often "seeing" you before you can even see their resting place? There are many interrelations between how and what trout see which are of *critical* importance to every angler. *Ring of the Rise* by Vincent Marinaro, *The Trout and the Fly* by Brian Clarke and John Goddard and Ernie Schwiebert's masterful *Trout* will give you invaluable insight about what fish see, their habits, reactions and how best to approach them.

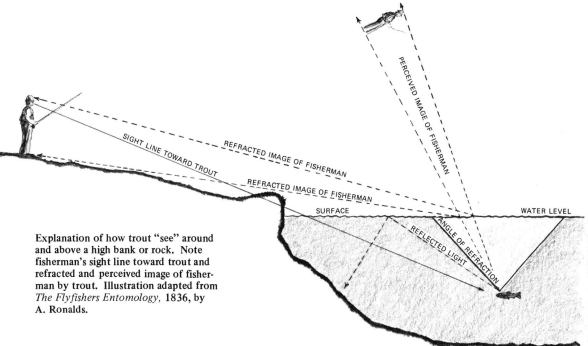

Explanation of how trout "see" around and above a high bank or rock. Note fisherman's sight line toward trout and refracted and perceived image of fisherman by trout. Illustration adapted from *The Flyfishers Entomology,* 1836, by A. Ronalds.

COLLECTING

Once you arrive along the inviting shoreline of a secluded lake it is difficult to constrain yourself from stumbling into the water with fly rod in hand, yet a few minutes of observation and collecting could mean the difference between success and failure.

When visiting any water, whether you are familiar with its heartbeat or not, collecting is mandatory before fishing. You never know when some unfamiliar hatch might be in progress or when you might chance upon a new discovery. For collecting, we carry a small dip net and a roll-up pocket screen in our vest. Roll some rocks, examine some weeds and explore the mud and sand but be careful not to desecrate the area. Treat these organisms kindly, returning them to their homes with as little disruption as possible.

Gently discover what is currently available as a food source. Remember, fish usually observe insects from below so pay close attention to the color of their underbodies. As you release them observe their swimming motion and speed. Such observations are invaluable and will ultimately lead to more productive and pleasurable hours of angling.

STALKING

Most anglers scare more fish than they ever see. We have often observed unthinking anglers rush and stumble into chest-deep water and immediately begin casting as far and as fast as possible, probably disturbing every fish in the area. These same anglers are probably wearing bright clothing. No doubt they took little or no notice of possible feeding fish or available food sources.

To be a consistently successful angler you must be very stealthy and you must understand that fish also have enemies and are easily put on guard or scared into hiding. Watch a heron fish. The same philosophy applies to your stalking techniques.

Fish rely heavily on their senses of sight and hearing. They consider the slightest abnormal disruptions or intrusions as danger signals. If any one of a number of alarms are sounded fish will rush for protective cover.

Normal human sounds created above the water will not penetrate water, so anglers need not be concerned about talking, for instance. Any sound created underwater or when in contact with water will be transmitted at five times the speed of sound above water. Outboard motors are out; float tubes are in. Stumbling, cleats, splashing and any boat noise quickly advertise your presence. Remember the last time you stumbled into a lake, sending out widening water rings (and noise vibrations) ahead of you? This did not go unnoticed by fish, for they can "feel" and hear such intrusions.

If you expect to be consistently successful you must be cautious and quiet.

FISH THE IMPOSSIBLE PLACES WITH FLOAT TUBES

Float tubes offer you a tremendous advantage over conventional boat fishermen by allowing you to quietly approach feeding fish which would otherwise be unapproachable. How often have you stood on the shoreline watching in helpless wonder as fish gorged themselves near a drop-off just beyond casting range? What about fish feeding on terrestrials on the other side of unreachable shoreline vegetation? You have probably suffered these circumstances more than once.

With a float tube boggy and brushy shorelines, offshore weedbeds, springs, ledges, islands, remote lakes and waters closed to motorized craft are all easily accessible. The pleasures of float tubing cannot be fully appreciated until you slip into the water and begin paddling about, half submerged in the water.

Aquatic insect collecting is easy and offers valuable insights to anglers. Randall Kaufmann surveys Idaho lake. Mike Reeves photo.

Ron Cordes "float tubing" California lake. R.C.

When buying a float tube do not settle on a "cut rate," stripped down or inferior tube. Select an American-made model with all the current state-of-the-art design features. Such refinements will pay for themselves many times over in comfort, peace of mind and durability. Look for a tube which is double and triple stitched, is constructed of nylon with nylon zippers, and has a quick draining/drying mesh bottom, stripping apron, double back rest, deep seat, suspender attachable "D" rings and ample pockets. More refinements will always be available and you will want to take advantage of them.

Paddling around in cold water even on a warm day can chill you to a point of numbness. Except for the warmest conditions we recommend you wear neoprene waders. For those who prefer lighter, stockingfoot style waders, you will want to wear pile or wool undergarments. Avoid standard boot-foot waders, they are clumsy, uncomfortable, collapse about you and tend to chafe your legs and wear out along the inseam. Neoprene booties are nice for added foot protection and warmth.

Locomotion is supplied by heavy-duty swim fins. You will only be able to propel yourself backwards but you will soon learn that this is the direction to travel. When entering and leaving the water you should walk backwards to avoid tripping on the fins. If you feel yourself falling merely sit down in the tube.

For safety reasons use an inflatable fishing vest. If you will be on the water at dark a waterproof flashlight is nice especially if you should need to warn motor boats of your presence. Float tubes are designed for still waters, not rivers, but you will be amazed at how stable they are in rough water. We feel much more comfortable in a tube than in a small boat.

There is no question that float tubing will open an entirely new dimension of lake fishing for you. Whether you become addicted or not, you should read *Float Tubes, Fly Rods and Other Essays* by Marv Taylor.

This ends Part I of *Lake Fishing . . . With A Fly*. Remember that these topics have been selected to quickly assist you in upgrading your lake fishing efforts while you begin your more prolonged study of Part II. In Part II you will learn what the fish eat, when and why and how to best imitate each food source, including mayflies, damselflies, scuds, leeches and many others. You will learn the significance of the various types of aquatic plants. In short, you will develop an understanding of lake fishing with a fly that heretofore has been achieved by only a few dedicated lake fly fishermen.

Float tubes allow access to otherwise untouchable trout.

Chapter Four

Origins and Forms of Lakes

Lakes are temporary phenomena from the geologists point of view. No sooner are their basins formed than the work of their destruction begins.
J. G. Needham & J. T. Lloyd, *The Life of Inland Waters* (1937)

How can you characterize the productivity or fishing potential of a lake you intend to fish? Unfortunately, not even lake biologists are particularly happy with the means now available for making such a determination. Over the years limnologists have tried to find a correlation between the ultimate production of numerous, healthy fish and such factors as the average depth of a lake, the amount of rooted submerged vegetation, the amount of plankton, the quality and quantity of the bottom fauna and various chemical factors. No single, satisfactory index of productivity has emerged although definite trends with occasional exceptions have been determined.

An understanding of the manner in which a lake was originally formed can frequently be reflected in an angler's ability to successfully "read" and fish that same lake. The form and structure of a lake as generally dictated by its origins is intimately related to the physical, chemical and biological processes which ultimately control the potential quality of the lake's sport fishery. The nature of the lake's drainage, the influx of nutrients and the stratification characteristics of the lake are controlled to a great extent by its form and structure. These factors control what we might refer to as the "metabolic process," the continual heartbeat underlying a lake's very existence. To understand the origins of a lake is to gain critical insight into the metabolic process itself.

Lakes are formed in numerous ways the principal ones of which include movements of the earth's crust, volcanic activity, landslides obstructing valleys, river activity, glacial activity, solution of underlying rock and organic activity by man or by beavers.

TECTONIC LAKE BASINS

Depressions created by the movement of deep portions of the earth's crust are referred to as tectonic basins, the most famous of which include Pyramid Lake in Nevada and Lake Tahoe in California.

VOLCANIC LAKE BASINS

Volcanic activity can result in the creation of lakes in any one of several different ways. The cavity of a quiescent volcanic peak may ultimately become filled with water as in the case of Oregon's spectacular Crater Lake. The cooling lava flows may collapse into voids, perhaps to be filled by rains and spring runoff or by groundwater seepage. Lava flows may also cut off pre-existing rivers by forming natural dams behind which the waters collect.

LAKES FORMED BY LANDSLIDES OBSTRUCTING VALLEYS

One of the most recent lakes to be formed by the sudden movement of large masses of dirt and rock is Quake Lake in Montana near Yellowstone Park. There, earthquake activity triggered a massive landslide which cascaded down upon the Madison River, blocking it and forming Quake Lake.

Frequently lakes which are formed in this manner are subject to rapid erosion by the action of the impinging river waters. In the case of Quake Lake, however, the materials dislodged from the mountainside were sufficiently compacted to form a reasonably secure dam, and a spillway was cut to alleviate pressure on the earthen dam.

LAKES FORMED BY RIVER ACTIVITY

Perhaps the primary way river activity results in the formation of lakes centers around the erosion and subsequent depositing of sediments. Larger rivers may deposit sufficient quantities of sediment at the mouths of tributaries until the flow of the tributary is totally obstructed and flooding occurs in the valley through which the tributary flowed.

Today in Alaska numerous examples exist of the formation of lakes resulting from a loop of a meandering, snake-like river being cut off from the main flow. Erosion and sedimentation are once again responsible for this phenomenon.

LAKES FORMED BY GLACIAL ACTIVITY

Glacial cirque lake, Wyoming. R.K.

The most significant means by which lakes are formed is by virtue of glacial activity. The catastrophic effects of glacial ice movements resulted in the formation of more lakes than any other process. Regions of the United States and Canada once covered by glaciers are today characterized by numerous lakes.

Basins destined to become lakes were literally dug out of mountainous regions by glacial activity. In the subarctic region of central Canada both Great Bear Lake and Great Slave Lake were created by this scouring process. The Great Lakes of the northern United States were likewise produced by glacial continental ice erosion.

Receding glaciers frequently left behind large deposits of rock and debris which dammed up depressions and valleys to form lake basins. The Finger Lakes of New York and many Wisconsin lakes, including Lake Mendota, were formed in this fashion.

Another frequent occurrence was the actual ice obstruction at the lower end of a mountain valley. The resulting ice barrier formed an effective dam behind which the lake basin formed.

Nearly all of our high lakes in the Sierras, Cascades and Rockies are of glacial origin. Many are spread out in broad basins while others are cirque lakes (lakes formed at the very head of a glacial head wall, filling the last depression of a melted glacier).

LAKES FORMED BY THE SOLUTION
OF UNDERLYING ROCK

Soluble rock deposits such as limestone or calcium carbonate may be slowly dissolved by the percolating of water. The resulting depression is referred to as a "solution lake," and such lakes are very common wherever limestone deposits predominate. In some cases tunnels formed by the percolation process collapse, thus forming the limestone depression. A common characteristic of solution lakes is a conically shaped basin generally very circular.

LAKES FORMED BY MAN

Although man has been actively damming rivers to form lakes for thousands of years it has only been during the last two hundred years that this activity has taken on any great significance. Today large reservoirs are being constructed for numerous purposes including flood control, power generation, irrigation, creation of municipal water supplies, and, in some cases, to artifically stimulate a lagging local economy or simply for profit at the expense of the resource and the general public. Smaller, shallower bodies of water in the forms of ponds and small lakes have been created by the thousands. In both cases, however, such lakes are relatively short-lived, generally because of the high rates of sedimentation and little or no purging of the basins' waters. High nutrient inputs relative to the small volume of water contained in these lakes frequently results in high productivity of the lake system. Properly protected, such waters can provide unusually good fishing not merely for bass and panfish but often for trout as well. Unfortunately, many such impoundments are not managed for fish and highly fluctuating water levels and temperatures usually preclude any great fishery.

To the avid outdoorsman, some of the most significant ponds have been constructed not by man but by the industrious beaver. In the Rocky Mountains in particular, as well as in some regions of the northeastern United States fishing these ponds is a very popular pastime.

Beautiful scenery is a constant companion of lake anglers. Crane Prairie Reservoir, Oregon. R.K.

Chapter Five

The Origins of Lake Waters

Twilight leaned mirrored in a pool
  Where willow boughs swept green and hoar,
Silk-clear the water, calm and cool,
  Silent the woody shore.
Excerpt from *The Old Angler*, Walter De La Mare

The origin, form and structure of a lake are significant factors in determining how a lake establishes its supply of water as well as how it maintains it. Both factors are of importance in assessing the nature and extent of nutrients entering the lake ecosystem to sustain aquatic organisms. Without an adequate supply of nutrients the potential of a lake for quality angling is quite limited.

The basic hydrological relationship governing the amount of water in a lake at any given time is referred to as the "hydrological cycle." This cycle is controlled by the climate peculiar to the region of the lake, by the surrounding countryside drained by the lake and by the form and structure of the lake itself. It reflects such considerations as rain, runoff, springs, effluents, seepage and evaporation. Of primary concern in considering the respective elements of the cycle are the chemical characteristics of the waters entering the lake basin, for the biotic metabolism of the lake is inextricably dependent upon their presence.

Most lakes receive a relatively small proportion of their water supply by direct precipitation. As lakes increase in size, however, this mechanism takes on greater significance. The groundwater seepage mechanism is a major source of water for lakes located in either glacial till or rock basins, as well as for the limestone "solution" lakes. Such water is effectively filtered before reaching the lake basin, limiting its potential for transporting nutrients and dissolved solids.

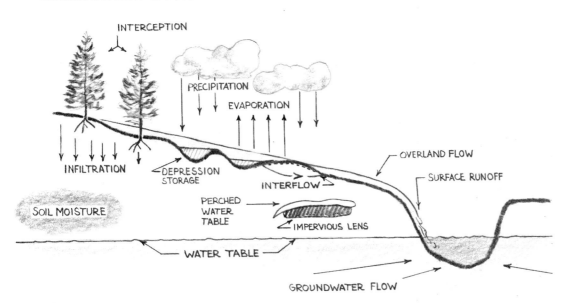

The most variable and in many instances the most significant source of water is runoff from the watershed drained by the lake. The rate of runoff is strongly influenced by the nature of both the solid and the vegetation characteristics of the watershed. If adjacent lands are grazed by cattle or fertilized for crop production the resulting chemicals are inevitably transported by the runoff into the lake basin sometimes making a very productive lake. In some cases this mix of organic and inorganic nutrients can be beneficial by forming an integral source of food for aquatic organisms attempting to survive in an otherwise nutrient-poor environment. On the other hand such a mix can lead to conditions conducive to the rapid growth of certain aquatic organisms detrimental to quality angling. Lakes choked with weeds and saturated with algae may be ideal for many insects but for just about anyone but the avid bass fisherman the lake may be completely undesirable to fish.

One of the most desirable sources of lake water is the underground spring, which is invariably cool and continual. Its presence often ensures an adequate water supply throughout the year, one which fish seek out during those periods when other waters in the lake become too warm.

Water losses from lakes occur in numerous ways, the most obvious resulting from outlet flows. Fishing such areas can often be quite productive particularly with surface patterns. Surface waters of a lake in the vicinity of the outflow are slowly drawn in a convergent "V" fashion to the point of the outflow where the trout wait.

Additional water losses result from direct evaporation as well as from what is referred to as "evapo-transpiration," the loss of water through the surface of aquatic vegetation having floating leaves or exposed portions. The rate of loss by both mechanisms is highly variable and dependent upon such factors as sunlight, air temperature, humidity and wind velocity.

Boat anglers anchor off springs at Henry's Lake, Idaho. R.C.

Chapter Six

Physical and Chemical Characteristics of Lakes

In the water, reflection and translucency, or one of them help to achieve the same end, and, I think, are more important than merely imitative colouring.
Col. E. W. Harding, *The Flyfisher and the Trout's Point of View* (1931)

Not all lake waters are capable of growing big fish, large numbers of small fish or sometimes *any* fish at all. There is an intricate relationship between the chemical and physical makeup of a lake and the number, size, condition and even the behavior of fish within a lake. Many outside influences including light, temperature and wind greatly influence habitat and fish. The more knowledge you have of these influences the better your understanding of the subtleties which ultimately control all fishing possibilities.

LIGHT

Light is of fundamental importance to the dynamics of the entire lake ecosystem including such biological phenomena as the growth of aquatic vegetation, the emergence of aquatic insects and even the rising of fish. The very metabolism of the lake is controlled to a great extent by the solar energy available to the lake ecosystem. Flora and fauna characteristic of lake productivity depend upon utilization of this energy to develop and flourish. Even behavior of aquatic organisms may be influenced by the nature and extent of available light.

Light is a form of energy which may be transformed into heat by absorption with the net result being a change in temperature of the lake waters. Or, light may become involved in various biochemical reactions thereby transforming it into potential energy to be utilized by aquatic organisms. The amount of light actually reaching the lake's surface depends upon numerous dynamic factors such as the season of the year, latitude, angle of contact, time of day and atmospheric conditions.

On a clear day with no atmospheric conditions such as the presence of clouds, the amount of light reaching the lake's surface is the sum total of the light coming directly from the sun and the light from the hemisphere of the sky. Assuming that the surface of the lake is undisturbed those light rays which strike the surface at right angles pass through it without deviating from their path. Light rays striking the surface at some angle less than 90°, however, are bent toward the perpendicular.

Light impinging upon the lake's surface does not penetrate the surface completely. A fraction is instead reflected and essentially lost unless the topography of the lands surrounding the lake or the sky reflect a portion back. If the surface is disturbed by waves the amount of light reflected may increase by approximately 20 percent.

Of the total amount of light that does pass through the lake's surface a portion is scattered and a portion is absorbed by the water itself as well as by organisms within the water. That portion of light ultimately scattered upward back toward the surface of the lake is what determines the observed color of the lake's water. Primary determinant is the presence of dissolved organic matter scattering back light in the green portion of the light spectrum with reds and yellows becoming more significant as concen-

Fish are best held and photographed in this manner. They should never be lifted above the water. Mark Weitz photo.

trations of organic matter increase. Presence of inorganic compounds such as clays can result in a yellow to reddish color. Large concentrations of blue-green algae may create a blue-green coloration. Iron compounds may produce shades of yellow while large quantities of calcium carbonate produce a green color.

The varied roles played by light in the dynamics of the lake ecosystem are quite amazing and only partially understood by even the most enthusiastic anglers. The water flea *Daphnia* uses the angular light distribution with depth as a means of orienting its body as it migrates daily from the depths of the lake to its surface. In doing so distribution of the *Daphnia* populations within the lake become determined by the vector of maximum light energy. In lakes where *Daphnia* are a major food source of fish at certain times of the year, such insight may lead to very productive angling by indicating where fish may be found. During times of intense lighting fish and other aquatic creatures usually seek deeper water or shaded areas. How such light affects the feeding habits of fish and movements of aquatic insects is not fully understood but bears consideration.

Light is almost certainly the factor which controls *when* fish will rise, other factors determine *if* fish will rise. The regularity of the evening rise is a very striking feature; it starts at almost the same time each evening after sundown and hence is later in the evening as the days lengthen, earlier as days become shorter. During cooler, cloudy days, fish will often feed and rise throughout the day. There are many interrelated reasons for such activity, the most obvious being cooler temperatures, increased insect activity and the fact that fish feel much more secure during times of dim light.

Fish may appreciate the longer infra-red light rays which, within limits, have the ability to penetrate clouds and fog. Red light from the visible spectrum is often very much appreciated by trout and adding red to an artificial fly frequently will improve its effectiveness, especially on forage fish imitations.

Thus it can be seen that light is of multifaceted significance to the angler. Understanding its role in the dynamics of the lake ecosystem enables him to analyze and explain that which he observes each day during his angling activities. And, of course, such knowledge gives him the advantage of calculated, intelligent preparation in his continued pursuit.

Twilight alpenglow colors mountain peaks shades of purple and snowbanks pink, signaling this High Sierra angler that the optimum fishing time has arrived. R.K.

HEAT AND TEMPERATURE

Temperature has many profound influences upon the aquatic environment. Some are quite direct while others are indirect and more subtle. For example, since fish are cold-blooded their body temperature is essentially controlled by the temperature of their external environment. Their body temperature in turn affects their bodily functions and their activities. Because of these significant influences each species of fish has certain temperature ranges in which it prefers to live. So sensitive are fish to the temperature of their environment that temperature changes as slight as $0.1°F$ ($0.05°C$) can be detected. Obviously, it is this capability that enables fish to follow a temperature gradient toward their preferred temperature! Migration patterns of such forage fish as the redside shiner are determined in this fashion.

Other influences of temperature upon the aquatic community include determining the locations of various insects, when insects begin to emerge, the quality of the rises exhibited by feeding trout and even the amount of terrestrial insects found upon a lake's surface. The temperature of lake water profoundly affects the condition of fish by affecting its eating habits, its susceptibility to disease and its sensitivity to the presence of toxic chemicals. It is because of the widespread, all pervasive influence of temperature upon aquatic organisms that the angler must learn to recognize not merely the effects of temperature changes but the very manner in which they occur. In many instances these changes will dictate where to fish and which techniques to employ, as well as when to fish.

Solar radiation is generally the single greatest source of heat in a lake. Water has the capacity to absorb this radiant energy in the form of heat directly. Some transfer of heat to the water from the air does occur, as does the transfer of heat from lake sediments which themselves have absorbed significant quantities of solar energy. Both of these mechanisms, however, are seldom as important as direct absorption itself.

Heat losses from lakes occur through the loss of water at outflows, by thermal radiation back to the sky, by conduction of heat to the air and even through the continual process of evaporation. That heat which is retained is ultimately distributed throughout the lake basin by several means, the most important of which is the action of wind upon the surface waters. As air currents move across the lake's surface, the friction between the air and the water cause the surface waters to move. The resulting current varies in magnitude according to the velocity of the wind and forces the lake waters to mix which in turn causes the heat contained in the warmer surface waters to be redistributed.

If it were not for this mechanism of the wind creating currents which result in the transfer of heat within a lake, the process whereby the water temperatures change would be very slow. Water has the capacity to absorb vast quantities of heat before its temperature will rise even $5°F$. It is this capability that explains why lake water warms up so slowly in spring as well as why in autumn lake water cools down so slowly. The vast quantities of heat involved in both heating and cooling processes make the response of a lake to even major changes in air temperatures a very deliberate one. Anglers should always keep in mind that water temperature lags far behind larger changes in air temperature. An awareness of this lag will help in particular in anticipation of the onset of various hatches.

One lake phenomenon that occurs as a result of temperature changes is so profound in its influence upon the aquatic community that it bears very close scrutiny. This phenomenon is referred to as "thermal stratification" and it includes both spring and fall overturn of lake waters. Few anglers understand the fact that fish are not found at every level of deep lakes. This is true because lakes divide into three distinct "layers" which are defined according to temperature and oxygen content.

Randall Kaufmann offered this bright Alaska silver salmon a minnow imitation and it promptly attacked it, perhaps out of natural aggression. R.K.

Ice out high in the Wyoming Rockies. Fish often cruise along the ice shelf and an offering cast upon and then pulled off the ice often produces a very quick grab. R.K.

When ice breaks in the spring lake waters are 32 degrees at the surface, warming slightly with increasing depth. As warmer, deeper water rises and mixes, the temperature of the entire lake will reach a uniform 39.2 degrees — when water is at it's greatest density, or weight. Winds easily circulate the entire mass, ending the oxygen depletion at deeper levels and transporting valuable nutrients, which have settled into the depths, to warmer food producing waters near the surface. This spring "overturn" can occur within 24 hours of ice out. At this time fish can be relatively scattered down to depths of 40 feet.

Summer temperatures soon warm surface areas and the difference in densities allow warmer surface water to sit on top of cooler, deeper water. Epilimnion is the name given this top layer of water. The entire epilimnion will be about the same temperature and circulate freely, responding quickly to wind, wave action and atmospheric pressure. Depending on the lake this top layer can extend down to five or perhaps over 50 feet, though 20 to 30 feet is generally the lower limit. The top layer will continue to deepen throughout the summer until a peak depth is reached in late summer at which time it will begin to cool (Figure I).

The middle layer of water is referred to as the thermocline. It is abruptly colder than the top layer and oxygen poor. This relatively narrow band of

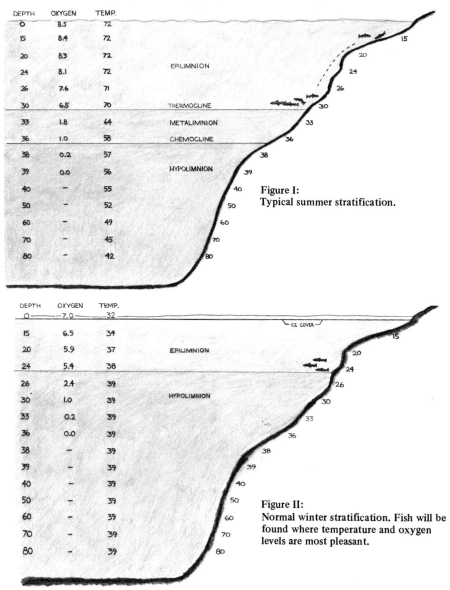

Figure I:
Typical summer stratification.

Figure II:
Normal winter stratification. Fish will be found where temperature and oxygen levels are most pleasant.

DEPTH	OXYGEN	TEMP.
0	2.0	32
15	1.0	34
20	0.0	34
24	–	39
26	–	39
30	–	39
33	–	39
36	–	39
38	–	39
39	–	39
40	–	39
50	–	39
60	–	39
70	–	39
80	–	39

SNOW COVER
ICE COVER
CHEMOCLINE
HYPOLIMNION

Figure III:
Extreme winter stratification. (Winter kill)
Temperatures might be fine but there is not
enough oxygen.

water is usually less than 10 feet from top to bottom but it can be further divided into the metalimnion and chemocline layers which are narrow transition zones of decreasing temperature and oxygen levels.

The hypolimnion is the bottom layer of water. During the summer it will be the coldest area of the lake and virtually void of oxygen and aquatic life.

In the fall cooler air temperatures lower the water temperature of the top layer of water until it matches that of the bottom layer. When the entire lake cools to 39.2 degrees the lake waters circulate freely, or "turnover" just as they do after ice out. At this time the entire lake is saturated with high levels of oxygen which seem to spur fish into gorging themselves.

Once a lake cools to its maximum density surface waters can freeze rather quickly, beginning an inverse thermal stratification whereby the coldest water is near the surface and warmest water near the bottom (Figure II). This occurs because lakes freeze from the top down. Small, shallow lakes freeze first because they lose their summer heat more quickly than large, deep lakes. Lakes that do not freeze continue to drop in temperature but continue to circulate and remain the same temperature from top to bottom, but may, however, drop below 39.2 degrees,

If light can penetrate winter ice cover lakes will remain reasonably well oxygenated, but excessive ice cover and especially heavy snow cover will drastically reduce photosynthesis, thus cutting off future oxygen supplies. When such is the case oxygen content is steadily depleted by organic decomposition and animal respiration. In lakes where oxygen has been severely depleted fish are driven to the cold, near icy waters of the surface in search of oxygen where they may become frozen or die of oxygen starvation (winter kill, Figure III). Many small, shallow waters cannot support fish for this reason. Other lakes are "on the border" and freeze kill only during extremely harsh winters.

The implication for anglers is simple. The top layer will have most of the oxygen, aquatic life and fish. The middle layer is cool but oxygen poor and the bottom layer is void of most life. Trout prefer cool temperatures but demand oxygen. During "summer dog days" or "slumps," fish will usually be found at the bottom of the top layer of water. They may, however, travel to shallower areas where food is more abundant, returning to the ideal comfort level with perhaps a full belly, or they may be able to do all their feeding at the optimum comfort level.

In the fall cooler weather lowers the temperature of the top layer increasing its density and sinking it lower and lower in the lake. Eventually the temperature (density) of the top equals that of the bottom and the entire lake "turns over," bringing fresh oxygen below and needed nutrients into the shallows. The entire lake is saturated with oxygen levels as high as 12 parts per million, making it ready for the lean winter. Such high levels of oxygen spur fish into gorging themselves. Perhaps they realize that the feast may be their last in open water until spring. Lakes which do not freeze continue to drop in temperature but circulate and remain the same temperature from top to bottom.

Understanding water temperatures is important in forecasting hatches. If springtime temperatures are above normal and waters warm sooner than usual, insect hatches will usually appear correspondingly earlier. This is important if you are planning to fish a particular hatch which normally appears June 15, but because of abnormal temperatures, is two weeks early or two weeks late. Temperatures also appear to have an indirect effect upon emerging insects in that the higher the water temperature the lower the amount of oxygen that is present particularly in lake waters which, unlike many streams, are not well aerated. A lack of oxygen may be particularly harmful to mature nymphs about to emerge. Before emergence a nymph requires a great amount of oxygen and the system by which the nymph transports oxygen loses its efficiency as the air-breathing adult forms beneath the skin of the aquatic nymph. An increase in temperature places an increased oxygen demand upon the tissues while at the same time reducing the amount of oxygen in solution in the water. Some aquatic species probably emerge at specific times to avoid this oxygen problem, even though slightly higher temperatures and resulting lower oxygen levels are harmless to immature nymphs of the same species.

Temperature is indeed an important parameter in one's angling activities yet very few individuals either take notice of it or record it along with other observations as a means of improving their future angling endeavors. In practice one should begin each period of angling with a temperature measurement. Subsequent measurements should be taken throughout the day to be later correlated with the anglers observations and angling successes or failures. It takes but a brief moment and yet provides at the same time a bit of rest and reflection. Like all other facets of fly fishing the rewards are commensurate with the effort.

Bill Bohannan demonstrates the easy release in Yosemite backcountry. R.K.

OXYGEN

Aside from the water itself oxygen dissolved in the water is one of the most important parameters of the lake ecosystem. Each aquatic organism including the fish themselves depends upon oxygen for its metabolic processes. The dynamics of oxygen distribution within the lake basin is thus of primary concern in understanding the distribution, behavior and physiological growth of aquatic organisms.

Presence of oxygen affects aquatic organisms not merely through metabolic demands but also by influencing the concentration of various inorganic nutrients essential to their growth and survival. As oxygen concentrations change so may the distribution of these nutrients.

There exists a marked difference in the amount of oxygen in the air and the amount in most natural waters. Air contains roughly 21 percent oxygen, an ample supply for the requirements of air-breathing organisms. Water on the other hand contains much less. One liter of water saturated with oxygen will contain only 9 cubic centimeters of this gas, whereas one liter of air will contain approximately 210 cubic centimeters of oxygen. In air the lack of oxygen is rarely a threat but the same cannot be said of water.

The small amounts frequently found in various lake waters provide but a tenuous margin of safety at best. For this reason disturbances in the lake ecosystem can lead to oxygen shortages resulting in the destruction of both the insects and the fish. Various parasitic and bacterial diseases are also related to inadequate supplies of dissolved oxygen.

The amount of dissolved oxygen in the water of a lake depends both on the altitude at which the lake is located and the temperature of the water, with solubility increasing with decreasing temperature and decreasing altitude. Its distribution throughout the lake occurs primarily by virtue of the spring and fall overturns transporting the more oxygen-rich surface waters into the deeper regions of the lake. Unfortunately, diffusion of oxygen into water is a very slow process, however it does continually occur at the surface of the lake.

From the viewpoint of the angler increasing water temperatures with resulting decrease in dissolved oxygen means that fish will seek out regions of the lake where adequate supplies of oxygen can be found. This generally occurs where cooler waters exist, such as at greater depths in the lake, or in close proximity to underwater springs or streams that flow directly into the lake without sufficient time to heat up significantly. Where cool, often well-oxygenated streams enter the lake basin these necessary conditions may be found. In late summer in particular the angler must give some thought to rising water temperatures or he may fail to recognize that fish have already responded by migrating out of those waters where angling success had previously been ensured.

Diffusion and thermal overturn are only two of at least five means by which oxygen is introduced into the lake's waters. Inflows, surface agitation by waves and the production of oxygen by green aquatic plants also make significant contributions. Wave action which is very effective in aerating water is probably unrivaled in oxygenating upper water layers. Photosynthetic processes of aquatic chlorophyll-bearing plants release oxygen directly into water with subsequent water movements distributing it throughout the lake basin.

The littoral, or shallow shore zone, and the limnetic or open-water zone both contain oxygen-producing green plants. In the littoral zone plants are rooted, whereas in the limnetic zone only green plants are the phytoplankton. Phytoplankton of course overlaps the littoral zone since it literally extends from shore to shore.

Depending upon the concentration of plant life and amount of light available for the photosynthetic process, the amount of oxygen introduced into the water will vary greatly. In regions of massive beds of plants or in areas of high phytoplankton concentrations, the amount of oxygen released can be quite large although water movement ultimately disperses it.

In light of both the capability of aquatic chlorophyll-bearing plants to release the necessary oxygen and at the same time to harbor large quantities of aquatic insects, it is no mystery why trout frequent such regions of a lake, temperature permitting.

ALKALINITY

Without becoming overly technical suffice it to say that biologists employ what is referred to as "ph" to characterize waters as being acidic, neutral or alkaline. The values of ph range only from 0 to 14, with 0 representing the greatest acidity and 14 representing an alkaline solution. The two primary conditions of acidity and alkalinity have long been recognized as being intimately associated with numerous biochemical processes many of which occur in the lake ecosystem. The property of alkalinity is frequently brought about by the presence of carbonates, bicarbonates and hydroxides, whereas natural waters rich in dissolved organic matter are generally acidic in nature.

Of importance to the angler is the fact that large, fast-growing trout tend to occur in hard, alkaline waters and small, slow-growing trout in soft, acid waters. Exceptions as always, do exist. As a general rule, however, where one can find alkaline waters, the fishing may well be exceptional.

MOVEMENT OF WATER IN LAKES

Water movements, which depend upon the winds and their magnitude and direction, the shape of the shoreline, and the relative amounts of deep and shallow water, are of major significance to the aquatic organisms in the lake ecosystem. The rhythmic motions initiated and sustained by the presence of winds are most obvious at the surface of the lake where the waves are visible. But beneath the surface these motions also occur. Water thrown up on shore rolls back into the lake creating an undertow. Mixing occurs resulting in changes in temperature and redistribution of nutrients and aquatic organisms.

Waves, however, are not the only important source of water movement. Currents are also significant in lakes — a fact which is generally unknown to lake fishermen. Three types may exist: vertical, horizontal and undertow currents, although the vertical current is generally restricted to large waters such as the Great Lakes. Horizontal currents occur frequently in lakes and are generated by winds and modified by the shape of the shoreline. In the northern hemisphere wind-driven currents below a low pressure system tend to move in a counterclockwise fashion. Beneath a high pressure system such currents tend to move in a clockwise fashion. In the southern hemisphere just the opposite occurs.

As mentioned above, an onshore wind may pile up water on an exposed shoreline thereby raising the water level at that point sufficiently to create a current of excess water escaping along the lake bottom. If the winds are strong enough an undertow may extend all the way to the opposite side of the lake! If the lake is stratified, however, the undertow will encounter the cooler, denser water of the metalimnion which will deflect the undertow and thereby create a circulation pattern at the center of which the water is essentially motionless.

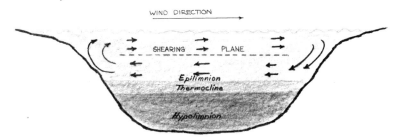

Currents within a lake may also be established by the entry of a river or stream whose waters will flow into the density layer within the lake which is most similar to its own density. Knowledge of where this current is located can be of importance to the angler when the fish are actively seeking it out.

The effects on the aquatic environment of these various forms of water movement are diverse. Continual wave action on the windward shore may ultimately prevent the rooting of aquatic vegetation and selectively eliminate those animals which are unable to burrow into the lake bottom. Organic bottom deposits can be removed thereby altering habitat and making it unsuitable for many organisms normally common to that region of the lake. On the other hand these same movements may assist the lake ecosystem by recirculating nutrients and renewing the supply of dissolved oxygen to the deeper lake waters. The presence of rooted aquatic vegetation as well as the configuration of the shoreline and the lake bottom often serves, however, to reduce these effects of water movement upon the aquatic ecosystem.

Once again, of primary importance is the ability of the angler to understand the underlying nature of the phenomenon that he is witnessing. With a fundamental insight into the nature of the lake ecosystem the angler can

Undertow current

Windy inlet and shoreline areas create currents and underwater "feed lanes" which few anglers understand. Randall Kaufmann wades remote Alaskan lake. Al Luray photo.

frequently analzye those happenings within the aquatic community which he recognizes are of importance to his angling endeavors. An understanding of water movement is one more tool with which the angler can delicately refine his skills.

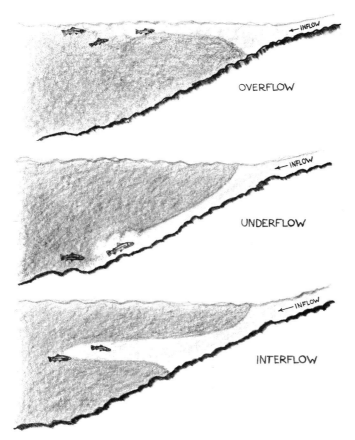

SURFACE-FILM

The surface-film phenomenon has some very interesting ramifications for the lake fly fisherman, particularly with regard to emerging insects and terrestrial insects. Paul Welch in his excellent book entitled *Liminology*, explained the phenomenon in the following fashion:

"When water is exposed to air, it acts as if it were encased within an extremely thin, elastic, surface membrane. This boundary is commonly known as the *surface film* and is interpreted as a manifestation of unbalanced molecular action. In the interior of the water the molecules do not exhibit any such phenomena, since in that position they are attracted to each other in all directions, neutralize the attraction of one another and are thus balanced. However, at the surface film a phenomenon called *surface tension* occurs, due to unbalanced attractions between molecules at the surface, since the surface molecules are attracted on one side only, and upward attraction is lacking because there are no water molecules above them. It happens, therefore, that a surface tension is produced which acts inwardly, and the molecules act as if they formed a tightly stretched, elastic membrane over the water. This surface tension diminishes with rise of temperature, and it is also lowered by organic substances in solution, although most salts increase it. In pure water, it is said to be greater than in any other liquid except mercury. Objects which do not wet may be supported on top of

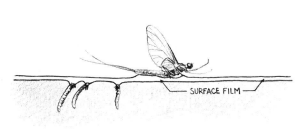

SURFACE FILM

this film, even though their specific gravity is several times greater than that of the underlying water. A time-honored demonstration is the supporting of a dry, steel needle on the surface film. The limnologist is accustomed to seeing, at times along sandy lake shores, patches of sand floating on the surface film. The under surface of the surface film also serves as a mechanical support for certain objects in nature. Light rays, impinging from above, penetrate it if the angle of incidence is not too great, but beyond a certain angle the surface film reflects light. Viewed from below, especially at an angle, it appears as an exceedingly smooth, somewhat silvery, opaque film. This film is now known to have many limnological relations . . ."

Several insects such as water striders, whirligig beetles and certain spiders actually live upon the surface film. Some even have the capability of breaking through it to swim below for short periods of time. Aquatic insects which emerge by swimming to the surface to undertake the transformation to the adult form must penetrate the surface film to utilize it to support their bodies. These insects are forced to drift upon this film while awaiting the full extension of their wings in preparation for flight.

Terrestrial insects which are either blown onto the surface of a lake or whose errant flight causes them to make contact with the surface often become prisoners of the film. Grasshoppers, crickets, adult caddisflies and mayflies, as well as midges, mosquitoes and others frequently become entrapped for days, drifting helplessly at the mercy of the winds, the currents and the cruising trout.

The underside of the surface film also supports, if only temporarily, certain other aquatic organisms. Midge and mosquito larvae and pupae are among the most important from the standpoint of angling. But even snails can be found literally clinging to the underside of the surface film. Trout will often take every advantage of the opportunity to feed upon organisms drifting at, on or below the surface film.

LITTORAL, SUBLITTORAL AND PROFUNDAL REGIONS

A good way to organize one's thoughts on a lake is in terms of water depth in relation to corresponding flora and fauna. The lake floor has been divided into three major zones referred to as the "littoral," "sublittoral" and the "profundal." It must be kept in mind, however, that although each of these zones has certain general distinguishing features they tend to blend into each other. Furthermore, although these zones are designated in terms of depths in the lake the depths will vary greatly from lake to lake depending upon the form of the lake basin. For example, some lakes such as Oregon's Mann Lake, are so uniformly shallow that the entire lake bottom is considered a littoral zone. Other lakes, such as Crater Lake, which drop off quickly into deep water have a very narrow littoral zone.

The littoral zone of the lake is generally thought of as extending from the edge of the lake to the lakeward limit of the rooted aquatic vegetation. The

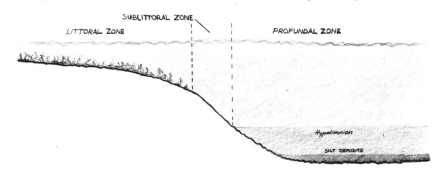

SUBLITTORAL ZONE

LITTORAL ZONE PROFUNDAL ZONE

Hypolimnion

SILT DEPOSITS

littoral bottom consists of the sorts of materials found along the shore, such as sand, stones and gravel. Organic deposits, plants and materials brought in by wave action also contribute to the final composition of the littoral zone. This zone is of greatest significance to the angler since it contains a much greater number of different animals than do the sublittoral or profundal zones. It is here, in the littoral zone, that the greatest concentration of insect hatches will occur, and as a partial result, foraging trout will also be present, supplying the best angling opportunities.

The sublittoral zone is a transition zone extending from the lakeward limit of the rooted aquatic vegetation down to the limit of the hypolimnion, the lowest temperature zone in a lake that stratifies each summer as discussed earlier. The bottom materials of this zone vary from those of the littoral to those of the profundal, with continual accumulations of those materials originally deposited upon the lake basin.

The profundal zone consists of very soft ooze which can become quite thick. Within the profundal zone lies the "shell zone" where dead shells from molluscan populations of the littoral zone accumulate. The profundal zone begins where the sublittoral zone ends and includes the remainder of the lake bottom.

Not only may a shallow lake have its entire bottom fall within the littoral zone, but a deeper lake with depths beyond the limit of rooted plants but which does not undergo thermal stratification would have littoral and sublittoral zones but no profundal zone.

The fact that the littoral zone starts at the water's edge and may characterize the entire bottom of a shallow lake should not be interpreted to mean that the littoral zone is only a few feet deep at best. On the contrary, the littoral may extend in some lakes to a depth of thirty feet. The key factor in defining its bounds is the limit of the rooted aquatic vegetation, which establishes not only the zone itself but that region of the lake with the greatest fishing promise.

While the tremendous diversity of lakes provides exceptions to virtually any statement made about them, in general it is true that *quantitatively* the fauna increases with increasing depth down to some optimum level somewhere within the lower littoral or upper sublittoral and then decreases with increasing depth to some minimum within the deepest portions of the lake.

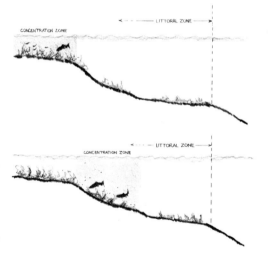

This region of high benthic bottom fauna concentration is referred to as the "concentration zone," a distinct zone in which the members of the benthic fauna are considerably more numerous than immediately above or below. Because of the emergence periods in the life cycles of the insect members of the fauna, as well as seasonal environmental changes, this zone will shift its position. But in general it will occur year after year, and one can only assume that the trout must respond accordingly. When their food sources are concentrated in one area more so than another it would seem that they would be much more successful foraging for food there. Other factors of which we are as of yet unaware, however, may offset this apparent advantage, such as greater protective cover for the organisms.

The implication for the angler is that he should consider whether the lake he intends to fish is a shallow one, perhaps having its lake bottom completely within the littoral zone, or a very large, deep one. And in both cases the supply of nutrients in the lake is at the same time very important. If a choice has to be made between various unknown and untested waters, you can now make a cursory inspection and arrive at an intelligent decision as to which would provide the better sport. You should also be considering at the same time other factors such as fishing pressure. There is unfortunately no clear-cut, single method for simply walking up to a body of water and predicting whether or not the fishing will be good. The more you understand about how lake organisms interact, however, the better you will be able to respond to whatever information is available.

Chapter Seven

Biological Characteristics of Lake Waters

For every insect a trout takes alive at the surface, a thousand are consumed drowned underwater or near the surface; and to one natural insect able to float on the surface, there are hundreds that cannot float.
L. Rhead, *American Trout Stream Insects* (1916)

A truly remarkable diversity of plants and animals exists within the lake's aquatic community, with tremendous variations from one body of water to the next. Each separate entity, no matter how small or seemingly inconsequential, is a structural and functional part of the composite whole. And the constant interplay of their physical, chemical and biological inter-dependencies weaves a complex design in the fabric of the life of the community as a whole. It is important for the angler to keep in mind that the behavior patterns of each organism of particular angling consequence, whether it be an insect or a fish, is everywhere determined by the external influences to which it is subjected. These external influences are controlled in turn by the intrinsic nature of the aquatic environment in which the organism lives. Life there is complex, ever changing and intricately inter-woven with that of the entire lake ecosystem. For this reason the angler must be aware of facets in the life of the aquatic community which bear not only directly upon issues of angling concern but indirectly as well. It is this understanding of an overview of the lake and its aquatic organisms that will ultimately provide the angler with exceptional insight into specific angling events as they occur.

PLANKTON

Plankton are minute organisms that have very little or no power of locomotion and are thus more or less subject to distribution by water movements. In fresh water these may include algae, fungi, protozoa, rotatoria and arthropoda. To the angler the arthropoda are probably of the greatest significance since they include certain crustaceans such as *daphnia* as well as certain insect larvae.

It is important to keep in mind that each plankter has its own particular physiology and ecological niche as well as a whole host of interdependencies. It should be remembered that many of the higher nonplankton animals depend extensively upon plankton for food either directly or indirectly. This includes many fish throughout their entire lives, or in some cases, only during particular stages of their lives.

Regardless whether or not the plankton is plant or animal it will invariably be found in all natural waters. Even high alpine lakes, frequently barren looking, produce small plankton.

While exploring Wyoming's Wind River Range, we witnessed golden trout which seemed to be feeding randomly but which were also "gulping" or "seining" something just subsurface. As we were carefully releasing a couple of these 15 inch beauties we noticed the inside of their mouths was speckled with numerous small red plankton. A dip of the collection net in the water revealed millions of tiny creatures. We assumed these to be *daphnia* or water fleas, and also assumed these minute creatures to be the object of

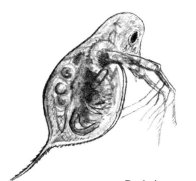

Daphnia

the trout's behavior. While we had observed these tiny pinhead creatures in alpine waters for years this was the first time we had actually observed them inside fish.

Plankton are so small (most people would not even notice them in their drinking water) that it would seem fish could only efficiently "seine" huge numbers, rather than feed on singular individuals. For this reason it would seem plankton must also be extremely concentrated and abundant to be of any value to fish over a few inches in size. Plankton can also be found along windward shores or in protected areas and may become so concentrated that the water will be altered in color.

Inflowing water from streams may have the effect of either enhancing plankton populations or diluting them, depending upon whether or not the water originates from a sluggish, weedy stream itself, a good producer of plankton, or from a fast stream perhaps maintaining only a scant plankton population.

With regard to the vertical distribution of plankton in a lake, the topic is too complex to go into in this book other than to point out that the depth to which the chlorophyll-bearing phytoplankton may be found is determined to a great extent by the depth to which sufficient light penetrates. No significant generalization can be made about the zooplankton, although several zooplankters actually migrate from various depths to the surface and back again at different times of the day.

The principle factors which influence this vertical distribution include the search for food, existence of certain light conditions, concentration of oxygen, water temperature, wind, gravity and even the age of the zooplankter in question.

Once again, what is important is not that the angler know and understand every nuance of the plankton community, but rather that he know that ultimately fish depend upon the presence of plankton. Its relationship to the plankton may be indirect in that plankton merely attract the organism of particular interest to the fish, such as some aquatic insect or smaller fish upon which it chooses to feed.

Nuphar

Vallisneria

Lily pads

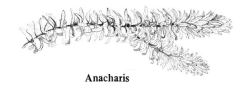

Anacharis

Chapter Eight

Aquatic Plants and Their Significance to Lake Fishermen

You will discover that plants in the lakes and streams are like the words in a book, revealing whether the water is rich or poor, and indicating what kind of fishing you have a right to anticipate. S. Gordon, *How To Fish From Top To Bottom* (1955)

Few waters are completely devoid of aquatic plants; in many cases they are present in great variety and vast quantities. The lake fisherman is, of course, familiar with many of them, having frequently paused to remove them from his fly. Occasionally the aquatic plants reciprocate by obligingly removing the fly from the fisherman's leader, thus sparing him the agony of once again stopping to strip away the weeds.

However frustrating this may be the angler is willing to subject himself to it knowing full well that there is ample reason for doing so. Aquatic vegetation frequently abounds with the food organisms continually sought after by foraging trout. Most aquatic animals upon which trout feed inhabit a wide variety of aquatic vegetation not merely to hide from their predators, but to feed as well. Numerous insects in their aquatic stage have been found to feed directly and extensively upon weeds. Ingenious methods of making use of these plants for complete life-history purposes characterize this insect-weed interdependency. So significant is the presence of abundant aquatic vegetation that many limnologists and seasoned lake fishermen feel it represents the very productivity of the entire lake. The greater the development of the larger aquatic vegetation the greater the biological productivity of the lake. There is no doubt that within limits the avid lake fisherman anticipates catching larger trout in those waters with the heavier weed growth, for it is those waters which have the greatest potential for harboring the greatest aquatic food supplies.

Aquatic plants can be loosely grouped into three general categories: emergent, floating and submerged. The emergent plants include those which are rooted in the lake bottom but which have portions projecting out of the water such as the common bulrush. Floating plants essentially lie upon the water's surface and may or may not be rooted to the bottom. Water lilies are representative of the rooted variety while certain duckweeds are representative of those floating plants which are unattached. Submerged plants, perhaps most important to the angler who should endeavor to seek them out and fish over or around them, include those such as the eelgrass which for all practical purposes are continuously under water. More complex classifications do exist, but they are of limited interest to the angler. Generally the normal development of submerged plants cannot take place at a depth where the light intensity is less than 2% or roughly ten to thirty feet. One feature of the larger aquatic plants noted and studied by many investigators is their tendency to be arranged in essentially parallel zones along the shorelines. The more protected a particular segment of shoreline is, the more likely that distinct zonation will occur. This phenomenon is of great value to the lake fisherman if he is aware not only of zonation but of the preferences shown by certain insects for specific types of weeds. If, for example, certain mayfly nymphs prefer a certain vegetation, the angler should position himself where he can continually present his imitation over that zone. Not only is this an area where free-swimming nymphs might be available to the trout, but during an emergence period this is the hotbed of cruising trout. To either side of the zone action would no doubt be less substantial. Such areas can be determined not only by witnessing hatching activity but by sampling the weeds with a small, narrow-mesh aquarium net.

The first zone consists of those plants which are rooted to the lake bottom but whose tops extend into the air. It can extend from the edge of the shore outward to a depth of approximately six feet and consist of cattails, bulrushes, reeds, wild rice and others. The next zone, which lies in deeper water beyond the first zone, is composed of plants rooted to the bottom but with an exposed portion floating on the surface of the lake. These plants may begin in very shallow water and extend lakeward to a depth of nine feet. Water lilies, pondweeds such as *Potamogeton natans*, and others characterize this zone.

The third zone, which lies in the deeper water beyond the first two zones, consists of the submerged plants including such varieties as the water weed, *Anacharis*, the pondweeds, *Potamogeton*, the eelgrass, *Vallisneria* and others. In general this zone extends to a depth of roughly 18 feet and often it forms large, dense areas of weed growth frequented by foraging trout. Because it may not be completely visible to the angler's scrutiny many will misjudge the nature and extent of its presence.

Depending upon the form and character of the lake and the basin it drains, overlapping of the zones may well occur. And because of the other factors such as wave action, certain zones may not exist at all.

As mentioned earlier, certain weeds inhabit specific zones within a lake and insects in turn inhabit certain weeds more so than they do others. The submerged aquatic plants are generally the most desirable to locate since the emergence of insects will occur above them where the angler can effectively present his imitation. Furthermore, it is in this sort of habitat that trout can be found cruising in search of free-swimming organisms either in search of food for their own use or simply dislodged by the disturbance of the foraging fish.

Of critical importance then is the ability to discern which weeds harbour the greater quantities of the insects sought after by the trout.

Various aquatic animals seek out specific weeds for protection from predators and because good footing is provided, a requirement for their own ability to successfully forage for food. In addition, some immature insect forms literally burrow into the plants for food and protection as well as merely rest on the plant's surface. As a general rule luxuriant plant growths with the greatest insect populations occur in the quiet, shallow waters of small lakes or in well-protected bays free from water disturbances caused by wave action or the use of outboard motors. Anglers should seek such areas out as one of their first steps in analyzing a lake fishery. Once found a sample of aquatic vegetation should be obtained to determine what organisms, insects in particular, inhabit that area. This information in turn is an excellent indication of which fly patterns the angler may choose to begin with.

P. Crispus

Myriophyllum

Potamogeton

Chapter Nine

Food Sources and Associated Fishing Strategy

The selection of the fly requires more judgement, experience, and patience than any other branch of the art. A. Ronalds, *The Flyfisher's Entomology* (1836)

The biological productivity of a lake, indicative of potentially quality angling, is, in part, the result of interaction of the multitude of aquatic organisms, and it may vary tremendously from lake to lake. Some lakes have been known to contain over 70,000 organisms in only one square meter of lake bottom! Others unfortunately contain only relatively few. It is the available food sources whose habitat is intrinsically tied to the chemical and physical makeup of a lake which ultimately produce a certain quality of angling.

In many lakes the aspiring angler would do well to first consider such factors as the average depth, the amount of submerged and rooted aquatic vegetation and the amount of permanent bottom fauna. These factors are interrelated in determining just how extensive the potential food sources may be. The more high energy food that is available to fish, the more likely that the lake can support a good population of large trout.

More than just a description of "food sources" is presented in the following chapters. Woven into the pages are critical insights into **food preferences, habitat** and **availability**, all very revealing pieces in the continuing watery puzzle of fly fishing lakes. A basic understanding of these critical factors will allow you to analyze and successfully fish almost any lake in the world.

Freshwater in general contains an extremely diverse array of organisms, with lakes harboring a variety frequently more extensive than rivers. Fish, as a result, often have a greater choice of food in lakes. These foods range from microscopic zooplankters such as cladocera and copepods, to the much larger and better known dragonfly nymphs, forage fishes and terrestrial insects which accidently become part of a lake's food supply. Except for isolated, local phenomena, fish in Alaska select from the same menu as fish in South America.

Generally, every food source and even specific species of aquatic insects require certain particulars for optimum survival. Learning to recognize these specific criteria will allow you to present an effective imitation in the proper area and to recognize the fishing possibilities and even to forecast the optimum fishing times of a lake!

Over the years we have been fortunate to fish a diverse array of lakes throughout the angling world. Those waters which offer outstanding sport always have one common denominator. They offer fish an abundant selection of food sources, or a mainstay food source, high in caloric value. It might be smelt in New Zealand, Pancora crab in Chile, salmon spawn and fry in Alaska, dragonfly nymphs in British Columbia or scuds in western America. Of hundreds of timberline lakes we have fished we cannot recall a single one which offers healthy fish over 15 inches *which does not contain scuds!*

Each lake will have its own "food print," but of the total number of available, or possible, food sources only a handful continually appear as the key food source in most lakes.

Food sources are presented in this book in their general order of importance to both fish and fishermen. This is our personal, arbitrary rating order and it is not based on any hard scientific data.

Midges are rated number one simply because of their great numbers and habitat diversity allowing fish to exist where they probably otherwise could not. However, we cannot recall observing a fishery sustained primarily on chironomids which offered oversized trout. Terrestrials are about equal to one another in importance as are mayflies and caddisflies. You will notice that most permanent organisms are rated at the top. Such organisms are available to trout 12 months out of the year, which is in sharp contrast to temporary organisms which during the winter months are usually composed of only very small individuals. Such organisms become important as food for fish in the spring when they are more fully grown and during times of emergence. Permanent food sources are often rich in calories and relatively easy to capture. The number of possible food sources is amazing in its length and diversity, but we will only concern ourselves with the most important ones, which include the following:

1. Midges, Chironomids, Mosquitos (Diptera)
2. Forage Fishes
3. Scuds, Crayfish (Crustacea)
4. Dragonflies and Damselflies (Odonata)
5. Leeches (Hirudinea)

6. Mayflies (Ephemeroptera)
7. Caddisflies (Trichoptera)
8. Terrestrials {Ants (Hymenoptera), Beetles (Coleoptera), Grasshoppers (Orthoptera)}
9. Eggs
10. Water Boatmen (Hemiptera)
11. Snails (Gastropoda)

It should be remembered that insects are divided into Orders, which are divided further into Families, then Genera and finally into individual species. Thus, when one speaks of Tricoptera, for example, one is referring to a multitude of species of caddisflies within that order, each varying somewhat in minor physical characteristics, size, color and choice of habitat within the aquatic community and ultimately perhaps in the manner in which they become available as food for trout. It is not necessary to learn each and every detail, but, obviously, the more you know the better you are. Broadly speaking one species of caddis looks like any other with the exception of size and color.

In the final analysis all that is required is that you be able to identify the food on which the trout are feeding — that is to say, that you know what it looks like so you can select an appropriate imitation and present it to trout in such a way that trout are convinced it is the real thing.

While the entire animal community living on or near the lake bottom has the potential to find its way into the diet of trout, only those organisms which somehow become available to trout ultimately will do so. Aquatic insects, like any other creatures, generally are well camouflaged for protection against predators. Unless they leave their protective housing or betray their presence by moving they often are difficult for trout to find.

From the standpoint of the angler in both lake and stream fishing one of the most important and fascinating topics is the manner in which various aquatic animals become "available" to trout as food.

1. Visually, by appearing at rest where trout may see and recognize them as a food source.

2. Fleeing in response to browsing trout in weeds or along the lake bottom.

3. General activities within their habitat which make them conspicuous, such as swimming from one location to another.

4. Emerging, or during that time when nymphs make their way toward the water's surface to change into winged adults.

5. Resting on or falling to the surface of the lake. This would include newly emerged or hatched insects resting on the surface prior to taking flight, returning egg-laying insects, or terrestrials which somehow find their way onto the water.

In general, it is when an insect emerges and makes its way to the surface or along the bottom toward shore that it becomes most available, not only in terms of numbers, but also in terms of vulnerability. If one were to correlate the number of food organisms available and the degree of difficulty associated with their capture by trout, emerging insects would represent the greatest numbers coupled with the least degree of difficulty to capture.

Hatches of aquatic insects such as midges, mayflies, caddisflies and damselflies can create periods of extensive availability and selective feeding. Certain lakes may have an unusual abundance of one or two organisms preferred throughout much of the season while others have a scarcity of most aquatic animals.

The general rule is to imitate those food sources which are most readily accessible to trout at any given time. Remember, however, that just because a particular food source is available does not necessarily mean that fish will be feeding on it. Don't conclude that such behavior occurs because "the fish aren't feeding." Feeding activity can be put off by any multitude of reasons. For example, the trout may simply be feeding on another food

Adult caddis at rest. R.K.

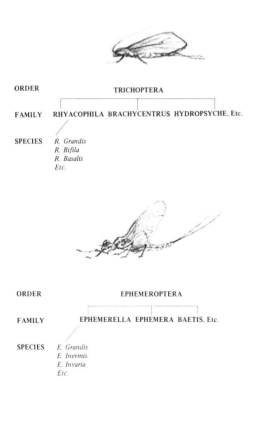

ORDER	TRICHOPTERA		
FAMILY	RHYACOPHILA	BRACHYCENTRUS	HYDROPSYCHE, Etc.
SPECIES	R. Grandis R. Bifila R. Basalis Etc.		

ORDER	EPHEMEROPTERA		
FAMILY	EPHEMERELLA	EPHEMERA	BAETIS, Etc.
SPECIES	E. Grandis E. Inermis E. Invaria Etc.		

source in another location, or on a food source that is not as conspicuous.

While availability plays the predominate role in determining what fish are feeding on, food preference must also be taken into consideration especially when there are multiple food sources available. While no one knows for certain, it would seem likely that when two or more food sources are equal in both availability and numbers that the largest food source will be preyed upon, for size is usually in direct proportion to calories or energy. From a survival point of view it makes little sense for trout to feed on emerging midges when large dragonfly nymphs are migrating along the bottom. Being highly sophisticated predators, fish are mainly concerned with obtaining the most food while expending the least energy.

Of interest to anglers in determining possible food preferences of trout is the following chart from a study of Castle Lake in northern California. The table lists the prominent food organisms in Castle Lake along with their respective calorie content per gram of dry weight. It also states the number of each type of organism required to produce a thousand calories.

ENERGY CONTENT OF FOOD ORGANISMS IN CASTLE LAKE

Food Organism	Calories Per Gram of Ash-Free Dry Weight	Number Per 1,000 Calories
Dragonfly nymphs	$5,514 \pm 285$	15
Beetles	$5,738 \pm 596$	26
Ants	$5,808 \pm 319$	70
Damselfly nymphs	$5,374 \pm 125$	85
Midge larvae/pupae	$5,542 \pm 104$	759
Caddisfly larvae	$4,409 \pm 871$	1,000
Snails	$3,484 \pm 229$	229

The above table reveals that one dragonfly nymph provides as many calories as roughly 67 caddisfly larvae. Unfortunately, the table fails to indicate which species are being compared; one species of caddisfly may vary tremendously in size and, hence, calories. Also, it fails to indicate whether or not mature species of insects are being compared. While the above data is far from conclusive and has many shortcomings, it does, however, remain of great value and offers a good insight to general and possible food preferences of trout.

Food preferences vary from one lake to another and with the time of year depending upon what food sources exist in the lake and which of those are more readily available. Trout concentrate on certain types of food which include the following:

1. Permanent subsurface organisms: scuds, leeches, minnows, etc.

2. Temporary subsurface organisms: midge and caddisfly larva and pupae, mayfly nymphs, dragonfly and damselfly nymphs, etc.

3. Surface organisms: Terrestrial insects (ants, beetles, grasshoppers) and adult aquatic insects such as mayflies, caddisflies, etc.

MIDGES (ORDER DIPTERA)

How often have you stood bewildered along a lake shore, changing flies in the dwindling twilight, frustrated and unable to entice a single fish even though the lake surface was covered with the widening rings of feeding trout? Chances are you have experienced this frustration and chances are equally good that whether you noticed or not, the lake surface was calm and littered with tiny, case-like nymphal "shucks," and perhaps numerous midge-like flies were resting on the water's surface. After a close inspection you were certain fish were feeding on the adult form of these midges . . . but

Adult midge at rest. John Goddard photo.

Lifecycle of a midge

Chironomid larvae

Chironomid pupa

were they really? A little knowledge of midge habitat and emergence characteristics will help overcome the frustrations of those all too common fishless evenings.

The order Diptera (which includes all two-winged insects) consists of mosquitoes, house flies, black flies, gnats, craneflies and hundreds of species of midges. A vast majority of Diptera are terrestrial in origin (not aquatic) and are of little value to fishermen. Of prime importance to fly fishermen, however, are chironomids. In an analysis of insect emergence from a small trout lake in Scotland, midge larvae numbered an astounding 16,047 per square meter at certain sampling sites. These figures compare to 1,069 mayfly and 108 caddisfly nymphs at the same sampling site. During this same study in April, 14 trout were found to contain 89 midge pupae per fish, with numbers varying from 28 to 174 per fish!

Another study on the food of trout in the Klamath River watershed in Northern California reported: "Chironomidae larvae and pupae contributed 41.8% by numbers of the organisms found and occurred in 80% of the stomachs examined."

In Strawberry Lake, Utah, it was determined that chironomidae pupae were found in 91% of stomachs containing food and were the most important item. In an Idaho sampling 670 chironomidae larvae and 730 pupae were found in a single trout. In another sampling two brook trout contained over 2,000 pupae between them.

Such statistics make it easy to understand why midges supply the largest number of food organisms for trout in lakes. Of all the aquatic insects which appear in lakes midges are certainly the most widely distributed and most abundant. Throughout the season hardly a day goes by without hatches of at least some species occurring sometime between dawn and dusk. All these factors combine to make midges the most important food organism for trout.

CHARACTERISTICS

Midge larvae are worm-like in shape and movement, their locomotion marked by sinuous undulations and crawling along the lake bottom and among weeds. The colors of larvae are diverse. The primary colors include black, gray, yellow, white, cream, ruby, amber, purple and all shades of green, olive and brown.

Waters which are alkaline and contain a good supply of dissolved oxygen often seem to contain many larvae in shades of green and brown. Acidic waters with little oxygen content contain reddish and purplish larvae. A

60   □   LAKE FISHING

species of red midge named *Tendipes* is common in many waters; the larva is often referred to as the "blood worm" because it is one of the few insects to contain hemoglobin.

Midge larvae all have nine segments. They usually measure between one-sixteenth inch or smaller to one inch in length. Appendages are few with a pair of short caudal fins on the first and last segments which facilitate swimming and several small respiratory protuberances along the body which somewhat resemble small legs. Larvae usually spend a year in the larval stage (molting four times) before they pupate and emerge into adults, although some species have shorter or longer life cycles.

Most midge larvae feed on small plants, animals and detritus. Detritus is any non-living organic matter, plant or animal, that has begun to be attacked by microconsumers. Some species, such as *Tanypodinae*, are carnivorous and swallow small prey. The larvae also feed by piercing the cuticle of other insects and sucking out the body contents. Many species known to be carnivorous also ingest algae and detritus.

HABITAT

Midge larvae being the most abundant of all bottom animals dwell in extremely diverse habitats. They are found in nearly every freshwater lake, pond, spring, slough, stream, bog hole, swamp and ditch on earth. Not all midge larvae are found in water, however; many species are found in mosses, dung, rotting wood, bases of plants and grasses. But these species are not aquatic and are of little or no value to the angler.

More than 5,000 species of midges have been identified, with large parts of Asia still virtually uninvestigated. In the Arctic alone, midges comprise one-fifth to one-half of the species in the insect fauna. Such statistics reveal to what extent other life forms in the ecosystem rely on midges, especially other insects and fish. It is the midges which mainly nurse tiny salmon to smolt size and send them toward the sea. Grayling continually ingest midges, certainly one reason they are such an eager quarry for fly fishermen.

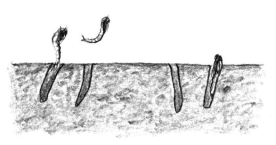

Many larva live below the mud-water interface

Most species or groups of midges prefer lake habitats to the extent that midge larvae often are used as indicators of different types of lakes. While certain species are characteristic of different types of lakes, species within a lake seek out and actually require specific habitats for survival. Types which are found in abundance in deeper waters are rare in the shallow shoreline areas, and vice versa.

Midges frequently can be found throughout an entire lake even at depths of several hundred feet. Under optimum conditions midge larvae may become as abundant as 20,000 per square meter (perhaps more), with counts of 2,000 per square meter being common.

While various species of midge larvae distribute themselves throughout the lake bottom at all depths the most important midge habitat is the shallow to moderately deep zone.

Except for some of the predacious species all midges build a larval case on or within the substrata on which they live. The case consists of particles from the substrata and is lined and held together with silk-like threads secreted by the salivary glands. The structure of the case varies with the genera and local environment. The carnivorous species *Lasiodiamesa, Corynoneurini* and *Tanypodinae* are believed to be free swimmers. These species move about freely seeking shelter from predators among bottom debris and weed beds.

From the moment the pupa leaves its protective case it can be captured

Most lake species of midges will be found buried in mud, sand and detritus, in algae, on rocks and in submerged weeds. The mud dwellers usually are the most common and construct "tubes" on or slightly below the surface of the mud, seldom ranging more than a few centimeters below the lake bottom.

Aside from the bottom-dwelling and free-swimming species, there are

High elevation lakes are noted for their often continual and prolific midge hatches. R.K.

some which inhabit aquatic vegetation. Midge larvae often will burrow or mine into aquatic vegetation for food and protection. Aquatic plants harboring large concentrations of larvae include *Nupharvarietgatum, Nuphara variagatum, Nymphaea odorata, Potamogeton crispus* and *Myriophyllym*. Some midge larvae will seek out particular aquatic growth while other species will be found almost anywhere. One ten-foot section of *Potamogeton crispus* was found to contain 970 midge larvae.

EMERGENCE

Midges emerge every month of the year where climatic conditions allow open, ice-free water, but the heaviest hatches occur from April through October with July and August showing a peak on many cooler waters.

There are two factors which most likely dictate the rate and time of emergence. These are *temperature* and the *length of daylight*. Though water temperature does play an integral part in emergence times, the number of daylight hours seems to dictate when, and even to what extent, midge pupae will emerge. As the number of daylight hours increases, so does the number of species hatching and the intensity of each hatch.

There are considerable differences in the emergence times of different species, which can be divided roughly into three groups:

1. Species which emerge in the period immediately following sunset.
2. Species which emerge during the period of high light intensity and maximum water temperature in the late morning and early afternoon.
3. Species which emerge more or less constantly during day and night.

Since midges populate virtually every area of a lake, they can emerge at almost any location. For example, species which inhabit deeper waters will be observed emerging over the deeper portions of the lake. At the same time it should be kept in mind that a substantial breeze can create considerable lake "drift" and carry the adults over shallow water and vice versa.

Prior to emergence all the energy required to complete the life cycle from the pupal stage through the adult mating period is built up in the larval stage because the adults, with few exceptions, do not feed. The pupal stage in which the insect develops the characteristics of the adult lasts up to a couple of weeks depending on conditions and the species. When the transformation is nearly complete a close inspection will reveal both the legs and folded wings of the adult fly. The wings may be seen through the skin in the vicinity of the thorax. The abdomen is slender with white breathing filaments protruding from the head, and small, whitish-lined caudal fins found at the tail end. The thorax of the pupa is bulky due to the formation of the wings and occupies one-third to one-half of the overall pupa length.

Before relinquishing its murky burrow the partly formed pupa will venture out of its home for short periods and wave its body about. Presumably this creates circulation of water around the insect and the whitish gills are able to assimilate a great deal of oxygen. Oxygen is a critical factor during emergence; it is believed that gases trapped within the pupal skin help split the pupal case so the adult insect can emerge.

After the pupa has nearly taken on the appearance of the adult it must shed its skin one more time before emergence can begin. During this penultimate molt the pupa can become trapped in its skin making it unable to swim to the surface. When this happens the pupa will become almost certain prey for other aquatic insects or for fish. This penultimate molting process may last anywhere from a few hours to a few days, again depending on conditions and species.

Once the molt is completed the pupa is ready to emerge at which time it must face the perils of open water. When the pupa reaches the surface film it is likely to remain there up to several minutes before completing its emergence into a winged adult. However, under hot, calm conditions with

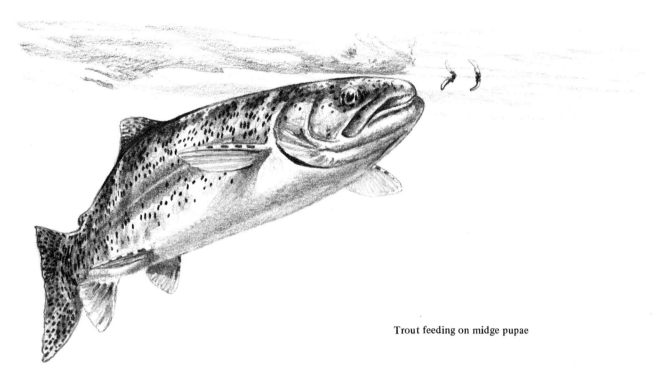

Trout feeding on midge pupae

a heavy surface film some species of midges may remain for two or three hours before breaking through to hatch. During this period the pupa either will swim back and forth with a strong wriggling action just under the surface or take up a vertical position with its head and filaments barely touching the surface film.

When the thorax of the emerging pupa splits down the middle the adult midge crawls out of its shuck and rests briefly on top of the water. If conditions are dry, warm and calm, the adult will be ready to fly in about ten seconds. If strong winds are churning up the lake the emerging pupa will hatch very quickly giving the trout little time to feed on them at the surface. Perfectly calm evenings will produce the largest midge activity as pupae become trapped under the surface film, granting trout easy access.

The appearance of adult midges should be familiar to most anglers. All are similar in appearance varying only in size and color. As a general rule the color of the adult also will be the color of the pupa. Adult midges are long-legged with bodies slightly longer than their wings which are mounted well forward, giving the insects a somewhat humpbacked appearance. Their wings are pale grayish to white in color and often are held flat over the body. Abdomens contain nine segments and the insect's overall length varies from one-sixteenth of an inch or smaller to one inch. Male adults have grayish-white "tuff" antennae splayed out from the head.

Most anglers can recall seeing small swarms of tiny, gnat-like insects hovering around shore vegetation and trees, disappearing with the slightest breeze, only to reappear as the wind dies down. Adult midges often are seen drifting lightly on the water's surface or "buzzing" in swarms, which helps them stay in position. Usually this phenomenon takes place at dusk or after dark but from time to time it occurs during midday. Large hatches may engulf whole buildings or spread out over several hundred feet.

The shoreward flight of the adult midge is governed by the direction of the wind. The selection of a favorable resting site for adult midges is related to wind and temperature. Humidity also is a main factor in selecting a resting site for adults; it is very important for the adult to avoid water loss, especially shortly after emergence when the body still is soft.

Swarms are almost completely composed of males, and females will enter them apparently for the purpose of selecting a mate. After a mate has been selected the pair will seek shelter in surrounding vegetation. The male usually will die within a day after mating has occurred but the female will live a few days longer while her eggs mature. At the time of egg maturation the female will return to the water's surface, preferring calm evening hours, and deposit her eggs which simply sink to the bottom thereby completing the life cycle.

AVAILABILITY

Midges become available to trout throughout the three stages of their life cycle — as larvae, pupae and adults. The larval form inhabits nearly the total lake bottom often in tremendous quantities. In relation to quantities of midge larvae available, however, trout make use of only a small fraction of the total.

In Castle Lake, northern California, midge larvae accounted for 83.8% of the total potential energy available to trout, but only a small fraction (5.8%) actually was utilized. This is due to the fact that the larvae seldom became available in large numbers because many larvae lived below the mud-water interface and were not subject to heavy predation.

The only chance trout have to feed on mud dwellers is when they venture out of their tube-like shelters which usually occurs during hours of darkness. Occasionally they will vacate their shelters to browse in weeds during the day when trout often feed upon them.

It is the weed dwellers, the species which live on bottom debris, and the free swimmers which constitute most of the larvae ingested by trout. Trout usually will take advantage of available midge larvae in the fall, and once again during the spring months. In the spring midge larvae are at their maximum size just prior to emergence and trout show a definite preference for the larger larvae. Also at this time of year the larvae frequently are outside their cases in preparation for emergence and are available to trout in fairly large numbers.

During summer months the larvae usually are neglected since fish are selecting more readily available emerging pupae which are available in astounding numbers. Exceptions to this trend occur in waters where an abundant selection of other food sources is not available. In such cases fish will feed heavily on larvae throughout the summer but select the pupae when they become available.

It is generally the emerging midge pupa which triggers the first real rise of fish in spring. It is also the emerging pupa which generally is the most important form of midge found in the stomachs of fish during both spring

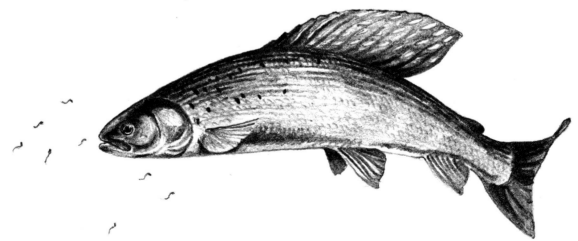

Grayling and midge larvae

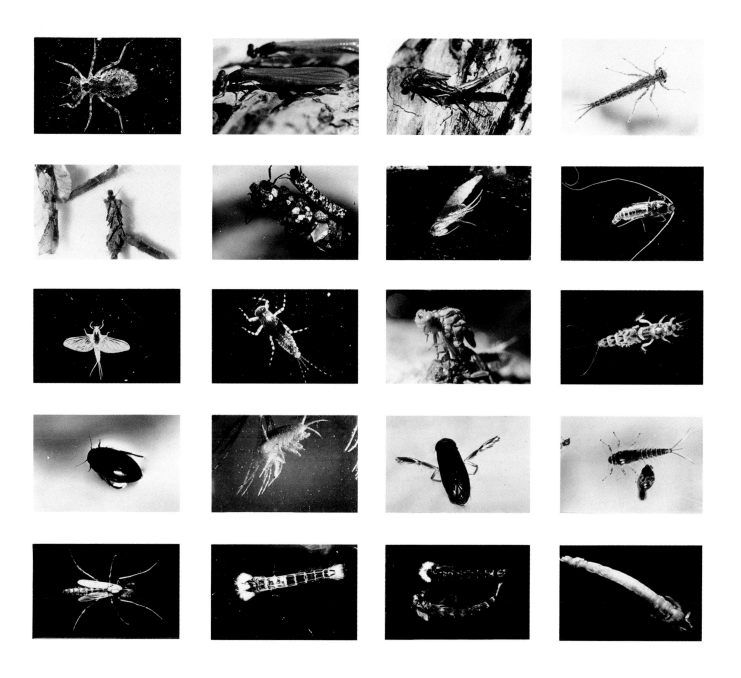

John Goddard photos unless otherwise indicated.

Row 1:   Dragon Fly Nymph (Libellulidae); Adult Damsel (Ceonagrionidae), R. C.; Emerging Damsel (Ceonagrionidae), R. C.; Damsel Nymph (Ceonagrionidae).

Row 2:   Various Case Making Caddis Larvae (Leptoceridae, Green Cased Caddis), (Limnephilidae, Leaf and Stick Cases); Caddis Larvae (In Stone Case), (Limnephilidae, Large Case), (Sericostomatidae, Small Case); Caddis Pupa (Swimming To Surface), (Unknown); Caddis Emerging From Pupal Case (Leptoceridae), R. C.

Row 3:   Mayfly Spinner (Caenidae, *Caenis*); Mayfly Nymph (Ephemerellidae, *Ephemerella*); Dragonfly Nymph (Gomphidae), R. K.; Mayfly Nymph (Ephemeridae, *Ephemera*).

Row 4:   Diving Beetle (Dytiscidae); Freshwater Scud (Amphipoda, *Gammarus*); Water Boatman Corixidae (Corixidae); Mayfly Nymph (Baetidae, *Baetis*)

Row 5:   Adult Banded Midge, Male (Chironomidae, *Chironomus*); Empty Pupal Case of Midge (Chironomidae, *Chironomus*); Mature Midge Pupa and Partly Emerged Pupa (Chironomidae, *Chironomus*); Immature Midge Pupa (Chironomidae, *Chironomus*).

John Muir Wilderness, High Sierra, California.

Grayling, southwest Alaska.

Lakes usually offer solitude, spectacular scenery and larger than average trout. Many productive lake waters will be found close to home, others across the planet. This pictorial reveals only a few of the many rewards enjoyed by lake anglers. (All photos by Randall Kaufmann unless otherwise noted.)

Rainbow, Lago Ranco, Chile.

Randall Kaufmann with 34 inch rainbow released back into small tributary stream of Lake Iliamna, Alaska. John Hickox photo.

Tom Judson, Mann Lake, Oregon.

Golden trout, Wind River Mountains, Wyoming.

Richard Henry, Crane Prarie, Oregon.

Jack Moore, Lake Taupo, New Zealand.

Jack Moore, Nonvianuk Lake, Alaska.

Lahontan cutthroat, Oregon.

Rainbow surface feeding on adult damsels, Idaho. Ron Cordes photo.

A typical Western America lake at sunset.

Mayflies, southwest Montana.

| Boatman/Backswimmer | Randall's Caddis Larva | Randall's Caddis Pupa | Soft Hackle | Emergent Sparkle Pupa | Diving Caddis |

| Stimulator | Elk Hair Caddis | Kaufmann Hare's Ear | Timberline | Timberline Emerger | Sawyer Pheasant Tail |

| Parachute/Paradun | Flying Ant | Callibaetis Spinner | Floating Nymph | No Hackle | Pale Morning Dun |

| Scud | Trueblood Otter | Mosquito Larva | Mosquito Pupa | Chironomid Pupa | Chironomid Adult |

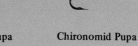    

| Marabou Damsel | Filo Plume Damsel | Randall's Dragon | Simulator | Threadfin Shad |

| Marabou Leech | Zonker | Crayfish | Woolly Bugger |

FLIES TIED BY RANDALL KAUFMANN

and summer months. In a survey of trout in Fish Lake, Utah, more than 90% of the midges were ingested while in the pupal state. This is explained by noting the secluded habitat preferred by most species of midge larvae, in contrast with the easy availability of the pupae over a considerable time. From the moment the pupa leaves its protective case on the bottom and rises toward the surface, until it is airborne, the pupa is running a good chance of being captured by trout and other predators.

The emergence process can last up to several hours; fish have ample time to ingest vast quantities of emerging pupae simply by cruising beneath the surface. Calorie studies show that it requires on the average 759 midges to produce 1,000 calories for a trout compared to only 15 dragonfly nymphs. From this data it is obvious that huge numbers of midges must be consumed by trout and indeed they are. During emergences you can enjoy outstanding fishing if the proper techniques and imitations are employed. Such techniques will be discussed shortly.

After emergence has taken place the recently emerged adult is ready to leave the water's surface in about ten seconds. Because of this time factor and the fact that other emerging pupae still are readily available, relatively few adult midges are ingested by trout — although in many lakes of the United Kingdom trout seem to prefer the adults.

Once airborne adult midges will not become available again until the female returns to the water's surface to deposit her eggs, unless a strong wind or rain forces the adults down to the water. Returning females can bring trout to the surface to feed.

MIDGE FISHING TECHNIQUES

Midges frequently are the most important organisms in a trout's diet. Except for isolated cases and unusual circumstances the midge stages — in order of importance to trout — are the *pupa, larva* and *adult.* Although the adult and larval stages of midges are consumed by trout, often in great quantities, the pupal stage receives the greatest attention. Consequently you should give it your greatest attention.

LARVAE

Midge larvae often inhabit lakes in huge numbers but even in those waters where they are prolific fish often show a preference for some other food source which may at particular times be more readily available. Thus, before considering the use of a midge larva imitation you should ask yourself if some other imitative food source might not be more productive. However, if you are fishing a lake where midge larvae are the predominant food source, which is often the case in high-altitude lakes, then you definitely should anticipate presenting a midge larva imitation.

The lift-off and settle techniques, when executed slowly will often produce when larvae are preparing to emerge. Larvae imitations fished along the bottom and designed to imitate burrowing species generally should be offered only during spring when trout frequently browse along the lake bottom or just prior to emergence.

The imitation of bottom-dwelling species will require an extremely slow crawl retrieve in conjunction with the sink and draw technique. The imitation is allowed to sink to the lake bottom and then is moved at the slowest possible speed. The fly is allowed to rest from time to time to ensure that it stays on or near the lake bottom. In this fashion the artificial will closely depict the motions of the natural larva moving about its watery domain. Be certain the line is always taut so delicate strikes may be detected.

The rise and fall technique will best emulate a free-swimming larva as it moves about. Be certain to retrieve the fly *very* slowly along shoreline areas.

The depth at which the fly is to be presented will determine what type of fly line and length of leader should be used. Knowing that midge larvae inhabit virtually every area of a lake you should be equipped with a selection of floating, sink-tip and full-sinking fly lines. Leaders generally should be six to 15 feet in length and since midge larvae imitations usually are comparatively small, light tippets, tapered to 5X or 6X will be most useful. If a quick penetration of the surface film is desired a slight amount of weight should be added to the fly. Keep in mind that strikes can occur at any time after the fly has penetrated the surface film so pay close attention for a delicate take.

Another effective technique, best executed from a boat when windy conditions occur on a lake and which is effective when free-swimming larvae are available, is simply to cast an unweighted imitation using a floating line and a 15-foot leader. Do not retrieve the cast, however. The fly eventually will settle below the surface and soon the rocking motion of the boat will impart the necessary action to the fly. You need only keep the line tight and pay close attention for a light, delicate pick up.

PUPAE

The angler who can successfully master the imitation and presentation of midge pupae will consistently take trout long after most other anglers have left the water in frustration. Midge pupae may be imitated by several deadly methods including the sink and draw and the dead drift techniques. Both are especially effective during an emergence of midges when the pupae are available in great numbers.

When fishing the sink and draw or the rise and fall technique you should use a very slow, steady retrieve with occasional pauses, allowing the imitation to rest and swim toward the surface in a long, ascending angle typical of the natural pupa. Strikes can occur at any time but generally trout will feed on pupae either near the lake bottom or close to the surface — seldom in-between. On occasion trout will take the imitation during the pause in your retrieve as the fly slowly settles back toward the bottom so be prepared!

It also is effective to present a pupa imitation to specific rising trout but in so doing you must either present the fly close to the trout as quickly as possible before the trout cruises away or swim your fly toward the surface in front of the trout. If no strike is forthcoming within a few feet strip in the line and cast again.

The dropper technique will assist in determining the trout's color

Grayling feed extensively on midge pupae. Jerry Swanson with a beautiful Alaska specimen. R.K.

preference and the preferred depth at which trout are feeding. The three pupae imitations may be fished dead-drift or they may be retrieved with very slight pulls and frequent pauses to simulate the slow rising and falling motion of the naturals.

When fishing a midge pupa imitation you should usually hold the rod tip perfectly still and devote complete concentration to the strike. The strikes seldom are dramatic, usually consisting only of a gentle sucking-in of the fly by a trout. For this reason you must watch closely for any sign of movement by the indicator fly or the fly line itself at the point where it enters the water. Frequently trout will accept and reject a midge imitation without the angler ever realizing it.

Dropper presentations are best during the early stages of the midge emergence, before trout have started to concentrate their efforts near the surface. During warm evenings when little wind is present the surface film often is heavier than normal and the emerging midges often have difficulty penetrating it. As a result pupae may hang in the film longer than usual. During such periods large concentrations of pupae build up just under the surface film and fish have an extended period of abundant feeding.

ADULT MIDGES

The adult stage of the midge is not nearly as important to fish as the pupal stage but winged midges occasionally are consumed freely by fish so it is necessary to have some insight into proper imitations and presentation.

Adult midges become available to trout immediately after emerging and when females return to the lake to deposit their eggs. The only other times these adult midges may be available is when they accidently become trapped in the surface film. You should thoroughly understand each of these situations in order to present a convincing imitation.

Those midges which remain on the surface for a long period before becoming airborne are most susceptible to feeding trout. Sometimes, when trying to become airborne, midges will fly low over a lake's surface trailing their long hind legs on the surface film and creating a small "V" wake behind them. When such behavior is observed you should use the skating or classic dry technique, presenting your imitation with a long rod, light fly line and a 15-foot leader tapered to 6X or 7X. A fly — especially a small one — always will appear more lifelike if it is fished from a light, soft leader. The reduced diameter and pliable features of a soft tippet allow the fly much more freedom of movement. A stiff, larger-diameter leader tippet tends to inhibit such movement. Such leaders also do not permit a natural rise and fall as the fly rests on the gently riffled lake surface. This is easily demonstrated by experimenting with one fly attached to a 7X leader tippet and another attached to a 4X leader tippet. Dangle the flies in front of you and observe which of the two bounces and dances in the most agile manner.

During the most opportune fishing periods and most prolific hatches the surface of the lake often is dead calm. A long rod and light line will help ensure a gentle presentation, an essential consideration when imitating adult midges. A longer rod and leader also will assist in skimming the fly across the water's surface and if a light breeze is blowing the fly can be skated or dapped over the riffled surface of the water in the manner of the natural. Be careful not to move the fly either too slowly or too quickly or there will be few, if any, strikes. Observe the speed and direction of the natural insects and attempt to duplicate these motions with your artificial.

When fish are feeding actively on adult midges you should cast to specific fish. Generally there will be such an abundance of adult insects on the water that "fishing the water" may prove disappointing.

Egg-laden females returning to the water's surface to deposit their eggs often trigger fine rises in the waning hours of evening or during the first light of morning. Females will alight gently on the water, deposit some eggs,

Female laying eggs

fly a short distance and deposit more eggs. Such activity can attract feeding trout in great numbers and you should present your imitation in much the same way as when attempting to imitate any other adult midge. Cast the imitation ahead of a cruising fish and allow it to remain motionless. Just prior to the point where the trout is likely to see your fly twitch the rod tip slightly. The motion will cause a tiny ring to spread from the imitation which may attract the cruising trout.

Swarms of midges sometimes become trapped in huge numbers in the surface film of lakes and often are carried about the lake by prevailing winds for days. Under such conditions they will become concentrated along feed lanes (foam lines) or deposited in vast numbers along windward shorelines. Remember, most of these adult midges are lifeless, often having been dead for several hours, and as a result the imitation should be presented in a corresponding manner. A partly submerged, lifeless imitation often will produce well and if it should slowly sink below the surface film so much the better. Fish often will see such isolated artificials and consume them readily. Imparting motion to an adult midge imitation usually detracts from its inherent fish appeal except under conditions described earlier.

You will need a large selection of adult midge patterns in several sizes and colors including some imitations of drowned adults. We suggest the Kaufmann Chironomid Larva, Kaufmann Chironomid Pupa and Kaufmann Chironomid Adult in sizes 12-24.

MOSQUITO (ORDER DIPTERA)

Before the snow has all melted and when fishing is often at its best regiments of mosquitoes rise up from slow streams, bogs and ponds in unbelievable numbers. Buzzing swarms can be devastating to humans and animals alike and have driven many early spring visitors back to lesser evils of civilization.

We have seen fishermen backpack ten miles to a campsite only to turn around immediately and retreat to the shelter of their car because of mosquitoes. We have even observed unprepared hikers running wildly down the trail close to mental collapse, their bodies covered with bloody welts! Once, in Wyoming's Bridger Wilderness, we counted more than 300 bites on the back and shoulders of a friend after he had spent a mere 30 minutes fishing in a light, long-sleeved shirt. Anglers visiting areas infested with mosquitoes must come prepared with head nets, gloves, tent, numerous containers of insect repellent and medicine to relieve itching and swelling.

It is little wonder most people consider mosquitoes a worthless insect but the lowly mosquito plays an integral part in reviving life in early spring. This is especially true in northern areas where mosquitoes provide food for the entire food chain at a time when the ecosystem needs a quick boost to snap out of its winter slumber.

Mosquitoes, like midges, belong to the insect order Diptera, which includes all insects having only one pair of wings. In scientific circles the mosquito is referred to as Culicidae.

ADULTS

Mosquitoes undergo a complete metamorphosis beginning as an egg and progressing to larva, pupa and finally into winged adult.

Adult mosquitoes have nearly cylindrical abdomens with ten segments, six legs and long, narrow, generally transparent black-veined wings. Male mosquitoes have a bushy plumose antennae. To many observers adult mosquitoes are difficult to distinguish from adult midges. However, adult

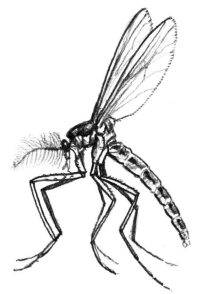

Male mosquito

Female mosquito

mosquitoes are easily distinguished from midges by the mosquitoes' habit of sitting with their hind legs in the air, while midges raise their forelegs — and do not bite.

All mosquitoes do not look alike. Indeed, they vary both in color and size. They usually range in size from one-eighth to one-half inch in length and you can be certain of encountering many swarms which will rate a size 10 hook! The most familiar color is the subtle black and white barred variety, but plain brown, buff, yellow and green-colored mosquitoes are all common. Many others are spotted or streaked with a wide range of colors.

Once, while driving along Crowley Lake in California, a tremendous hatch of unknown insects nearly obliterated the view out of the car's windshield. Stopping the car to clean the windshield and inspect the unknown insect phenomenon was a mistake for once outside we were mercilessly attacked by millions of pale green mosquitoes. That explained the boxes of green mosquito patterns we had recently observed in local sport shops!

Male mosquitoes do not bite. This is not because they do not want to but because their mouth parts are unable to penetrate human and animal skin. Male mosquitoes, however, will drink blood if offered to them or if readily available.

Most northern species of mosquitoes hibernate through the winter seeking shelter in attics, outbuildings or anywhere they can find protection and semidarkness. As many as 100,000 hibernating mosquitoes have been observed in a cellar measuring only four by six by seven feet! In the spring the females seek a suitable spot to lay their eggs fertilized the previous summer. Other species will mate, deposit their eggs and die in the same summer season. Females deposit 100 to 400 eggs on the surface of standing water preferably in areas protected from wind. Favorite areas include pools and ponds with lots of vegetation, especially lilies and algae, slow meadow streams, stagnant water and catch basins. Waters which are covered with "green scum" are usually avoided. Such waters are not conducive to mosquito propagation because the larva and pupa become entangled and drown in such scum. Mosquito eggs resist drying almost indefinitely and this accounts for the appearance of larvae in a pool freshly formed by rain or run-off in a place where there had been no water for perhaps months or even years.

LARVAE

Mosquito larvae are easily recognized by their minute worm-like bodies and slender abdomens of nine or ten segments. A prominent siphon, or respiratory tube, rises from the dorsal side of the eighth segment. Mosquito larvae have a disproportionately large head, a pair of prominent black eyes, short antennae, tufts of hair at their head and lateral tufts along their abdomen. Mosquito larvae have no legs so they swim or maneuver with vigorous body undulations. Larvae undergo four stages, the fourth stage disclosing the pupa, which, depending upon temperature, can be reached in seven to ten days. If the weather and water remain cold the transformation of the pupal stage will be greatly delayed.

PUPAE

The pupa differs markedly from larva in appearance. The head and thorax seemingly become one and are enclosed in a common chitinous sheath resembling a giant comma. Within this sheath the head can be distinguished along with legs and developing wings. The abdomen is fully moveable and when at rest it is curved under the bulky cephalo-thorax. The pupa no longer sports the rear respiratory tube but obtains air by means of two hornlike tubes which are located on top of the thorax area.

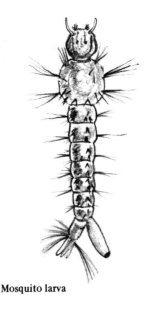

Mosquito larva

Mosquito pupa hanging in surface film

Mosquito pupa

The pupae are only slightly heavier than water and can easily rise to the surface by means of a rapid wriggling of the body from side to side. Pupae break through the surface film with their air tubes and rest with their bodies often sloping at an angle. Pupae spend their entire two- to three-day life span at rest hanging in this downward position just below the water's surface waiting for emergence time. When disturbed they will swim rapidly toward the bottom by means of violent abdominal contractions. They are extremely sensitive to light and will dart downward immediately if a shadow falls upon them. As actual emergence time approaches the pupa straightens out its abdomen allowing air to gather between the pupal skin and the newly forming adult. Due to the trapped air the pupa cannot swim very rapidly, descending with difficulty and rising much more rapidly to the surface. The pupa now appears silvery white in color and the entire thorax area of the mosquito will touch the water's surface. The actual period of transformation from pupa to adult is very short. The pupal skin splits at the thorax and the adult works itself out using the pupal skin as a float. Shortly thereafter the mosquito is poised for flight.

AVAILABILITY AND IMPORTANCE TO TROUT

Because of their short aquatic life and limited distribution in larger, well-aerated waters, mosquitoes play a somewhat limited role as a food source for trout. For the fly fisherman mosquitoes are important in small lakes and ponds scattered across North America, especially in the north woods. Here mosquitoes thrive virtually unchallenged by man and propagate in unbelievable numbers. Trout inhabiting such small waters gorge themselves on both the larvae and pupae but usually concentrate on the more vulnerable pupal stage. Feeding sprees usually last two to three weeks in the spring. Trout feeding in this manner will virtually ignore all other food sources. Thus it is very important to present a lifelike imitation.

The value of adult mosquito imitations is questionable; trout usually will avoid egg-laying adults, preferring more easily obtainable food sources.

Because midges and mosquitoes belong to the same aquatic insect order and are indeed very close in habits to one another, the same fishing techniques employed when presenting midge imitations are applicable to mosquito imitations.

PATTERNS

The Mosquito Larva, Mosquito Pupa and California Mosquito are all useful imitations. Common sizes are 14-18.

Mosquito Pupa

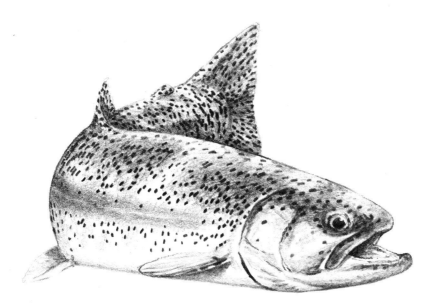

FORAGE FISH

In many waters small forage fish contribute a very significant part of the overall food intake of trout, especially larger trout. An August study of Paul Lake in British Columbia revealed that trout under ten inches consumed only six percent shiners by volume. For trout between ten and 14 inches the figure was 79 percent and for trout over 14 inches the figure jumped to 94 percent. The August shiner take was by far the most significant and predation the greatest on hot, clear days when the lake was calm and exceptionally clear. During this time the sun's reflection off the silvery scales of shiners was clearly visible at 25 feet and perhaps even further. The study concluded visibility seemed to be a strong reason for such predation.

Fishing streamers is quite effective for imitating all types of forage fish yet it is probably one of the most underrated aspects of fly fishing. The basic elements of successful streamer fly fishing include an understanding of the particular forage fish inhabiting a lake and an understanding of where and how to best present an appropriate imitation. Such an imitation must act lifelike and be similar in size and color to the natural.

Keep in mind, however, that trout do not always attack a small fish out of hunger. Sometimes they attack out of aggression or curiosity. When such is the case the retrieve should be calculated to make the imitation look like a terrified fish attempting to escape a predator. Such frantic motions often trigger the instinctive, aggressive response of large trout.

Your rod tip can be used to great advantage when fishing minnow imitations. You can dart and swim an imitation or change its direction with simple movements of the rod tip. Rapid stripping also will impart necessary movements to your fly. Remember that smaller fish are capable of quick, erratic bursts of speed, ready at any time to take evasive action. Work your pattern in the same manner — fast, slow, up and down, keeping it moving and turning constantly. Dart it around cover, such as rocks, logs, weeds and snags.

Each time you use your rod tip to impart motion to the fly you create a bit of slack line. This slack should be gathered in quickly with your stripping hand. Be certain to cover the water thoroughly and alternate the depth of your retrieves.

When you are fishing lake inlets where a strong current is present a very effective technique is dead drifting a minnow imitation downstream into the lake. This technique often requires a long cast and stealthy approach to avoid spooking any trout which might be facing upstream into the current.

When fishing larger inlets a boat or float tube is helpful. Anchor your boat well back from either side of the incoming current and cast your fly as far upstream as possible, allowing your fly to swim downstream in full view of any waiting trout.

Another technique employed by steelhead and Atlantic salmon fishermen is the greased line method. In this presentation a floating line is used and the fly is cast quartering upstream. The fly is allowed to drift downstream sideways to the current and slightly below the surface of the water. When a fish is hooked lead it away from the area you are fishing to avoid alerting other fish.

Perhaps the easiest method of covering an inlet area with fish imitations (streamers) is to take position along the shore but well back from where the stream enters the lake. Begin with short casts gradually lengthening them until all the water has been covered. Present your fly from both sides of the inlet stream and even from midstream itself if possible using both floating and sinking lines. Allow your fly to cross the current, rise, fall and swim over any drop-off. In lakes with fluctuating water levels drop-offs occur at the end of a "deposition bar," the outlying buildup where silt is dropped during high water periods. Often large trout will be present just off the bar for safety, cruising in to feed in the shallows and you may have to be patient, trying a variety of presentations until you come upon the right one.

On occasion a very long sinking line will have to be paid out in order to reach trout. This technique paid off for us in Chile one memorable fall morning at the boca of Lago Ranco. Scattered low clouds skirted the mountains exposing remote Andes summits protected from visitors by dense foothill vegetation. Filtered sunshine turned the wandering river bottom at the inlet into a fairyland of misty riffles and hidden pools. We began probing the unknown waters of Lago Ranco with Marabou Muddlers, our minds continually wandering to the distant hillside farms tended by men and oxen. Two hours passed without a bonafide strike but we were certain that large trout were lurking beyond the drop-off, so we continued experimenting. Besides, we were stranded there until the shuttle boat returned for us.

While we relaxed along the shore a local fisherman appeared and cast a heavy spoon into the current. His reel consisted of nothing more than a rusty tin can with some heavy monofilament wound around it. He used no rod but, using his arm, the visitor cast and allowed the lure to sink beyond the deep drop-off for perhaps a minute before beginning a quick hand retrieve of the line. Moments later a silvery, arm-long rainbow began a series of salmon-like leaps toward a distant island, the bright spoon plainly visible hanging from its lower jaw. There was little doubt that this fish had taken on the bottom — apparently we had not been reaching the proper depth. Wading into midstream we paid out our shooting heads, 200 feet of running line and many yards of backing and still the underwater currents of Lago Ranco tugged for more. The second effort produced a rainbow identical to the trout the native angler had just lost. The strong rainbow grudgingly gave up after a series of reel-screaming runs. After a few photos we gently placed the eight-pound trout back in the current and held it there to assure it would revive and regain the strength lost in battle. Soon the beautiful fish turned and headed back into the depths from which it had come.

From time to time you probably have noticed crippled or sick minnows swimming in a dazed manner close to the surface. Such fish will drift and falter, occasionally summoning strength in an attempt to swim, only to exhaust themselves, keel over to one side and drift helplessly away. These injured fish offer an easy meal to trout so keep an eye open for trout feeding at such times. Should you witness such an event present your imitation immediately either directly beyond or to either side of the surface disturbance. Chances are good the trout will attack your streamer. The skating technique is useful under such circumstances and the wind drift is also of value.

Kurt Zahner, Lago Ranco, Chile. R.K.

Blacknose Dace

Sculpin

Many times, particularly late in the day and during hours of darkness, trout will invade shallow areas where huge concentrations of forage fish assemble to feed. Trout dash into these schools, pick out a minnow, chase it down, then turn their attention to another minnow. Such action is commonplace in many New Zealand lakes where smelt comprise the main diet of rainbow and brown trout. In waters where large numbers of smelt are available it is common for trout to gain two to three pounds per year. Lake Taupo, located on the North Island, is the mecca for anglers wishing to fish the smelt run. When smelt are in the shallows trout are not far away. On many occasions we have observed three to five-pound trout pursue schools of several thousand smelt in shallow areas, the smelt erupting in terror-stricken panic across the surface of the lake as trout slash through their ranks.

In Paul Lake, B.C., researchers have observed trout swimming in from open water at a depth of about 15 to 20 feet. It often was possible to identify individual trout by marks, scars or injured fins. The trout would characteristically swim slowly under a school of shiners and then swim off out of sight into open water causing no apparent alarm on behalf of the shiners. Soon, it would return at the same depth but with far greater speed. Once near or beneath the school the trout would rise toward the surface. It was during this rise that the shiners would disperse and leap out of the water. The trout would follow them to the surface and there would be two clearly audible splashes in close succession as if the trout had thrust very vigorously with its tail. While at the surface it would engulf one or two shiners.

At times a trout would chase a shiner over the surface for 15 feet before capturing it. Then the trout would dive and return to deeper water.

In all cases observed the trout appeared to be pursuing individual shiners rather than attempting to catch one at random by rushing through the center of the school. Typically, trout came to the surface at the edge of the school rather than in the center of it. Around the fringe of a school there would commonly be five to ten three- to four-inch shiners that were less active than the others and somewhat isolated from the main group. These shiners were the victims of predation. In this particular instance trout did not stun one or more shiners with its tail, then turn and engulf the injured prey. This same sort of feeding phenomenon probably occurs in trout lakes containing any silvery schooling fish. When trout attack in this fashion it is generally with force and conviction for they realize that to be successful they must hit the minnow with sufficient force to capture it. Your imitation, moving at a fair speed, coupled with the speed of the trout closing quickly to intercept it, can produce some rod-shattering results.

Brook trout inhabit many lakes and ponds across North America and are known for their almost continual appetite. R.K.

Matuka

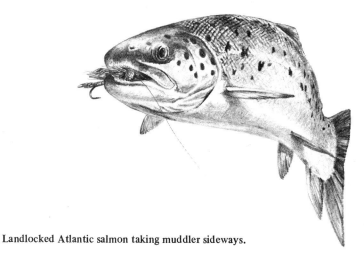

Spruce

Use a floating line when fishing the shallow areas. Skipping the streamer across the surface is a good technique to attract trout to your area. Another similar attracting technique is to lunge your fly toward the surface by lifting the rod tip and pulling in line with your retrieve hand allowing the fly line to create the disturbance.

Keep in mind that when trout are feeding on forage fish in this manner some specialized techniques may be required to set the hook although if you smash down the hook barb and sharpen the hook your chances of solidly hooking a fish will improve immensely. Once we were fishing rather over-sized streamers in an Oregon lake in hopes of enticing some of the large brookies known to inhabit the lake's weedy areas. Morning mist was rising from the lake's cool waters and shimmering in the frosty dawn, nearly obliterating the volcanic cone of a mountain rising 4,000 feet above the lake. In the eerie mist the reed-lined shore of the lake seemed locked in perpetual secrecy but we knew that huge brookies and bullet-shaped landlocked Atlantic salmon were searching the shoreline for food.

We were anchored a long cast from the reeds. We began casting our streamers toward the shoreline, retrieving them quickly near the surface, away from the reedy snags. We both had jolting strikes almost immediately but neither of us hooked up. Our barbs were filed down and we had sharpened our hooks only moments before so we were rather puzzled why we both missed the fish. This frustration continued for another hour and a half. At that time we risked spooking the fish and stood up in our boat to peer toward the weeds where most of our strikes were occurring. The early morning glare was now off the water and our polaroid glasses easily cut the reflection from the surface of the water. A few casts later the puzzle was solved. Salmon were attacking the fly sideways carrying it off much like a dog would a bone. By paying close attention to our flies and lines we could easily judge when our flies were being attacked. A simple twitch of the rod tip at right angles to the line easily hooked the fish. Once the puzzle was solved we settled back for a fantastic, action-packed morning during which we wore out half a dozen Muddlers and lost twice that many on the menacing reeds — but it was well worth it!

The lure and wait technique is an interesting one which we find invaluable, especially in lakes which contain large trout which often act more curious than hungry. This technique has saved the day for us on many occasions and should be attempted whenever you notice fish following your streamer imitations toward shore.

Be inventive and experiment. We know of anglers who will fish a nymph dropper and streamer point fly. This can perhaps look like a minnow chasing a nymph. A greedy fish might decide to eat both of them.

Landlocked Atlantic salmon taking muddler sideways.

Not all streamers are tied and fished as exact imitations. Many patterns are attractors or patterns which do not represent any particular fish, but which still command the attention of trout, perhaps appealing to their curiosity or natural aggression. Studies have shown that streamer patterns dressed with some red around the throat produce much better than the same patterns without red.

The color of streamers can be very important in relation to light and water conditions. Bright colors fished near the surface, especially in bright sunlight, lost very little of their color-reflective properties. The greater the depth, however, the less light there is to pick up such bright colors and some colors become nearly invisible in zones with very little light perception. Ernie Schwiebert, in his book *Trout*, presents a very enlightening chart which depicts subsurface color wavelengths. Black and purple are most visible; even in very low light they project a visible silhouette. As a result, if you are fishing under a dark, cloudy sky or at twilight, a black fly will be most visible to trout. A simple test of this is to hold a light-colored fly and a dark-colored fly up to the sky. You will readily observe that the dark fly stands out markedly while lighter colors lose their silhouette against the light sky.

When you wish to fish a streamer deep you can use either a sinking line, a floating line, a heavily weighted fly, some split shot a foot or two above the fly or a combination. Weighting the fly extremely heavily can nullify much of its natural swimming action especially if it is not being retrieved very quickly. Furthermore, in the case of weighted marabou streamers the heavy body will separate quite a distance from the more buoyant wing, and when a trout grabs the fly it invariably mouths the wing, not the body. Thus, while strikes may be felt you will experience difficulty hooking the trout. If you do weight a marabou-style streamer be certain to place the lead wire as far forward on the shank of the hook as possible.

The construction of streamer flies has much to do with their action in the water and their fish-catching abilities. Consider using a 36620 or 9575 Mustad hook for all but the smallest of imitations. Both are 6X long, limerick-bend hooks with either a turned down, loop, or ring, eye. Both hooks give you the length needed for a minnow imitation along with a narrow hook gap thus eliminating the likelihood of hooking trout through the eye, a common problem with weighted wide-gap hooks. The 9575 loop eye assures a strong, smooth leader connection, and there will not be any rough edges to saw through your leader when you are playing a large trout. They are also a joy to tie with.

The position of streamer wings is very important to the streamer's effectiveness. A wing positioned low over the body will provide more action during a slow retrieve. A high wing is better for a fast retrieve or when fishing fast inlet water. Streamers also should be dressed sparsely. A fly dressed in this manner will not only penetrate the water more easily but will react and come to life much better than a bulky, heavily dressed fly which also tends to be more buoyant. Sometimes such subtleties as a gently swaying motion imparted to the imitation will attract fish while the same pattern encumbered with too many materials will not draw any attention.

Streamers should have a minnow-like shape tapered toward the tail. A fly constructed in this manner will swim and breathe in a very lifelike fashion and subsequently produce more trout. Whatever streamer pattern you choose before you start to fish it try gripping the leader a few feet above the fly and draw the fly through the water the same way you intend to retrieve it. If the fly tilts to one side it may be weighted wrong, improperly constructed or not tied properly to the leader. Tie it on again making sure the leader has been straightened, stretched and is not twisted. A tilted streamer simply does not look realistic.

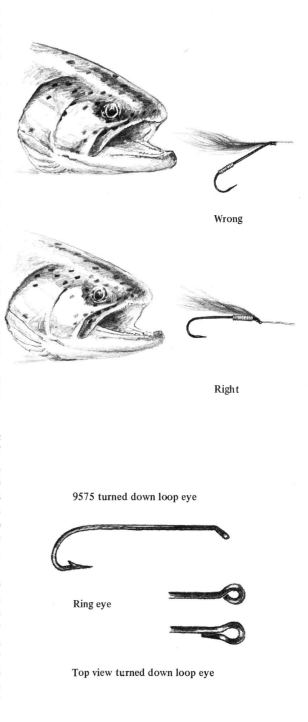

Wrong

Right

9575 turned down loop eye

Ring eye

Top view turned down loop eye

We like to use a Turle knot. This knot will allow the leader to be an extension of the hook shank because it is secured *behind* the eye and exits *through* the eye. This knot is very effective for all styles of fishing and is the only knot we use except in the case of a ring eye hook where a swivel or Duncan loop is used.

Always keep in mind that bait fish can be roughly divided into bottom dwellers and open water school fish. Bottom dwellers usually are smaller and swim more slowly while depending upon concealment for protection. School fish usually are fast swimmers depending upon large numbers and speed for protection. As a result in creating an imitation of the correct color, size and shape, tying materials and methods must be chosen to approximate either the more clumsy, less active motions of bottom dwellers, such as sculpins, or the swift motion of more open-water school minnows such as threadfin shad.

The following streamer patterns are of value to the lake fisherman and a selection in sizes 2 through 10 should be stocked in your fly box: Muddler Minnow, Sculpin, Spuddler, Spruce, Matuka, Threadfin Shad, Dace, Roach, Chub, Royal Coachman.

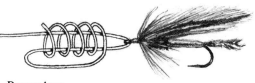

Duncan loop

Finished Duncan loop

Turle knot

THREADFIN SHAD

Closer to home threadfin shad provide angling thrills similar to New Zealand smelting. Fish feed heavily on prolific threadfin shad throughout the year but spring and fall provide best surface action.

We had arrived at Lake Berryessa one fall morning, assembled our float tubes and paddled out into the lake towing a comfortable casting length of line behind us while watching for the sudden appearance of trout feeding on surfacing threadfin shad.

Soon a small school of shad surfaced about a hundred yards from us, moving away quickly. Several good-sized trout slashed at the edges of the school picking up stragglers. Unfortunately, we were no match for their speed even with swim fins and float tubes and the school soon faded into the distant ripples and disappeared. Chasing schools of shad can be tiring, exasperating and fruitless but we paddled on in the hope of locating another school.

Suddenly a boiling school of little threadfin shad erupted in front of us with several large trout in quick pursuit. As the panicky shad approached we cast our imitations into their midst and rapidly stripped line to imitate the motion of the darting shad. Almost immediately we were fast to leaping trout. Meanwhile, the school of shad continued on a frantic collision course with us suddenly exploding and swirling about in a hasty retreat from both us and pursuing trout. After a few exciting moments it was all over. The school had passed leaving two wet, grinning float tubers to land and gently release two beautiful brown trout.

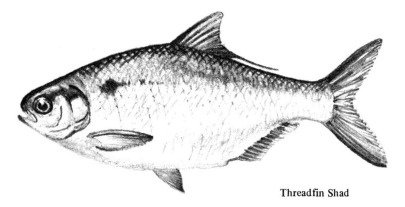

Threadfin Shad

Threadfin shad do not always travel with such reckless abandon and often you are able to stay within casting distance for a greater length of time. Trout bold enough to rise from the security of the subsurface depths in pursuit of shad frequently are of good size and attack on the run so use 3X or 4X tippets and be prepared for bone-jarring strikes. Your imitation should have a silvery appearance that is best obtained by using silver mylar tubing to construct the fly.

Many lowland reservoirs were plagued for years with very poor fishing for a variety of reasons. Such impoundments usually became quite warm in the summer and fluctuating water levels discouraged good insect hatches but recently many state agencies have started planting threadfin shad in an effort to provide fish with a substantial and reliable food source. In most cases the introductions seem to have been extremely successful at least as far as fishermen are concerned. All predatory fish species gorge themselves on these silvery morsels and during peak feeding periods large fish will ingest a few hundred at a time.

Threadfin were introduced to the lower Colorado River system of impoundments in the 1950's. Two initial plants of about 1,500 shad were made and within 18 months they had multiplied and spread from Davis Dam all the way south to the Mexican border and even into the Salton Sea.

Lake Powell, Utah, that unfortunate impoundment which destroyed the finest desert wilderness in North America, received a plant of threadfin shad a few years after it was filled. Accurate records were kept as to the size of the trout before and after the shad became established. The results were amazing. Rainbow trout averaged 14 inches in length before shad were introduced and 19 inches after the shad were established. The increase in the weight of rainbow trout was even more dramatic. Before shad were introduced the average weight of a rainbow was roughly 26 ounces. One year later the average weight had increased to 59 ounces.

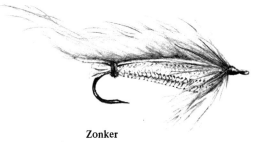

Zonker

Once successfully planted shad often virtually replace all other food sources in the diets of fish. This was the case in Lake Powell where for all practical purposes the shad formed nearly 100 percent of the trout's diet. In an impoundment on the Feather River in California, it was found that rainbow began feeding on shad when the trout were only eight to ten inches long and their reliance on shad had become extensive by the time they reached a length of 12 inches.

HABITAT

Threadfin shad are widely distributed throughout the United States, particularly in the warmer southern states. A high mortality rate occurs at temperatures below 45 degrees. Waters less than 50 feet deep are preferred and the shad like to hang out in the vicinity of currents or over and alongside smooth objects such as rocks and dam walls. They also seek out steep banks but avoid brushy areas. Threadfin shad do not do well in crowded spaces but thrive in large waters.

CHARACTERISTICS

Their appearance is silvery in color with occasional black spots. Under ideal conditions they grow quite rapidly, as much as an inch per month, until they reach a length of three inches. After that their growth rate tails off rapidly. Two-year-old fish usually are a maximum of four inches in length although some reach seven inches.

Shad are a school fish sometimes moving about in groups numbering in the tens of thousands. Such schools appear as silvery black clouds in the water ranging from one or two feet in diameter to more than several yards across.

Spawning usually occurs in the spring when the water warms to between 60 and 70 degrees. The females lay between 6,000 and 12,000 eggs in open water near shoreline vegetation or around obstructions. With high water temperatures the eggs can hatch in just a few days. Very few threadfins survive to spawn twice but those that hatch from the spring spawning can spawn in the fall. Under optimum conditions biologists claim that three generations can be produced in one season.

PATTERNS

When retrieved properly almost any silvery minnow-type imitation of the proper size will produce fish. The Zonker, Hornberg, Threadfin Shad and various Matuka-style flies are some of the better patterns available.

Threadfin Shad

CRUSTACEA

Crustaceans are permanent organisms of the lake spending their entire lives under water and frequently supplying the primary food source for trout throughout the year. Crustaceans are hatched from eggs, grow into adults, mate and die without ever leaving their underwater domain. They often are readily available to trout as a key food source and thus are of great importance to anglers.

SCUDS (Amphipoda — *Gammarus* and *Hyalella*)

Scuds belong to the order Amphipoda of the class Crustacea. Within the order Amphipoda are several genera the most common being *Gammarus* and *Hyalella*. *Hyalella* are difficult to distinguish from *Gammarus* except for their smaller size. *Gammarus*, however, can be distinguished from other scud genera by its first antennae which are longer than the second pair. However, it is doubtful trout can tell the difference. Since the two genera differ little visibly, we will refer to both simply as scuds. Many anglers use scuds as an indicator of the quality of fishing in a lake; such waters usually support many other high-energy foods. Lakes containing a good population of scuds usually support exceptional populations of large trout. All our "secret" golden trout lakes throughout the Sierras and the Rockies contain good populations of scuds as do nearly all the famous trout lakes of the West including the legendary Kamloops waters in British Columbia.

Waters containing scuds often produce fast-growing trout and lakes stocked with fingerling trout in the fall may produce fish in excess of a pound by the following spring. In some waters trout will gain more than two pounds per season! Because of the number of lakes containing scuds and the quality of fishing often encountered in such lakes we rate the scud third in importance to the midges as a food source for trout and first from the angling standpoint of producing nice, well-conditioned fish.

Hyalella and *Gammarus* often are found in the same waters including small lakes, ponds, seeps and springs which offer a wide range of aquatic

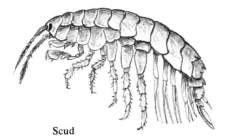

Scud

vegetation such as chara, elodea and watercress. Both genera also seek out stones, gravel, dead leaves, detritus, debris and moss for cover and for food. *Hyalella*, however, can tolerate wider chemical and temperature variations than *Gammarus* and is, therefore, more widely distributed. *Hyalella* thrives in both acid and alkaline environments of either cold or warm water while *Gammarus* prefers relatively cold waters.

Scuds cannot tolerate polluted waters and since they prefer shallow shoreline areas they are seldom able to prosper in reservoirs with widely fluctuating water levels. Often the first three feet of a lake will harbor the largest concentrations of scuds but they commonly are found in large numbers to 20 feet. Beyond a depth of 20 feet scud populations drop off drastically.

Despite the wider distribution of *Hyalella*, *Gammarus* is perhaps the more important of the two primarily because of its larger size. Typically, *Gammarus* will range in size from one-third to one inch in length while *Hyalella* seldom reaches lengths greater than one-third inch.

We have observed scuds in waters from sea level all the way up to 12,000 feet. Many of the known scud species inhabit subterranean environments such as caves, wells and seeps. This may explain their shyness toward light and their tendency to seek shadowy, dark areas during daylight hours. All scuds display this preference for darkness and great numbers of scuds usually can be observed feeding in the shallows at night, migrating downward into the shadowy depths of weeds beds as daylight approaches.

We approached a typical high-elevation lake one morning long before the sun had climbed over the steep talus cliff to the east. A careful approach to the shoreline revealed several fat golden trout feeding on scuds at various points along the tundra-lined shore. The very instant the sun appeared on the water both scuds and goldens vanished into the ice-blue water.

When disturbed during daylight hours scuds instinctively swim downward not only for protection but to avoid bright light. During overcast days and early or late evening hours scuds can be observed swimming and darting along lake margins.

Scuds are omnivorous feeding on small invertebrates and assorted vegetation. They are extremely prolific with some species being known to produce 20,000 offspring during their fertile season which lasts from about April to December. During this time, *Gammarus* can produce offspring every ten to 15 days! Scuds may populate lake bottoms to the extent of 2,000 individuals per square meter. Populations of 4,000 per square meter of bottom are not uncommon and Hot Creek Fish Hatchery in eastern California once reported a population of more than 5,000 per square foot!

Gammarus pulex is a species especially well-suited to high mountain lakes since it can tolerate both muddy and rocky bottoms characteristic of such lakes. *Gammarus* has even been reported in a lake in Tibet. We have sampled several hundred lakes throughout the West and simply by picking up a handful of aquatic vegetation it is frequently possible to count a couple of dozen scuds wriggling about.

Male scuds generally are larger than females. When mating, males carry the female underneath them, sometimes for days until the female is ready to lay her eggs. Such activity can easily be observed throughout the mating season.

Scuds commonly are found in many different colors including grays, browns, olives, tans, creams and combinations of all the above. *Hyalella* sometimes is bright green, opalescent blue or even bright red, although in all our observations we have seen very few of the latter color. Some anglers have reported seeing them frequently in British Columbia waters.

The abdominal gills, by which scuds breathe, often are mistaken for legs. The actual legs, however, are located along the underside of their bodies and at the thorax. The front legs are used for climbing and grasping while

Randall Kaufmann and Steve Peeters camped at a favorite High Sierra lake, elevation about 11,500 feet. R.K.

the appendages located under the belly behind the thorax are predominately used for jumping and swimming. Scud bodies are somewhat curved and are enclosed in a hard exoskeleton which they outgrow and change during their growth much like aquatic nymph "molts." While the very nature of their bodies seems curved or humped scuds generally swim with their body *completely outstretched*. At times scuds swim steadily for some distance usually heading for some type of shelter or visible food source. At other times they swim aimlessly for a few inches, settle, then rise in an upward motion or dart rhythmically in various directions, sometimes in a very erratic manner.

SCUDS AS A FOOD SOURCE FOR TROUT

Because of their ready availability, great numbers and high caloric value, trout often forage eagerly for scuds especially during winter months. In many waters trout subsist almost entirely on scuds during the winter, putting on weight throughout this normally lean time. In waters rich with a multitude of aquatic insects trout still will rely on scuds for up to 50 percent of their food intake. In many waters scuds are an important food item during the summer as well, except during times of prolific insect emergence or when some other food source is more readily available. Henry's Lake is a classic example of trout alternating between various food sources depending upon availability. Sometimes the trout ignore scuds for two to four weeks only to switch back suddenly to a steady diet of scuds. Yellowstone Lake in Wyoming is another example of a scud lake which produces excellent angling, an example which we verified during a trip to Yellowstone Park.

Rising before dawn we walked through the crowded campground amid several hundred sleeping people. Cutthroat trout were the reason we were up so early. Soon we rendezvoused with four other fly fishermen at the boat dock. Within five minutes we were gliding across a quiet, deserted Yellowstone Lake, the largest high-elevation body of water in North America. Our destination was the Southeast Arm of the lake where several secluded streams flow in.

An osprey suddenly appeared out of a fog bank making its way toward Steamboat Island, its talons tightly gripping what seemed to be a 14-inch trout. We watched until it faded into the distance, our thoughts quickly turning to cutthroat trout which according to the skipper were only 60 minutes away.

Yellowstone Lake can provide excellent fishing just about anywhere along its 300-mile shoreline but we wanted to explore a little-fished section along the wild east bank. Having fished the lake several times before we knew what to expect. In fact we curtailed the after-dinner drinks the night before in favor of tying an extensive selection of scud imitations spanning several color and size possibilities. Actually, *Gammarus pulex* is the predominant scud found in Yellowstone Lake but we hoped to do a little experimenting on other lesser-known waters for the balance of the week so we took the opportunity to tie a good supply of six dozen scuds.

The other fishermen in our group were less informed and while they were accomplished fly fishermen only a few minutes of fishing were needed to determine who had the right pattern. In less than 20 minutes two of us had released six brightly-colored cutthroat between 14 and 18 inches while the other four fishermen had not had a strike! Fortunately, we had tied up enough patterns for all. During such times trout can be extremely selective, not only to the degree of accepting only scuds, but only a scud imitation of a certain color and size! The degree of selectivity can best be demonstrated by the fact that a rainbow-cutthroat hybrid once taken from Henry's Lake had nothing but *Gammarus pulex* scuds in its stomach — 473 of them. Such selectivity can and usually does change from day to day and week to week.

On this particular day the cutthroat of Yellowstone Lake were demanding a size 10, 1X long olive-gray scud, slightly weighted and fished with a slow, steady hand-twist retrieve.

Since scuds vary their swimming characteristics you should experiment with several retrieves at various depths and with different color and size combinations until the right combination is found. This may sound difficult and time-consuming, but scuds actually are rather simple to fish effectively because of their abundance and availability. Generally you stumble quickly onto the right combination or one that produces reasonably well. The best approach is to check to see what color and size scuds are most abundant in the water you intend to fish and begin from there. During bright daylight concentrate on shadowy areas along weed beds, around rocks and anywhere a shadow might be present. We have found that a very slow, hand-twist retrieve is most consistent. Often a relatively slow, steady retrieve interspersed with frequent stops and quick, short movements will produce well, as will short, smooth pulls which simulate the steady swimming motion of the scud. You should cover the intended fishing area with casts placed a couple of feet apart around an imaginary clock face. This method of covering the water should be employed whenever you are "probing" or "fishing the water." By utilizing this method you can effectively cover all the water and intercept any cruising trout.

The spacing of your casts should be determined by water clarity. The cleaner the water the better the trout's vision, hence you might space your casts ten or even 15 feet apart. Such tactics will allow you to cover water quickly while allowing every trout a view and not spooking fish with too many casts. Less clear water or dim light may require casts only two to three feet apart and perhaps even a darker colored, larger fly and a slower retrieve.

Almost all of the subsurface techniques described earlier are applicable to scud presentation. Lakes which contain an abundance of aquatic growth usually are best fished with an intermediate or floating line, the length of the leader being determined by the depth at which you wish to present your pattern. Normally a nine to 15-foot leader will be ideal as you will be fishing water no deeper than 20 feet with masses of weeds growing up from the bottom. When you need to present a scud at a depth deeper than about seven feet, we suggest you use a sink-tip line. The floating section of a sink-tip line usually will allow you to reach the greater depth while preventing entanglements with dense bottom vegetation. A sink-tip or sinking belly line can be used to fish a wide variety of depths, the depth being dictated by how long you allow the line to sink and by the length of your leader. Deeper waters, or adverse wind conditions, may require a slow-sinking line. This will allow a longer presentation at the desired depth. When fishing a sinking line and slightly weighted scud you probably will want to shorten your leader to three to nine feet.

Clockface cast should extend in half circle in front of angler, thereby covering all the water.

A shallow British Columbia lake produced this fat brookie for Ed Delatte. R.K.

R.K. Scud

Keep in mind the preferred habitat of scuds when presenting an imitation. Work it over springs, dense weed beds and in shallow water. When fishing over submerged weed beds it is best to present your imitation just above or to the side of the weeds. To be certain your fly is just above the weed bed use the countdown method of retrieve described earlier.

Drop-offs also are good places to present a scud imitation since the shallow water is fine habitat for scuds and fish feel secure when deeper water is close at hand. Trout feeding on scuds often cruise in from deeper water, swallow a few scuds and then retreat for a minute or two into deeper water. The best approach for presenting a scud imitation under such circumstances is to cast your imitation into shallow water and slowly swim it into the deeper water. A boat or a float tube will be necessary for this technique but if neither are available cast your fly over the drop-off, allow it to sink, then slowly swim it along the bottom over the lip of the drop-off. Most of your strikes will occur at or near the lip.

Once while fishing such an area a member of our party was hooking fat brook trout on almost every cast. Though we all were using the same pattern, same type of line and the same retrieve the rest of us were not getting any action. It soon became apparent that the successful angler was allowing his fly to sink an extra ten seconds just as the fly approached the drop-off. We estimated the fly sank about two feet in that time and the extra depth meant the difference between success and failure. Don't be afraid to experiment and observe other successful anglers. If they are catching fish and you are not there often is no more than some very subtle reason for the difference.

SCUD IMITATIONS

Most scud or "shrimp" imitations available in sport shops today are poor representations at best. The ever-present wildly curved "pink" shrimp commonly sold for a shrimp or a scud imitation is not very effective. This dressing probably came into existence through some tyer's observation of fish-market shrimp. Scuds do have a natural tendency to turn tan or slightly rosy in color when dead and they sometimes turn an orange-tan when propagating, but we have not seen any bright pink ones. Scud patterns generally should not be tied with a drastic curve to the body. You will do much better presenting a "swimming" scud. When swimming, these prolific little creatures are completely stretched out and it is at this time that scuds are most freely ingested. For special effect a slightly elongated body or very slight curve wouldn't hurt, but nothing approaching the exaggerated half-circle patterns which have been perpetuated over the years.

If we were to count all the possible fly patterns in use today we would not find time to fish. Every fishing area in the world (and even most anglers) have their favorite patterns and everyone is constantly searching for the one "killer fly." We are of the belief that the more realistic the fly in regard to size, shape, color and lifelikeness, the more fish you will deceive. Rather than carrying a scattering of various scud patterns, for instance, we carry one or perhaps two patterns in about five sizes and six colors. Such a selection will usually allow us to cover the spectrum of scud species relatively well almost any place in the world. The fly patterns we mention throughout this book are our current favorites. Do not short yourself on flies, or, for that matter, on anything else. Fly fishing can be frustrating enough without adding to your difficulties by being ill-prepared. You are on the water to enjoy yourself so make things easy — be prepared for almost any eventuality.

Once the pattern has been decided upon you only need to be concerned with the proper size and color and that will be determined by what is present in the water you are fishing. Scud patterns should have a fur body picked out along the underside to simulate legs and gills. Imitations usually have a smooth, well-segmented back and very short rear appendages and antennae. Scud patterns may be weighted or unweighted. We recommend the Scud and Trueblood Otter in sizes 8 to 18.

Trueblood Otter

CRAYFISH

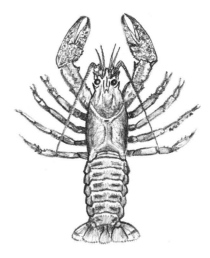

Crayfish also belong to the order Crustacea, the most common crayfish being classified in the genus *Cambarus*. Most anglers familiar with inland waters have seen these elusive freshwater inhabitants at one time or another. Crayfish are the freshwater counterpart of the lobster and they use their pinchers for protection and for grasping prey which includes insects and plant life. Primarily a scavenger, crayfish will attempt to devour anything left unattended on the lake bottom.

Those crayfish which are wary enough to survive a year or two may reach an overall length up to five inches although two to four inches is average. They have five pairs of legs with the front pair actually functioning as pinchers. Young crayfish, up to two inches in length, are easily imitated and no trout in its right mind would turn down such an offering.

Crayfish lurk in dark, sheltered places. They are rusty brown to orangish in color and are capable of quick bursts of speed, often creating a cloud of mud in their haste to reach shelter or elude an attacker. Imitations should be presented along shoreline areas, weed beds, bottom debris and particularly around roots and snags. Allow your pattern to sink to the bottom and retrieve it very slowly, making every effort to keep it on the bottom. A sinking line is best for this type of presentation. From time to time foot-long bursts of speed will serve well to imitate a startled crayfish and hopefully will attract the attention of a nearby trout. Four to six-foot leaders tapered to 2X and 4X are well suited for presenting such imitations.

Some of the best brook trout fishing in the country is in the state of Maine and one of the most effective patterns for big brookies is a crayfish imitation. Since crayfish are nocturnal, dawn and dusk are when they are most vulnerable.

There is one special technique for fishing a crayfish imitation called "mooching." In using this technique concentrate your efforts on steep, rocky banks, casting a sinking line and weighed fly. Let the fly settle to the bottom. Then, combining a pull of the line hand with a big sweep of the rod, start the fly off the bottom with a violent burst of speed (mimicking the spurt of a frightened crayfish). Follow this with three or four quick strips and then let the fly sink again. This procedure is repeated until the retrieve is finished.

Strikes often come while the fly is sinking so pay close attention.

Patterns we recommend are Crayfish in sizes 2 to 10.

DRAGONFLIES AND DAMSELFLIES (ODONATA)

The large order Odonata includes two suborders, Anisoptera (Dragonflies) and Zygoptera (Damselflies). These aquatic insects are two of the most conspicuous groups to be seen around inland waters, especially lakes, although many species frequent streams as well.

Even the most casual observer can hardly fail to notice the quick, erratic flight of the amazing adult forms of these insects as they dart in an incredible aerobatic fashion in search of food. Their two sets of wings operate independently of one another, allowing them to turn at right angles, hover and reverse direction instantly. Their iridescent blues and greens look rather out of place in nature's scheme of normally subdued insect colors but they do add a welcome sparkle to a warm summer day.

DRAGONFLIES

Dragonflies have changed little over the millenia and at first glance the aquatic stage, the nymph, appears to be well armored and rather menacing. Abdomens are much wider than the head. Three very short, flat appendages are found at the tip of the abdomen. Six legs originate out of the thorax and the eyes are rather large but always narrower than the widest part of the abdomen.

Nymphs range in size up to two inches. One unique feature of both the dragonfly and damselfly is the lower lip, or labium. The labium is able to reach out beyond the body to grasp prey. Another interesting feature unique to the dragonfly nymph is its ability to propel itself through the water by means of a water jet system. Water is taken through the anus for breathing, but when necessary it can be ejected forcefully as an effective means of propelling the nymph up to five inches in one burst.

DRAGONFLY HABITAT

Dragonflies are most abundant in slow streams and lakes where aquatic vegetation is lush and the water alkaline and comparatively warm but they may be found just about anywhere where there is adequate water for their simple existence from lowland bogs to alpine tarns.

There are two basic types of dragonfly nymphs, the mud dwellers and the weed dwellers. The mud dwellers include burrowing nymphs whose legs are fashioned for digging and whose siphon-like tails enable them to breathe while buried beneath the mud. Also included in this group are the bottom dwellers. These particular dragonfly nymphs have long, spider-like legs and flat abdomens which allow them to slip under or lie flush with rocks while still maintaining a firm hold. Their colors which vary from light to dark chocolate brown provide excellent camouflage allowing them to go unnoticed by their predators.

The weed dwellers, however, differ considerably from the mud dwellers. Their comparatively slender bodies and longer legs are designed for climbing and their colors range from light sand and yellow to several shades of green, depending on the surrounding fauna. During the molting process the species *Anax* even will change colors to match its last surroundings. Most species have superimposed mottling ranging anywhere from dark brown to black depending upon the particular species. The weed dwellers especially require pure waters for survival. They expose their heads and thoraxes to the air. Other individuals literally poke the tip of their abdomen above the water.

Dragonfly nymphs often seek out river inlets, drop-offs and shallower areas of lakes where they frequently may be found among exposed roots, sticks, rocks, vegetation and other debris. Weed-inhabiting nymphs are commonly found clinging to such aquatic plants as *Elodea* and *Cerato-phyllum*, particularly where the main stems fork. Often they hang head downward, providing a wide-angle view of the lower lake domain while still maintaining concealment.

It is here in the aquatic jungle that the stealthy dragonfly nymph lies in wait for its prey. Occasionally it actually stalks its victim but more often than not it simply waits for an unsuspecting organism to come within striking range.

FOOD SOURCES OF DRAGONFLY NYMPHS

The appetite of dragonfly nymphs is nearly insatiable and they are not particularly selective in their choice of food, requiring only that it be alive and moving. They will attack and devour virtually anything they can get within their grasp including small fish fry and even their own kind, if possible. This cannibalistic nature probably is a safety valve for survival of the species when rapid population growth occurs in a confined area.

The nine to 18-month life span of the nymph is spent catching and digesting such aquatic organisms as fish fry, scuds and the larvae of midges and mosquitoes. Under ideal food conditions a nymph seldom moves more than a few centimeters for days, relying heavily upon its camouflage and labium for close-in food gathering, usually feeding at a distance no greater than its body length. In the absence of sunlight, dragonfly nymphs often head for deeper water.

DRAGONFLY EMERGENCE

Dragonfly nymphs emerge each month of the angling season until frost occurs in the fall. They are most abundant during the months of May through August, depending upon local weather and water conditions. The burrowing species leave their shelters and begin crawling toward the shoreline. Once there they crawl out of the water and attach themselves to a

Mud dweller

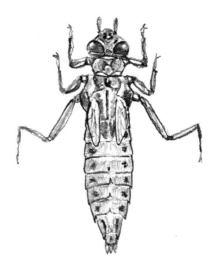

Weed dweller

A dragonfly completes its metamorphosis in meadow grass. R.K.

Dragonfly adult

Lake Dragon

solid foundation, including anything from rocks, roots and plants to floating debris. The weed dwellers emerge by crawling along submerged stems and leaves, sometimes for several minutes, until the water's surface is reached.

The spectacle of the dragonfly's metamorphosis from the nymph to the adult form is fascinating but seldom seen. Upon emerging from the lake the nymph grasps a solid object very firmly and remains motionless for up to a few minutes while its nymphal case dries. When the sunlight has penetrated the nymphal case sufficiently a split occurs just behind the head. At this time the back of the adult fly pushes its way out. Then the head, legs, wings and finally the long abdomen are freed. After emerging it takes about an hour for the adult to completely unfold its wings, fully extend its abdomen and gain the necessary strength to fly into its new environment. During this entire period the young adult is extremely vulnerable to birds and other predators. Fortunately, the brilliant colors associated with dragonflies do not develop until later in life.

Adult dragonflies are much larger than damselflies and occasionally have a wing span of up to six inches. The appearance of the adult dragonfly is more massive than delicate. Their wings are held horizontally in repose, sometimes tilted up or down. Their legs are crowded together under the thorax and are not used for walking but form a sort of basket to catch insects in flight. They have even been known to go from flower to flower while eating bees. Many believe dragonflies to be one of nature's most efficient hunters.

During mating the males are extremely territorial often driving off all smaller intruders. After mating the female returns to the site of emergence and either deposits her eggs in the water or in the fiber substance of aquatic vegetation. When depositing eggs in the water the female flies low over the surface periodically descending to the water where she simply drops her eggs. In some instances the female crawls beneath the water and attaches eggs to subsurface vegetation.

DRAGONFLY AVAILABILITY

Fish seldom have the opportunity to feed on dragonfly nymphs. Though they are available throughout the year their stealthy nature and usually small numbers keep them fairly well protected from foraging fish. It is during the time of emergence when the nymphs are crawling toward the water's edge that trout are most able to take advantage of their availability. Even though there is seldom active feeding on the nymphs, this is not meant to imply that trout will turn down a properly presented imitation. Quite the contrary. Rainbow trout in particular are extremely opportunistic feeders and find it difficult to turn down a well-presented dragonfly nymph imitation. Brook trout also enjoy "cruise feeding" and respond similarly.

There is no question about the nutritional value of dragonfly nymphs. The number of nymphs required to produce 1,000 calories for a trout is only 15, thus making dragonfly nymphs one of the most energy-rich food sources available.

The adult dragonfly seldom is easy prey for trout but on two occasions we have seen trout leap out of the water to bring down an adult dragonfly in flight. We have witnessed two to four-pound brook and rainbow trout gobbling migratory dragonfly nymphs in water so shallow that their tails were often exposed as they turned downward to feed. Such action is common in the more fertile waters of the West and British Columbia. Dragonfly nymphs inhabiting Tasmania's Lake Pedder migrate just under the surface toward shoreline areas much like a damselfly does. Such migrations provide wild surface action on browns from two to ten pounds.

Dragonfly nymph patterns should be tied in sizes 2 to 10, 3X to 6X long hooks, in assorted colors. A few recommended patterns are Lake Dragonfly, Assam Dragon and Randall's Dragon.

DRAGONFLY FISHING TECHNIQUES

Most aquatic insects including the dragonfly nymph, rely heavily on camouflage for protection and the motionless dragonfly nymph often goes unnoticed. When alarmed, however, the dragonfly nymph ejects water from its posterior orifice in order to propel itself in short, rapid four to six-inch spurts. This unusual trait, in sharp contrast to the nymph's slow, bottom-walking gait and frequent motionless periods, can be put to use by an angler since it generally represents the manner in which the dragonfly nymph is most likely to be seen by a trout.

The sink and draw in conjunction with the count-down technique are the best to employ. After your imitation sinks to the bottom give a light twitch to the rod tip imparting a slight movement to your imitation. This short, abrupt motion often will kick up a puff of sand or silt along the bottom, or create a slight but revealing movement alerting nearby fish to the location of the imitation. On the assumption that a nearby fish has seen and perhaps approached the imitation the angler should retrieve the fly with a series of sharp four to six-inch strips. With luck the fish will respond by attacking the imitation. This technique is very effective when used in combination with pauses that allow the fly to sink again to the bottom where the whole process is repeated.

Dragonfly nymph imitations are generally weighted although this depends on the hook size, water depth and fly line being used.

When dragonfly nymphs are active over or within aquatic weed beds near the water's surface a floating line with an unweighted fly often will prove effective. Under such conditions the sink and draw technique, incorporating a variable retrieve, should be tried.

Due to the size of dragonfly nymphs and because such imitations often entice large fish nine-foot leaders tapered to 3X or 4X generally should be used. Water clarity, fish size and weight, the size of the imitation and hazards presented by underwater snags will further dictate the size of the leader tippet. The strike itself may be extremely forceful or it may simply seem as if the fly has come to an abrupt halt in the water. You should remain attentive and watch the fly line at the point where it enters the water for any slight movement indicating a strike. The rod tip should remain at or slightly below the surface of the water to avoid a slack line which makes soft strikes difficult to detect.

DAMSELFLIES

At first glance adult damselflies are similar in appearance to adult dragonflies, but there are several distinct differences. When at rest a damselfly folds its wings together over the top of its abdomen. The damselfly also is much smaller and more delicate in appearance than the robust dragonfly.

The nymph of the species varies in size from roughly one-half to one inch in length with a very thin, streamlined body and a thorax area only slightly larger in diameter than the abdomen. All damselfly nymphs have three distinctive blade-like tails which serve as gills and which are about one-fourth the overall length of the nymph. The nymph has six legs tucked under the thorax area which are adapted for climbing.

The damselfly nymph also has an extendable labium which allows these fragile-looking but efficient predators to reach out for prey in the same way as the more aggressive dragonfly nymph. When swimming the nymphs move with a rhythmic wiggle swimming from side to side with a grace only nature could provide. Their side-to-side wiggle ceases only when the nymph stops to rest. When resting occurs in mid-water the nymphs either settle slowly toward bottom or spiral downward. These nymphs, like chameleons, tend to change their colors to blend into their chosen environment. Colors vary from browns to greens with olive being most common.

Randall's Dragon

Assam Dragon

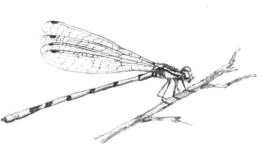

Adult damselfly

HABITAT

Shallow, spring-fed lakes with a good deal of aquatic vegetation and alkalinity often support huge populations of damselflies. In Parvin Lake, Colorado, it was calculated that there were over 2,500 damselfly nymphs per square meter at a depth of only one meter. Damselfly nymphs frequently are attracted to cool inlets and are prolific in some slow, unpolluted streams which offer proper feed and cover. They are seldom bottom dwellers but instead spend their underwater lives among the weeds.

Any sizable quantity of damselfly nymphs requires dense aquatic vegetation, with *Potamogeton Crispus, Potamogeton Richardsonii, Myriophyllum* and *Elodea Canadensis* providing the most sought-after habitat. Floating "mats" of *Elodea* also support dense populations of damselfly nymphs. It is not uncommon to observe "rafts" of adult damselflies skimming, resting and mating over floating weeds. They will often number in the thousands. If an environment is conducive to good damselfly nymph populations, closely examining a handful of weeds should be quite revealing. Damselfly nymphs require pollution-free water and an abundance of oxygen.

FOOD SOURCES OF DAMSELFLY NYMPHS

Damselfly nymphs, like dragonfly nymphs, consume huge quantities of living prey. Thus their chosen habitat also must harbor large quantities of other aquatic life. Crustaceans, midges and mosquito larvae are favorites of the damselfly but they will consume almost anything. Under less than ideal conditions damselflies will devour their own kind.

If required, damselfly nymphs will stalk through their weedy environment relentlessly searching for food but they prefer to remain motionless and let the prey come to them. Their natural coloring blends well with their surroundings and it is merely a matter of time before some unsuspecting prey happens along.

Damselfly nymphs are clearly a high-energy food source for fish. It takes roughly 85 damselfly nymphs to produce 1,000 calories.

DAMSELFLY EMERGENCE

Damselfly nymphs have an average life span in their underwater domain of three to five months and two to three generations are produced each year. Peak emergence occurs between May and July depending on local conditions. Peak emergence will generally last a couple of weeks.

When the time of emergence is at hand the damselfly nymph swims slowly and vulnerably to the water's surface where it crawls out on weed growth protruding above the water. In the absence of floating weeds, exposed rocks or trees or when wind and wave action submerge the exposed plants, the nymphs will migrate toward shore, leaving themselves unusually susceptible to predatory trout. The nymph sheds its case in the manner of the dragonfly and the adult emerges.

After mating has taken place egg-laying females deposit their eggs by dropping them onto the surface of the water thereby allowing the eggs to sink to the lake bottom or by crawling down the stem of an aquatic plant and depositing the eggs in the fibrous plant tissue. The cycle begins anew with the subsequent hatching of more damselfly nymphs.

DAMSELFLY AVAILABILITY

It is during emergence when the damselfly nymphs are swimming slowly toward the surface and the shoreline or crawling along the lake bottom toward shore, that they are most vulnerable and fish feed upon them in

Adult damselfly. R.K.

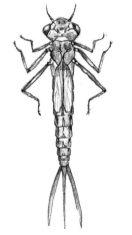

Damselfly nymph

large numbers. To underscore their availability, damsel nymphs in Henry's Lake accounted for seven percent of the cutthroat's food intake during June and 92 percent during July when their annual migration takes place. As many as 1,445 damselfly nymphs have been found in a single trout during such migrations! We once walked a 50 yard stretch of shoreline on a small Idaho lake, and counted over 50 rainbows each facing shore in about 2 to 3 feet of water. They were waiting for damselfly nymphs to leave the nearby submerged weed beds and cross the 5 feet of exposed, rocky lake bottom where they would be easily captured. When one considers that such large quantities can be consumed in a very short time the importance of the damselfly emergence and the selectivity with which trout feed on them becomes apparent.

DAMSELFLY FISHING TECHNIQUES

Damselfly imitations are employed under a variety of circumstances. The most productive involves the nymph stage either during periods of migration prior to emergence or during the daily movement of naturals among the weeds.

Damselfly nymphs for the most part prefer shallow areas of lakes in and among aquatic vegetation but also are found occasionally in deeper weedy water particularly in the spring and early summer. Anglers have reason to present damselfly nymph patterns throughout the entire shallow water zone of a lake with productive depths ranging from roughly 30 feet up to and including the surface film itself. Depending on current conditions all subsurface methods of presentation can be effective.

Depending upon the depth at which the damselfly nymph is to be presented and keeping in mind that the retrieve will be a slow to moderate one the choice of fly line is very important. The rate at which the line sinks must be balanced against the rate at which it is being pulled back toward the surface in order to ensure that the fly remains at the desired depth.

When probing the deeper habitat frequented by damselfly nymphs fast-sinking and extra-fast-sinking fly lines generally are employed with nine-foot leaders tapered to 5X. The leader tippet will vary according to specific conditions including water clarity and pattern size. Clear water and smaller patterns require more delicate tippets. The retrieve should be around or just above the weeds.

When casting damselfly nymphs over known submerged weed beds the imitation should be allowed to sink to the very top of the submerged vegetation. In this manner the slowly-moving imitation will appear to have just begun its pre-emergence migration or to be simply moving about among the aquatic vegetation, depending upon the type of fly line being used. With a slow-sinking or floating line, the fly will rise slowly as if migrating toward the surface or toward shore. An imitation leaving its aquatic habitat frequently is quite conspicuous and attracts the immediate attention of nearby fish often provoking a savage strike.

If damselfly nymphs are concentrated in very shallow water as they often are just prior to emergence a floating line should be used in conjunction with a nine to 12-foot leader.

No retrieve will exactly imitate the seductive wiggle of the natural damselfly nymph but a retrieve imitating the slow to moderate speed, the direction and the occasional motionless, sinking periods of damselfly nymphs usually will deceive fish. Introducing an occasional erratic motion to the retrieve sometimes can provoke a strike. Perhaps this sudden motion captures the trout's attention and momentarily separates the imitation from the multitude of naturals. Keep this technique of deliberate variation in mind when fishing the damselfly hatch and experiment until you hit upon a retrieve that gets results.

The principal technique is simply a succession of short, slow, one-inch

Large trout are attracted to the high energy content and availability of migrating dragon and damselfly nymphs. This 7-pound rainbow was captured while feeding over submerged weeds. R.K.

Extensive aquatic vegetation is usually synonymous with good populations of dragon and damselflies. Pictured is Agency Lake in Oregon. R.K.

Drowned timber can provide good emergent sites for damselflies. Here anglers cast among snags at Quake Lake in Montana. R.C.

Marabou Damsel

pulls of the fly line coupled with regular pauses. When applicable, retrieves always should be executed in the direction of migrating damselflies which is usually toward floating weed beds or shoreline vegetation.

If you are fortunate enough to happen upon a surface migration of emerging damselflies you should be prepared to cast to fish working a specific area. Select rises that produce the largest swirls; these frequently are created by the largest fish. The artificial should be cast within the ring of the swirl immediately after the fish has made its presence known. Large fish seldom travel very far when feeding under conditions of great abundance. If your offering is presented quickly fish are often looking downward and the surface rise disturbance helps camouflage your offering.

Upon casting to the immediate vicinity of a rising fish you should be ready for a strike shortly after having commenced the retrieve. If no strike occurs after the fly has been retrieved a few feet and no other rise form has appeared within the line of your present retrieve it is best to pick up the line and make another cast. When picking up your fly line in preparation for another cast do it smoothly being careful not to spook any fish in the area.

A long line is best picked up with a water haul, which simply entails loading the rod by using the resistance of the water before the back cast is made. This technique builds up immediate line speed thereby allowing the angler to cast to another fish without wasting time false casting to work out more line. The water haul is executed as follows: Gently strip in line until a comfortable casting length of line is left on the water. Point the rod tip down toward the water and with your line-retrieve hand strip in all slack. Pick up the fly line by lifting the rod tip toward the ten o'clock position while at the same time stripping in a long haul of line. Carry through with the back cast and the water haul is complete. No false cast should be necessary and a long forward cast is ensured. It should be remembered that such a cast will probably spook any fish in the immediate area of the fly line hence the water haul is best used when casting behind you or in a much different direction.

While fishing Crane Prairie Reservoir in central Oregon, we witnessed a rather interesting phenomenon which occurs during windy conditions when damselflies are emerging onto floating vegetation. Under such conditions newly-emerged and highly vulnerable adults often are blown onto the water before they have fully extended and dried their wings. Their color at this time is not fully developed and they appear a little on the dull side. This stage of the damselfly is sometimes accepted by fish and a well designed, immature adult imitation should be presented with a floating line and a nine to 12-foot leader among floating aquatic vegetation or near other areas where emergent activity is occurring.

One final consideration that frequently spells the difference between success and failure among anglers fishing a damselfly hatch is the position of the rod tip during the retrieve. Keep it at or even below the water's surface to avoid the slack belly of line that inevitably hangs from a rod tip held above the surface during a slow retrieve. The slack makes it more difficult to detect a strike and only by eliminating it will it be possible to feel more delicate strikes.

TERRESTRIAL ADULTS AND OVIPOSITING FEMALES

Once damselflies have hatched into adults their importance to fishermen dwindles considerably. There are times, however, when adult damselflies can provide some exceptional sport if the proper patterns and techniques are used.

Adult damselflies can be crippled or sometimes appear on the water's surface for reasons connected with weather, mating or other natural circumstances. When adult damselflies become available on the surface cruising fish take them eagerly. At other times fish must exercise a bit of finesse to obtain such flies. Canadian angler Jack Shaw observed that trout sometimes knock adult damselflies onto the water by brushing against the stems of reeds and rushes where the flies are resting. The fish then devour the struggling victims.

A floating line and nine-foot or longer leader should be used to present imitations of the adult damselfly. Cast the imitation toward shoreline vegetation in such a manner as to represent an adult damselfly which has fallen onto the water. If the cast can be executed so that the fly lands on exposed vegetation and then is carefully pulled into the water without hooking the vegetation any trout in the vicinity is likely to be convinced the imitation is genuine. Allow the fly to sit motionless for a few seconds then twitch it by lifting the rod tip to simulate the struggle of the natural damselfly adult trapped in the surface film.

When depositing eggs over the surface of water, the females sometimes are vulnerable to fish and may be imitated successfully.

Damselfly imitations should be tied in shades of olive, brown, tan, and combinations thereof. Two suggested patterns are Kaufmann's Green Mountain Damsel and Kaufmann's Marabou Damsel, both in sizes 8 to 12.

Mountain Damsel

LEECHES (Order Hirudinea)

Distant rumbling warned us of an approaching thunderstorm. A funnel-like cloud suddenly raced across Yellowstone Lake sweeping up water from its wild surface. Earlier, the day had been exceptionally pleasant so we had elected to wade wet rather than put on waders. But the sight of the gods tossing lightning bolts along the low, timbered ridges prompted us to exit the exposed sweep of the Yellowstone River where we had been fishing below the lake. Besides, we had spent a very enjoyable morning releasing numerous cutthroat and were ready for lunch and a cold brew.

We made our way through the chest-high meadow grass, wading into the "black bog," splashing water around our waists as we headed toward the car. No sooner had we reached the highway than we heard a succession of anxious screams. Turning quickly we found one of our cohorts dancing and screaming frantically along the edge of the highway no doubt entertaining passing motorists. Panic was spread across his boyish face as he jumped madly in an effort to rid himself of a black, devilish creature which was clinging to his thigh. Close inspection revealed a leech and a wide stream of blood trickling down his leg. We dispatched the little beast with a solid swat and after calming our friend vowed never to wade the "black bog" unprotected by waders!

To some, leeches might be loathsome creatures especially when one attaches itself to you. But they also are very much misunderstood, much like the wolf and grizzly bear which also inhabit the more remote reaches of Yellowstone Park. Few species of leech actually seek blood as their primary food, and those that do focus most of their attention on birds or fish.

Rainbow trout from Oregon lake with leech imitation in its mouth. R.K.

HABITAT

Leeches live virtually everywhere on land and in fresh and saltwater. They are most numerous in shallow lakes and ponds which contain an abundance of bottom debris, dead organisms, logs and vegetation. Waters which appear dark or brown in color generally seem to be conducive to leech propagation. While leeches can be observed swimming about at all hours, instinctively they are nocturnal creatures, plying the surface of waters during the hours of darkness.

After a slow day of fishing on Peterhope Lake in British Columbia a friend of ours went out after dark and anchored his boat off the edge of a weed bed. The sky was clear and a full moon illuminated the lake. He fished a black leech pattern just below the surface and quickly boated numerous rainbow trout, including four over three pounds each!

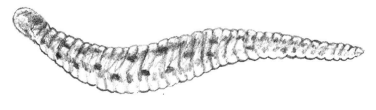

Leech

CHARACTERISTICS

Leeches are annelid worms and are easily recognized by their flattened, ribbon-like bodies, disc-shaped mouths and steady undulating swimming motion. Often they grow more than six inches in length though two to four inches is most common. Their colors vary drastically ranging from light cream to nearly black with many species appearing brown, gray or olive, sometimes with lateral stripes, spots or mottled markings. They usually are lighter on the underside much like most aquatic insects. When swimming their bodies elongate up to two times and move in a wave-like up-and-down motion, traveling about one foot every two or three seconds, but often they will hang in a nearly vertical position under the surface or crawl along the bottom in search of food or cover.

Leeches can go for great lengths of time without food and blood seldom is the mainstay of their diet. Many species are carnivorous, feeding on aquatic insects, earthworms, snails and other underwater creatures. Other species prefer to dine on detritus and other dead organic matter.

While most species of trout seldom ingest leeches in large numbers, there are exceptions in individual waters and at different times of year. For example, a 1.4-pound trout captured from Fish Lake, Utah, contained 192 leeches! Brook trout in Henry's Lake, Idaho, are known to focus attention on leeches only during September when leeches account for nearly 50 percent of their diet. In contrast the cutthroat and rainbow-cutthroat hybrids of Henry's Lake seldom ingest leeches even in September. The angler armed with such information recognizes immediately that the best chance of enticing large brookies is to fish leech patterns in the month of September. In many waters trout ingest numerous leeches whenever they can.

LEECH FISHING TECHNIQUES

There are several leech patterns of value. We have experimented with patterns incorporating marabou, feathers, hair and fur left on the skin and cut into long strips in an effort to effectively duplicate the waving action of the natural leech. In all cases, a long, extended body is desirable, but this frequently leads to short strikes or hook and fly foul-ups unless a long-shank hook is used. We recommend a 6X long shank, limerick bend, Mustad 9575.

It generally is believed that short strikes are the result of trout nipping the tail of the fly. This probably is true some of the time but there also is another reason. Trout do not always strike a fly. They often take naturals as well as artificials by flaring their gills to suck in both water and their prey. An insect, a crawfish, or a leech is pulled deep into the throat before the fish even tries to close its mouth. A fly on a taut line, however, does not get sucked backwards due to the inherent restraint of the line.

Osprey looks over Oregon Cascade lake noted for its leech population. R.K.

Gary LaFontaine told us that while scuba diving he once witnessed a friend get four strikes in a half hour with the trout actually pulling the fly into their mouths. But his friend never tightened up because he never realized the fish were taking. Sometimes the opposite problem occurs with anglers trying to set the hook too quickly just as the fly is being drawn backwards by the fish. Fly fishermen are indeed very observant in noticing the slight pull on the line when this happens but they often react too soon and take the fly away before the fish closes its mouth resulting in a missed strike. Whenever you are missing strikes experiment striking both faster and slower than usual until you find the proper reaction time for the particular type of feeding style.

Since a leech swims in a fairly consistent fashion, a long, rhythmic retrieve is appropriate. The hand-twist method is of value as is a steady, short-strip retrieve, allowing the imitation to move progressively forward while still imparting the undulating motion an imitation ideally should portray. Even so short strikes still will occur. Resist the urge to quickly strip in your imitation. Continue your retrieve, for trout often will turn and savagely attack the fly from another angle.

Another useful presentation, one which must be executed from a floating device, is referred to as the "wind drift" technique. When practiced correctly this technique creates the natural illusion of a leech drifting aimlessly with the lake drift, or windward current. We often employ a quick succession of four-inch strips which imparts a purposeful speed with enough exertion to allow marabou to breathe.

If you are presenting a leech imitation in a lake with a silty or muddy bottom let the leech come to rest before imparting any motion. Let it lie on the lake bottom for a second then give it a short, sharp jerk. Invariably this sudden motion will kick up a small cloud of mud, realistically revealing the presence of the imitation to any nearby fish. In some waters this is precisely what will trigger the trout into striking.

This New Zealand rainbow couldn't resist a well presented Lake Leech pattern. R.K.

LEECH PATTERNS

Some suggested patterns include Lake Leech, Marabou Leech and Woolly Bugger in sizes 2 to 10, 4X to 6X long in assorted colors.

Marabou Leech

Woolly Bugger

MAYFLIES (Order Ephemeroptera)

While walking through a pristine alpine meadow in search of a remote lake high in the Rocky Mountains known only as lake 11,024 on our topo maps, we stumbled onto a small, unmapped alpine tarn. Flowering meadows and granite slabs long since polished by a retreating glacier bordered the pond. And though the season was mid-summer and the intense alpine sun climbed high in the noonday sky, there were still snow banks hidden in the shaded pockets along the north face of the mountain basin. A flower garden of colorful shooting stars marched down to the sandy shoreline of the tarn.

For a while the glassy surface of the tarn was absolutely still, mirroring perfectly the intricate shoreline of rock and flowers. While preparing lunch and enjoying the distant vista of unending mountain peaks piercing the sky at more than 12,000 feet we suddenly saw a delicate mayfly drifting along the shoreline. Then, as if by magical command, several dozen more appeared and paraded along the smooth surface of the water each creating a slight, light-reflecting ring of disturbance. The newly-formed adults were crawling from their floating nymphal skins.

Near the shoreline we noticed several mayfly nymphs moving along the bottom of the tarn. One of the nymphs "popped up" to the surface film, wriggling and turning in an effort to break through the rubbery film. Shortly after penetrating the surface film the nymphal skin split at the top of the thorax and a slate-colored adult mayfly, shimmering in the intense light, crawled free and waited patiently for the alpine heat to evaporate moisture from its fragile wings.

A short distance from shore we observed a recently emerged dun disappear in a slow, deliberate swirl, and the unmistakable flash of a golden trout dissipated within the widening rings spreading over the surface of the tarn. Then, two goldens, apparently unaware of our presence, began a rhythmic cruising pattern which brought them to within an arm's length of us. We remained motionless, frozen into the timberline background, while every rise, every muscle and every black parr mark of the trout became plainly visible as mayfly after mayfly was gently selected from the calm, blue surface of the water.

The highly visible dun-colored mayflies which were now available by the hundreds were carefully selected by the two goldens and an occasional subsurface flash indicated the take of a rising nymph as well.

There was no need to assemble our rods, for angling at that time would have been anti-climatic and almost certainly would have disrupted the scene before nature began its final act. Perhaps 30 minutes passed before the nymphs ended their quest for the surface. Finally, the last adult mayfly vanished into the high mountain air and the golden trout faded back into the depths of the magical tarn ending a brief act in a continuing play on nature's fascinating stage.

We finished our lunch and continued along the pleasant shore of the tarn picking a route toward our ultimate destination, lake 11,024, with confident thoughts of finding a fleet of hatching mayflies and giant, swirling golden trout.

Mayflies are the insects most familiar to fly fishermen, and you probably have seen them on many occasions over lakes and streams. Throughout angling history these delicate insects were thought to be the single most important insect to trout.

While mayflies are of considerable importance to the stream angler they seldom match the sheer numbers of midges in lakes. This is not to imply that mayflies are of little value to the lake angler but in the overall insect community of the lake mayflies generally rank somewhere behind permanent organisms in importance to trout. Nevertheless, mayflies provide some very exciting action for lake anglers.

Mayflies can provide excellent midday angling. Here Randall Kaufmann fishes an inlet of a quiet New Zealand lake. R.K.

HABITAT

The dispersal of mayfly nymphs like other aquatic organisms in lakes depends on the existence and location of aquatic vegetation, temperature, oxygen saturation, geological environment and availability of food sources.

Mayfly nymphs are able to inhabit virtually any clean, unpolluted water. While they usually are not nearly as prolific as caddisflies or as widespread as midges they nevertheless play an integral role as a food source for trout in lakes.

Mayfly nymphs probably are the most fragile nymphs found in any considerable quantity in aquatic habitat. They cannot tolerate high pollution and have trouble enough meeting nature's own challenge. Severe waves can dislodge nymphs in shallow water. Rocky bottoms can become silted in inlet areas destroying habitat. Drought is another factor which can eliminate the mayfly. While many other aquatic forms can survive simply by staying in the proximity of moisture, mayfly nymphs cannot. Shallow lakes and ponds which dry up from time to time are unlikely to support any population of mayflies.

Mayfly nymphs do not build cases and are for the most part crawlers and free-swimmers. Adult mayflies lay about 6,000 eggs. The chances that an egg will hatch, grow into an adult, mate and produce offspring are very remote.

Mayfly nymphs generally can be categorized into two groups: those which inhabit slow or still water and those which inhabit fast water. These two categories can be broken down further according to the shape and behavior of the nymph. Flat-bodied nymphs are adapted to sneaking under rocks and into cracks; swimming nymphs roam freely among weeds and bottom fauna; and burrowing and crawling nymphs inhabit bottom mud and aquatic weed beds. Various types of nymphs are well adapted to their

Siphlonurus

Isonychia

Heptagenia

particular types of habitat. The following classifications are based on body form and other adaptations which show close correlation with particular habitats.

A. *Still-water forms* — Swimmers amid vegetation (*Siphlonurus, Callibaetis*); Silt crawlers on the bottom (*Choroterpese, Tricorythodes*); burrowers in the bottom (*Hexagenia*).

B. *Rapid-water forms* — Agile, darters, free roaming, streamlined forms (*Isonychia, Ameletus, Baetis*); stone clingers (*Heptagenia, Ironodes*); stiff-legged, trash, silt and moss-inhabiting forms (some *Ephemerella*).

While many species of mayflies inhabit various types of aquatic vegetation certain preferences are displayed for some types of vegetation over others. This is explained by the fact that some vegetation offers better conceal-ment and food for various insects depending on their particular requirements.

In general the vegetation frequently sought by most mayfly nymphs includes *Myriophyllum spicatum, Naias flexilus* and *Potamogeton* with *Myriophyllum* the most densely populated. Shallow, weedy areas along the shore of one lake were found to harbor 1,069 mayfly nymphs per square meter. While such numbers do occur in some waters populations of 500 per square meter are considered dense and even populations of 100 per square meter will yield a tremendous hatch. Mayflies as a general rule do not populate as densely as other aquatic insects.

FOOD SOURCES AND PREDATORS OF MAYFLY NYMPHS

Most mayfly nymphs are vegetarians, living off aquatic matter, including plankton, detritus, aquatic vegetation and algae. Some species, however, are omnivorous and also prey on other insect larvae. Such species will forage along the bottom or through weed beds, ingesting almost any living organism which they can catch, being especially adapted to catch mosquito larvae. Mayfly nymphs can easily be observed feeding along shallow lake shores especially where midge or mosquito larvae are present. Take the time to observe the underwater movements of these nymphs for such observation will give you insight into proper presentation of your imitation.

For protection against enemies mayfly nymphs rely on agility and color. Their natural coloring blends so well with the background that nymphs can lie exposed on top of stones and go completely unnoticed by their enemies. When disturbed the quick-swimming mayfly nymph will dart away very rapidly for a short distance then stop abruptly and remain perfectly motion-less in an effort to confuse and elude its attacker. Mayfly nymphs also seek protective shelter on the undersides of rocks or burrow into dense weed beds. A few species even will excavate burrows in mud or sand.

CHARACTERISTICS OF MAYFLY NYMPHS

The development of mayflies progresses from egg to nymph to dun and finally to the spinner stage. Because a pupal stage is lacking in their development their life cycle is considered an incomplete metamorphosis.

After hatching from the egg nymphs are so small as to be nearly invisible to the unaided eye. As the nymph develops it must molt or shed its skin. The molting is necessary to accommodate the nymph's increasing size. The number of molts undergone by various species of mayflies is not certain, but one species of *Baetis* was observed to pass through 27!

The nymphal stage of the mayfly can last anywhere from two months to a couple of years, depending on the species and the water temperature but most species complete their underwater development in a single year.

Once the nymph has matured beyond its infant stage wing cases can be plainly seen on the thorax. Probably the most prominent identifying features of the mayfly are the rear abdominal segments of which four to seven will bear gills. The gills are wavy filaments along the abdominal segments. No other aquatic insect displays this unique feature. The shape of the gills varies among different species with some species having longer, flowing gills and others having gills that are barely visible.

Six legs protrude from the thorax area of the nymph with the front legs usually being longer than the other four. The front legs of the male usually are a little longer than those of the female and in the spinner stage they often are longer still. Each leg has five main joints.

Tails generally are long and slender. Some species have two and others three. The tails vary in length from one-quarter to one-and-a-half times the overall length of the nymph.

Mayfly nymphs occur in an extremely wide range of colors and sizes. Some nymphs are so tiny they can hardly be identified while others, such as *Hexagenia*, approach the size of the dragonfly nymph, reaching lengths of up to one-and-a-half inches. The color of the newly-molted nymph is whitish at first, but it soon darkens to the normal color scheme of the species. Nymphs usually appear somewhat brownish in appearance but a close inspection will reveal a variety of colors including blackish brown, dirty claret, tan, yellowish brown, all shades of olive and combinations of all the foregoing. The undersides of nymphs always are lighter in color than the top and the angler should remember that trout often inspect rising nymphs from below.

Ephemerella

EMERGENCE

Mayflies do not emerge in the actual sense of the word. There is no pupal stage in the development of mayflies and they do not have a case to abandon like a caddisfly before finding their way to the surface. The only visible change in the nymph is that its wing pads darken and are more pronounced and in those species in which adults possess three tails the middle tail of the nymph becomes pale and translucent. For these reasons the transformation of nymph into adult, or dun, usually is referred to as "hatching" rather than emerging. Just prior to hatching mayfly nymphs create gas or air which is stored in the nymphal case allowing the nymph to float or swim easily toward the surface.

Mayfly nymphs hatch in one of three ways. Some float and swim to the surface; others crawl out of their nymphal shucks, abandoning them on the bottom or in mid-water, and swim the remaining distance to the surface and still others crawl out on nearby vegetation to hatch. The hatching often takes place so quickly that the adult fly seems to appear on the water's surface as if by magic. The newly-hatched duns wait on the surface for their wings to dry before taking to the air. At times the dun will fail to emerge completely from its nymphal shuck or will become trapped in the surface film. When trapped in this manner the insect is referred to as a "stillborn dun." Stillborns either will struggle until dead or until a trout is attracted to them by the surface commotion they make. Trout often concentrate their feeding efforts on stillborn duns because they are easily located and cannot escape at the last moment.

Hexagenia

Stillborn dun

Floating nymphs also offer trout an easy meal, due to their high availability and their inability to escape easily. On many occasions trout will feed exclusively on these unhatched nymphs, baffling uninitiated fishermen. At other times trout will feed on every stage of the mayfly hatch showing little selectivity or preference.

The sail-like wings of mayfly duns make them particularly susceptible to wind. They turn readily in the direction of the wind, both while floating on the surface and when first taking flight. When you are imitating duns your imitation should proceed in the same direction as the naturals.

On hot, dry days or during windy conditions you also will notice that duns are able to fly very quickly after hatching but flight often is delayed much longer on cool, damp days or when there is a heavy surface film. For these reasons surface feeding activity could be affected to the degree that trout might avoid duns on a hot, windy day in preference for a stillborn dun or floating nymph.

Surface tension plays a very important part in the hatching of mayfly nymphs. Briefly, the thorax of the emerging dun possesses water-repellent properties, so that water will actually retreat from this area, thus exerting a slight upward pull on the nymph. This upward pull allows the fly to break through to the surface and, once it is there, holds it in position so the dun can safely hatch. When the surface film is heavy or thick, hatching flies often struggle for some time in an attempt to break through to the surface. During these times we have seen trout cruise along and feed just under the surface on the multitudes of insects which were unable to penetrate the surface film.

CHARACTERISTICS OF THE MAYFLY DUN

When adult mayflies first hatch out from their nymphal cases they are rather dull in appearance and are known as subimagoes or "duns." The dun stage of the mayfly is extremely short; the mayfly will undergo one more molt to become the "spinner," generally within 24 hours after hatching.

The body of the dun consists of three main sections — head, thorax and abdomen. The head is relatively small and compact. Eyes are large and compound with the antennae usually rather short, about the length of the head.

The thorax consists of three segments with the posterior being closely fused together. The foremost section is the smallest and carries the front two legs. The second section is the largest and supports the large forewings and the center pair of legs. The third segment carries the hind legs and, when present, the small hind wings.

The abdomen, which is attached to the thorax, consists of ten segments and is the largest section of the mayfly often being one to two times as long as the head and thorax combined. Anglers and fly tiers often refer to the abdomen as the "body."

Two or three tails extend from the last body segment and the tails will often be one to three times the overall length of the body. Bodies range in size from near microscopic to more than two inches in some *Hexagenia* species. Most species, however, measure about one-half to three-quarters of an inch in length. Size seldom varies within the same species.

Some anglers feel the adult mayfly is the most beautiful of all winged insects and their colors certainly stretch the imagination. While the colors of the duns are somewhat on the dull, opaque side, even the casual observer can hardly fail to notice the creams, coal blacks, grays, olives, rusts, duns, pale yellow, browns and various combinations thereof on the fragile insects gracefully riding the whispering currents of air above the waters of the lake.

Wings and tails are mostly a dull dun color with some species displaying rusty-dun or olive-dun wings lightly veined with black. Other wings are

Spider webs often reveal what insects have recently transformed into adults. These *tricorythodes* were photographed in Montana. R.K.

An adult mayfly dun sheds its outer skin, becoming a spinner. Spent spinners are those adults which have mated and lie dying in a spent position on the water's surface. R.K.

nearly transparent and seem so fragile one wonders how they can survive.

Keep in mind that colors may vary even within the same species. This little-known facet of the mayfly can frustrate identification and pose a considerable problem when fishing over extremely selective trout. Males generally are darker than females, and, generally speaking, the colder and darker the day, the darker the overall color of the fly will be. Hence a *Baetis* species hatching out in warm days of mid-summer could be lighter in color than the same fly hatching out during the colder days of autumn. The color of the same species also may vary from lake to lake; hence, you should capture a specimen and observe the color closely when fish appear to be selective.

CHARACTERISTICS OF MAYFLY SPINNERS

A dun becomes a spinner after it sheds its outer skin, which, depending on the species, may occur at any time from a few minutes up to a few days after the dun hatches from its nymphal case. This process is unique to mayflies. Upon shedding its outer skin the spinner assumes the same color as the dun, but with a bright, shiny appearance. Most wings of spinners take on a transparent blue-gray coloring while others appear iridescent bronze or olive. Still other species, *Tricorythodes* in particular, appear to have transparent white wings with perhaps a hint of blue-gray. It is during this stage that the mayfly will mate.

Spinners, because of their bright, glossy wings and bodies, are truly beautiful, especially in filtered sunlight and when they are present you will have a difficult time keeping your attention on your fishing. The smooth, delicate flight and vivid coloring of mayfly spinners have captured the attention of countless artists and poets not to mention trout!

Besides color there are two other noticeable changes associated with the final spinner molt. The tails and legs of the spinner often are considerably longer than those of the dun and during the transformation (except on the species of *Caenis*) the microscopic hairs on the wing will disappear.

There are several famous hatches of mayflies on lakes throughout the country occurring at various times throughout the season. The most famous hatches usually are quite prolific and during these hatches trout go on a feeding binge which is perhaps unparalleled by any other insect hatch.

Lakes which support above-average populations of mayflies should be watched closely for the "spinner fall," as some unbelievable angling will be available during this time.

MATING AND FLIGHT

The sole purpose in life of the adult mayfly is to perpetuate the species. After the dun has molted and become a spinner it is ready to mate. Males take up a position in swarms of a few dozen to several hundred, holding position in the air, usually over land. The swarm hovers or glides up and down flying against the wind for a short distance.

The purpose of the swarms is to enable the male and female to locate each other. The female flies into the swarm and the male makes visual contact and pursues her. Copulation takes place in the air after which time the male returns to the swarm to possibly mate again, dying shortly thereafter. For this reason males seldom are observed lying spent on the water's surface since they usually mate and die over land.

After copulation females either immediately commence their egg-laying flights or seek temporary shelter along the shore. Most species will return to the water for ovipositing within one or two hours, but unsettled weather can prolong this rest period for a day or longer. The chief deterrents to the egg-laying flight are heavy rain, high winds or low temperatures. The

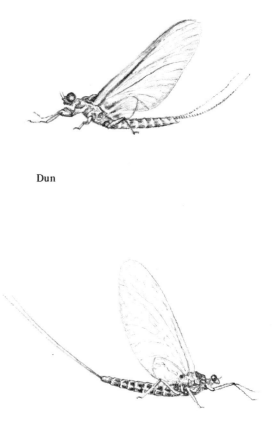

Dun

Spinner

female deposits her eggs either by flying low over the water's surface or resting briefly on the water's surface and dipping her abdomen into the water, releasing her eggs to sink to the lake bottom. Some species, notably *Baetis*, crawl underwater and deposit their eggs on weeds or under stones or rocks. After depositing her eggs the female usually will fall spent on the water's surface, and except for an occasional wing flutter will lie in that position until dead. The dead and dying flies are picked off the water by birds, driven on shore by the wind, sink slowly to the bottom or fall prey to trout.

We have witnessed spinner falls on many lakes where trout simply went berserk scooping spinners off the lake surface. This aspect of lake fishing is so important to fly fishermen that we have devoted a section to what is called the "gulper phenomenon," an event where brown and rainbow trout splurge for weeks on *Callibaetis* and *Tricorythodes* spinners, making an audible "gulp" as they literally scoop up and gulp down the thousands of spinners which litter the water.

AVAILABILITY

As with other aquatic insects mayflies are only available to trout in sizeable quantities during certain times of the year which correspond to the developmental cycle of the insect. Mayfly nymphs inhabit a wide variety of areas in a lake, and their availability as a food source depends on what habitat each species is adapted to. Some species, such as burrowers, are seldom available in large quantities while bottom crawlers or free swimmers are far more vulnerable to cruising trout. However, all species of mayfly nymphs are most readily available to trout just prior to and during emergence.

Up to a week before the actual emergence takes place mayfly nymphs will leave their burrows or protective shelter for short periods, moving about restlessly near the lake bottom. It is important to be familiar with individual hatches in order to determine when such activity is about to take place for trout often will focus their attention on such restless nymphs, and consequently a properly presented imitation can prove deadly.

Many species of mayfly nymphs migrate toward shore in preparation for emergence seeking out optimum sites which afford protection from predators. During such times trout will focus their attention on conspicuous swimming and crawling insects. As such migrations come to an end nymphs emerge into adult duns and fish continue to feed on hatching nymphs and adults until the hatch is over.

The species *E. simulans* spends its early life deeply imbedded in the lake bottom and seldom is available to trout. One study found only six dates between late May and early August when this nymph was found in trout stomachs. However, on May 23, when a mass emergence of *E. simulans* took place, an average of 507 nymphs and 106 duns were found in each stomach checked. One 18-inch rainbow contained 789 nymphs and 232 duns!

Aside from the times of migration and emergence mayfly nymphs also become available to trout foraging along lake bottoms and in weed beds. When trout swim through weed beds some nymphs are likely to become dislodged and these are freely taken by fish. Other nymphs are taken by fish as they expose themselves while foraging among weed beds and along bottom rocks and sand. When food is not readily available in large quantities trout are forced to forage. Mayfly nymphs, along with a host of other aquatic types, are taken by trout wherever they are encountered in a lake.

Burrowing species are known to shun light. They crawl deep within their burrows during daylight hours but often venture toward the surface during hours of darkness. Little is known about why such species leave their protective cover in this manner but trout do indeed prey on them after dark. You should investigate what burrowing species, if any, are available in the waters you intend to fish and, perhaps, present an appropriate nymph imitation toward dark, retrieving it slightly below the water's surface.

The idea that fishing isn't very productive during the middle of the day is not always the case particularly in regard to mayflies. If you were to plot emergence times of insects during a 24-hour period you would find that trout are feeding almost continuously around the clock. On many lakes we have consistently taken plump trout gorging themselves on mayflies during the brightest part of the day. As always the trick is to have your fly in the right place at the right time.

Many mayfly species hatch from about ten in the morning until two in the afternoon at which time trout often can be seen feeding on duns and are almost certain to also be feeding under the surface on rising nymphs. Some lakes support such tremendous mayfly populations that you can fish the spinner falls beginning early in the morning, switching to rising nymphs before noon and then to duns after noon as the trout select different stages of the insect until the daily cycle ceases about mid-afternoon. Cold or windy weather can put off such hatches and if adverse weather continues for a few days a very prolific hatch often will follow on the first day of good weather.

When trout feed on duns they often will be selective to the point of ingesting only males or females and it is necessary to pay close attention to determine the exact preferences of the trout.

The length of time a dun is on the water also is critical to both trout and fisherman. The longer a dun rests on the water the more appealing it is to a feeding trout. If a dun spends only a few seconds on the water's surface before taking flight trout usually will select the floating or hatching nymph. Floating nymphs and stillborn duns require little energy to capture and often are the prime targets of feeding trout.

LAKE MAYFLIES OF SPECIAL INTEREST

Two species of mayflies, *Callibaetis* and *Tricorythodes*, are of special interest to lake fly fishermen due to their widespread distribution, incredible numbers and prolonged hatches.

CALLIBAETIS

The brilliant desert dawn was blinding as the four-wheel drive rig negotiated the twisting, hairpin turns that looked as if they had been

Callibaetis

Callibaetis dun

Spent Callibaetis spinner

designed by some insidious engineer seeking the most tortuous route across the high desert. Climbing steadily we finally reached the dry desert summit and the low light of the early morning caught and illuminated a vast array of mountain peaks behind us to the west, peaks still wrapped tightly in snow.

Turning east once again we descended into a broad valley inhabited only by underfed cattle, sheep and a few Basques and their loyal dogs. Directly in front of us a flock of about 2,000 sheep huddled in a white line, refusing to move despite nipping antics of the dogs and the prod of the shepherd's crooked staff. Eventually the "hoofed locusts," as John Muir called them, ambled onto the dusty shoulder, leaving behind a trail of hoof-trodden sand, droppings and stench. A tortuous washboard road like you would expect to encounter in Baja, California, forced us to hang on to the overhead roll bar. Finally we reached our remote destination, a little body of water we call "Callibaetis Pond," partly out of respect for the beautiful mayflies which inhabit its shallow, weedy depth but mostly to disguise it from wandering ears that might overhear a "private" conversation about its fine, secluded fishing. It's not that we are a selfish lot; it's just that we are a bit protective about who fishes "our" pond. If only ten anglers killed a limit of trout from that little lake more than half the fish population might be absent upon our next visit. We guard this little jewel religiously, never taking anyone to its secluded shore unless we have complete confidence that he will use barbless hooks, carefully return every fish landed, and never, absolutely never, take anyone else there. Needless to say, we have never found a fisherman quite like that; hence, we never have taken anyone to Callibaetis Pond.

Our timing that morning was perfect. Thousands of mayfly spinners already were in the air and beginning to light on the weed-pocked surface of the pond. A scattering of widening rings were visible along the edges of the weedbeds as several large brown trout slowly cruised their shadowy lair among the rich, food-lined weedbeds.

Before we could rig up our graphite rods, slip on our waders and crawl along the boggy shoreline the spinners were in full fall. Trout were slurping in earnest and their loud, unrestrained feeding reminded us of "gulpers" of other western lakes.

Upon reaching the wide-open, boggy margin of the small lake, we each crouched low in an effort to hide our silhouette from the nearby trout. Observing for ten minutes we each selected one particularly voracious feeder, counted its rises per minute and calculated its feeding pattern and general movements. Only after we had a good idea of a particular trout's feeding rhythm and cruise pattern did we proceed to cast our size 14 spinner imitations. In this manner we were fairly certain to cover a trout and at least have a chance of enticing a rise. Such fishing can be slow in that you are not always casting but it is extremely rewarding fishing. This particular morning we each hooked about five fish during the three-hour spinner fall, losing most of them in the weeds.

Callibaetis belong to the enormous family Baetidae, perhaps the most widespread of all lake and pond mayfly species, being especially abundant throughout the western states, British Columbia and Alaska. *Callibaetis* also are found in most sluggish streams and some faster brooks. We have seen these beautifully fragile insects from sea level to alpine waters where spinner falls occurred at more than 10,000 feet.

The *Callibaetis* are very prolific, and under ideal conditions nymphs can hatch within six weeks. This means as many as three or four hatches a season, beginning in late May and continuing into September. The nymphs prefer shallow water and shoreline vegetation where they usually can be observed crawling about feeding on decaying stems, leaves and various plants. *Callibaetis* nymphs are slim in appearance, very agile and one-fourth to one-half-inch in length. Their protective, mottled brown to tannish and olive coloring allows them to avoid predatory trout for most of their early existence.

Nymphs seldom are found deeper than 20 feet and hatching generally takes place in water no deeper than ten feet unless there are adequate weedbeds near or protruding from the water's surface. When hatching they prefer to climb to the surface of exposed vegetation where the adult dun eventually will emerge, dry its wings and take flight. Those nymphs forced by a lack of exposed vegetation to hatch in open water do so quickly, ascending to the surface in short bursts of speed.

When attempting to imitate emerging *Callibaetis* nymphs you should employ a floating line, a 12- to 18-foot leader and a slightly weighted imitation. Allow your fly to sink to the desired depth and retrieve it in three- to four-inch strips, pausing for a second or two between each such strip.

Depending upon the water temperature *Callibaetis* begins hatching in May on some waters, but July and August will provide the best action on most. While both the nymphs and emergers can provide some fine angling during these hatches it is the spinner fall that offers the most consistent action. Spinner falls generally occur from 7:00 to 11:00 a.m., but they also may take place in the evening. During an emergence nymphs fished in the surface film often provide excellent results especially if trout seem a little hesitant about accepting a subsurface emerger or high-riding dun.

Unlike the nymph which has three tails adults have only two tails. Adult duns are easily recognized by their tan mottled body and wings. In the spinner stage the wings become transparent with dark mottlings on the leading edges. Many anglers refer to *Callibaetis* spinner imitations as "speckled spinners." Some of the best imitations incorporate fur bodies and partridge hackle tied "spent" for wings.

TRICORYTHODES

The soundless hush of a chilly dawn filled the basin as visions of slurping trout splashed through our sleepy minds. Finally, unable to sleep, we crawled from our sleeping bags in much the same manner as an emerging insect might crawl from its nymphal case on a cool, damp morning. We soon had a small sagebrush fire glowing warmly, sending a pleasant haze of smoke curling up through the scattered canopy of aspen trees overhead.

While huddling around the fire we kept a sleepy eye in the direction of the lake for the first sign of feeding trout. Nothing. Too early. We knew that within the hour, however, tens of thousands of mayflies would descend onto the lake to deposit their eggs.

Soon the first rays of sunlight crested the perimeter of timber surrounding the lake, revealing millions of miniscule *Tricorythodes* spinners, their transparent wings silver in the light.

The tiny acrobats danced in clouds, rising and falling around the edges of the lake, seemingly oblivious to the dangers lurking beneath the surface. These *Tricorythodes* adults had hatched out the evening before, molting in the fading twilight and taking refuge in nearby vegetation for the night. Usually though, the tiny nymphs hatch at daylight, molt into spinners in an hour or so and begin their mating ritual shortly thereafter. Within a few minutes hordes of spinners covered every inch of the lake's surface within casting distance. Almost immediately trout began to rise, nosing out with gentle swirls to grab the floating flies. Then, as the concentration of mayflies increased, the trout began to display a rather unusual feeding technique, surging forward to inhale many mayflies simultaneously.

Such "gulping" trout are found in lakes where large mayfly spinner falls occur and the prolific *Tricorythodes* hatches are particularly conducive to such feeding characteristics. Trout often travel in schools cruising about looking for masses of spinners to feed on. A school might consist of three to

Trico nymph

Trico dun

Trico spinner

a dozen trout feeding in a 15-foot radius, each giving off a resounding and totally disconcerting "gulp." Such trout often feed in a circle or even a straight line, surfacing and submerging in frequently predictable patterns. This makes it possible to cast to the point where you have calculated they will reappear next. Catching these heavy feeders, however, is not as easy as you might expect.

On this particular morning the multitude of spinners on the water made it necessary for us to "read the rise form" and estimate the time and location of the next rise of a specific trout, then place the cast exactly in the path of the trout. If this had not been done correctly few trout would have been landed. It often is possible to do well at the beginning of a *Tricorythodes* spinner fall before the water becomes too littered with the flies. Fishing also may be good at the end of the fall when the trout have lost much of their natural caution and are looking for one last mouthful.

Our first strike came shortly after the spinner fall had gotten under way when a 15-inch rainbow sucked in a size 24 spinner along with about six naturals and continued feeding, completely unaware of the bogus spinner until the line was tightened. After shattering the surface with several leaps and runs the colorful trout was carefully released. After the spinner fall had been in progress for an hour or so the rainbows we released were bulging with hundreds, perhaps thousands, of tiny spinners. A couple of fish had gorged themselves to the point that spinners were spilling out of their throats! During such feeding sprees it is easy to believe that trout can, and do, ingest hundreds of insects in a very short period of time, completely ignoring any other food source. At such times 12- to 15-foot leaders tapered to 6X, 7X or even 8X are a must. If you do not have a reasonably representative imitation, particularly in size and shape, you might as well sit back and observe the spectacle.

The spinner falls of *Tricorythodes*, and, perhaps, *Caenis*, offer one of the longest fishable hatches of mayflies. These minute insects can be commonly found in profusion daily for up to two months! Many lakes and streams in North America play host to these hatches and while many do not have hatches of such intensity, trout still will come to the surface for lesser falls of spinners. The slightest breeze, however, will put an instant end to the event, scattering the flies or creating a riffle on which the tiny insects are next to impossible to see, both for you and the trout. A wind of short duration can be beneficial, however, concentrating helpless spinners in drift lines or washing hordes of them against floating weedbeds.

Fortunately for us these micro-mayflies usually appear in the early morning, usually before the wind comes up; otherwise this incomparable hatch would be hopelessly lost to whimsical breezes. Many anglers who have fished lakes for years are not even aware that such hatches exist, for the spinners have come and gone before they have made it to the lake. Other anglers who have fished this maddening hatch become frustrated at their inability to meet the demands imposed by normally wary trout suddenly feeding with apparent but misleading abandon. Those who have met with success, however, return year after year to test their skills.

Anglers searching for such hatches should check lakes for *Tricorythodes* nymphs or watch for a fall of spinners. The nymphs are easily identified by their small size and the triangular gill covers attached to the second segment of the abdomen. This triangular configuration is the origin of the insect's Latin name. Nymphs seek out a habitat of silty bottoms, fine sand and aquatic vegetation such as *Elodea*, algae growths and the base of aquatic root structures. They can be observed crawling and climbing about but because of their mostly secluded habitat they are seldom available to trout except when they rise to the surface to hatch.

The nymphs are incapable of swimming; hence during emergence they wriggle and undulate toward the surface. When attempting to fish such an emergence it is best not to fish blind. Instead, pick out a specific feeding trout and concentrate on it. Trout often work along the borders of weedbeds but such areas present a danger to the long (12 to 15 feet) leaders and delicate 6X, 7X or 8X tippets that are best for presenting small flies. Emerging patterns should be fished very slowly with a slight twitching, rising motion. When trout are cruising just under the surface taking emerging or "hatching" nymphs as they often do, you should fish the nymph exactly like a dry fly, presenting your imitation in advance of the feeding trout with a 12- to 15-foot leader tapered to 5X to 7X. If you suspect a "take," simply tighten the line. If no fish is there and other feeders are nearby allow your fly to remain on the water. Otherwise, retrieve gently and cast to another feeder.

Tricorythodes adults formerly were classified in the family Caenidae, but many entomologists now agree they represent a separate family and should be recognized as such. However, the angler's concern is mainly with their shape, size and color. Generally, the newly-hatched duns are three to five millimeters in length and have smoky, transparent wings and black or chocolate-colored bodies, though some may be lighter with a hint of gray or pale yellow. Many spinners have a spot of white at the rear of their bodies. There may be either two or three tails, and the legs are pale dun in color.

Life cycle of a mayfly

Note the gills along the abdominal segments of these mayfly nymphs. No other aquatic insect displays this unique feature. John Goddard photo.

Floating Nymph

MAYFLY FISHING TECHNIQUES

It has been shown that trout feed on every stage of the mayfly, from nymph to spinner, and in order to imitate the various cycles of these insects you must master an extensive variety of presentations and have a wide selection of fly patterns. There follows an examination of the most productive fishing techniques for each stage of the insect.

NYMPH TECHNIQUES

Nymph imitations should be presented along the bottom and in areas around weedbeds frequented by mayfly nymphs. The sink-and-draw is the perfect method to employ here. If the water is shallow a floating line and a nine-foot or longer leader will be in order. If you are fishing in water over six or eight feet deep a combination floating-sinking line would be best and should the water depth range below ten feet a sinking line would probably be best. Remember, when you are attempting to imitate a nymph foraging along the bottom you want the fly to reach the desired depth quickly and *stay* there, hence the use of a sinking line and short leader in relatively shallow water. This is especially important when a migration is in progress. At that time nearly all the nymphs are on the bottom which is where your fly should be. Another consideration is the direction in which the nymphs are moving. If they are moving directly toward shore then obviously you should retrieve your fly in the same direction.

The speed of the retrieve should vary according to the species being imitated. As a general rule mayfly nymphs move fairly slowly unless scurrying for cover. A slow, steady hand-twist retrieve with frequent pauses is a good bet. Or you can imitate a frightened nymph by a quick short pull, after which you should allow the fly to remain motionless for a few seconds then repeat the maneuver. Such quick, evasive actions often will attract the attention of nearby trout and a jarring strike could be forthcoming.

The rise-and-fall technique is perfect for imitating nymphs swimming all the way to the surface to hatch into adults. During this phase of the nymphs' lives, they often will swim steadily until the surface has been reached but more often than not they will swim a short distance, rest, then slowly settle a bit before again starting their ascent.

When utilizing the rise-and-fall method it is best to incorporate a floating line, weighted nymph and a length of leader just long enough to reach the bottom. When the fly is cast and allowed to sink it should just touch the bottom. Retrieve the fly at a moderate speed for about three feet then allow it to sink back to the bottom, imitating a false start for the surface. The sink-and-draw technique also is useful at such times, but, unlike the method just described, it allows the fly to swim up at a gradual angle.

Don't be afraid to experiment during the hatch for fish often concentrate on nymphs just above the bottom or just below the surface and sometimes halfway between. One or two droppers can be attached to your leader to assist in locating the preferred feeding depth. When using this technique the point fly should be weighted.

FLOATING NYMPH TECHNIQUES

Once the nymphs have reached the surface they may float in, or just below, the surface film before hatching. At this time the nymphs frequently are motionless and present a highly visible outline for trout. As a result, trout ingest numerous "floating nymphs."

Imitations should look much like the actual nymph but as a visual aid for those who need it a tuft or ball of fluorescent poly yarn can be added to the top of the thorox. This will not be too noticeable to fish inspecting the fly from below but will be highly visible to you, allowing you to follow the fly much more easily. These imitations should be fished dead drift in the surface film employing the classic dry fly technique. Strikes often will be subtle with trout simply sucking the imitation under. When this happens there is no need to set the hook. Simply tighten up your line and the trout will be on. By using such a light pick-up a much smaller diameter leader may be employed to assist in deceiving typically wary fish. When fishing a floating nymph especially in low, clear water and under windless conditions a 12- to 20-foot leader may be required. When trout are feeding on floating nymphs they often settle into a rise pattern. You should attempt to decipher such feeding patterns and present your fly at the most advantageous time and place.

STILLBORN DUN TECHNIQUES

The technique of fishing a stillborn dun imitation is much the same as that used for floating nymphs but the stillborn duns are almost always on top of the surface film half emerged from the nymphal shuck or tangled up in their wings. Their struggles on the surface attract the attention of nearby trout so the imitation should not only look like the natural in shape, size and color, but also *act* like it. Dress the fly with floatant and occasionally twitch it slightly to represent the struggles of the natural.

ADULT DUN TECHNIQUES

When fish are selecting duns it is imperative to have a good imitation. Under extremely selective conditions the no-hackle patterns work well, as do the Lempke-Cordes extended body flies and the parachute style flies. During times when trout are not so selective standard dry fly patterns in the proper size and color also will work well, especially when there is a slight breeze rippling the lake's surface. The classic dry fly technique is obviously in order and many techniques and strategies associated with fishing floating nymphs and stillborn duns apply to adult duns. Be certain to present your fly in such a manner that it drifts in the same direction as the naturals.

No Hackle

SPINNER TECHNIQUES

During the spinner fall trout can become unbelievably selective and lakes are generally dead calm, taxing the skills of the fly angler to the limit. There is little room for error and exact imitation frequently is required along with a long, light leader and thorough knowledge of rise-forms. Your imitation must float flush on the surface film and your leader must be sunk or unnatural surface vibrations and shadows probably will warn off any interested trout. Do not be afraid to use 7X or even 8X tippet material keeping in mind that fish usually take several insects at once on a directional feeding path and all that is needed to hook fish is a lift of the rod tip. When trout are handled in this manner you can hook and land comparatively large ones with very light leaders, assuming, of course, the trout do not get into weeds.

The spent mayfly spinner always has been one of the ultimate challenges of imitation. Fish have such an unhurried and clear view of the fly that all the important characteristics of the pattern have to be just right. With the prone spinner imitation where there is little or no motion other factors become more important.

The main characteristics of the natural, the first features that a fish recognizes, are the transparent wings lying flush upon the water. In sunshine they are especially important because the transparent wings not

Partridge Spinner

only make an imprint on the meniscus but they also act like a prism and refract the light. The result is shimmering variations of color visible to the trout.

Materials such as polypropylene or hackle fibers fail to duplicate this refraction of light because they are not translucent. In very selective situations flies winged with such opaque strands often are refused. Dupont's Antron (trilobal nylon) works perfectly in this situation. The fibers are clear, reflecting and breaking up light just like the natural wings of the spinner, and even more important they do not mat into a sodden lump on the water. Every strand remains separate to duplicate the intricate veination and color streaks of the natural's wings.

MAYFLY PATTERNS

Suggested nymph patterns are Hare's Ear, Timberline, Pheasant Tail Nymph and Cate's Turkey in sizes 8 to 20.

Emergers should be tied in sizes 10 to 18. Suggested patterns are Timberline Emerger and soft hackles in assorted colors.

Floating nymphs should be tied in sizes 10 to 22 in an assortment of colors.

Stillborn duns should be tied in assorted colors on size 8 to 20 hooks.

Suggested patterns for duns are No-Hackles in assorted colors and sizes 10 to 24; Parachutes in assorted colors and sizes 10 to 24; and standard patterns such as Adams, Cahill, Hendrickson, Blue Dun and March Brown in sizes 10 to 24, and the Lempke-Cordes extended-body patterns.

Spinners should be tied on size 10 to 26 hooks in an assortment of colors.

Timberline mountain areas of the West offer some of the most spectacular fishing and scenery to be found. R.K.

Lempke-Cordes Extended Body

Hares Ear

Adams

Timberline Emerger

Pheasant Tail

CADDISFLIES (Order Trichoptera)

The next time you visit a waterway during a bright day take a few seconds to shake a tree or willow branch. A small cloud of moth-like insects should rise into the sky and quickly settle back to the cool, shaded protection on the undersides of the leaves. These are caddisflies of the order Trichoptera, which translated means, "hairy wings."

Adult caddisfly hatches can be amazingly prolific. During a visit to Hells Canyon, Oregon, millions of adults were observed flying along with the steady wind currents during the closing hours of daylight. Spent adult caddisflies have been known to collect up to depths of several inches in back eddies or to completely cover wind-washed lake shores.

Some species of caddisflies are completely nocturnal and are seldom seen. For example, one summer evening while sitting around a Sierra campfire the unmistakable sound of rising fish aroused our curiosity. A close inspection with the flashlight revealed a fine caddisfly hatch in progress under total darkness. The fish were splashing on the surface, taking the large, green, newly-emerged adults as they sat on the water's surface drying their wings before flying into the cool evening.

Many anglers have difficulty identifying the caddisfly when they see it fluttering against a pale evening sky. This insect has two sets of slightly hairy wings which allow for a great deal of maneuverability, thereby explaining in part its quick and often erratic flight. When at rest the wings of caddisflies fold back over and alongside their bodies in a tent-like inverted "V" fashion. In this position the wings usually extend about 30 percent beyond the actual length of the body which is somewhat obscured.

Most caddisflies display rather long antennae with some species having antennae two or three times their body length. The size of the adult caddisfly ranges from tiny, minute insects to specimens up to two inches in length with the average being about one-half to one inch in length. The abdomen is formed by nine segments while the thorax consists of three. Adult caddisflies appear to take on several mottled colors, the most common of which are browns, olives, tans, grays and yellows. Over 1,200 species of adult caddisflies have been identified, but only 350 have been associated with the appropriate larval form.

Tent-like wings of caddisfly at rest

LARVAE

Caddisfly larvae are extremely delicate and subject to fierce predation by other underwater life forms. For these reasons nature has endowed many species with the instinct and the means to construct a protective case. Cases are assembled with sticky silk webs which the larvae exude from their salivary glands and to which various particles are adhered, including sand, stones, sticks and leaves. Case builders are perhaps the most conspicuous of caddisfly species and they freely inhabit both lakes and streams. Stream inhabitants generally require a heavier case than lake dwellers, both for protection and weight, which helps keep the caddis case from being swept away.

Other species of caddisflies build nets in much the same manner as a spider. Food particles are caught in the funnel-shaped nets and later are consumed by the larvae. Net builders, however, are mostly confined to running water and are of little importance to the lake fisherman.

Another type of caddisfly larva is the "free swimmer." These build neither net nor case, but simply drift and swim about the water and seek shelter among aquatic plants and bottom debris.

The larva appears worm-like in appearance with definite body segments which often will be slightly hairy. The thorax will be about 25 percent of the overall body length. Larvae use their six legs which are all located under the thorax for grasping prey and for crawling.

For locomotion the cased caddisfly larva simply protrudes its thorax and legs and drags itself along case and all. When frightened the larva easily withdraws into the safe confines of its case although trout frequently will consume the case along with the larva. Some larvae when frightened will abandon their case and take off. Larva sizes range up to one-and-a-half inches in length, and larva colors include grays, greens, olives, creams, yellows, tans, browns and orange.

LARVAE HABITAT

Caddisflies are found in most freshwater environments. The larvae do not like deep water, however, preferring to inhabit depths of ten feet or less. Caddisfly larvae cannot tolerate fluctuating water levels mainly due to their lack of mobility and their tendency to occupy shallow areas of the lake.

Of particular importance to the fisherman is knowledge of which species of caddisflies are most likely to be found emerging from particular areas of a lake. Since different species do indeed inhabit selected benthic (bottom) regions, varying sizes and colors of caddisflies will be observed emerging at different locations on the lake. Some close observation of habitat and emergence patterns will pay large dividends to the patient angler season after season.

The preferred habitat of many species of caddisfly larvae is aquatic vegetation which provides both shelter and forage. *Myriophyllum* and *Potamogeton crispus* have been found to harbor large concentrations of caddisfly larvae. *Ceratophyllum* is the common habitat for the caddisfly *Leptocerus americanus*. Caddisfly larvae will attach themselves to such vegetation and possibly attract attention as their rigid cases wave about in the ebb and flow of the water.

Other species of caddis larvae seek out shallow lake bottoms where they can hide in the bottom debris. During the winter, caddis larvae in Marion Lake, British Columbia, select submerged and marginal vegetation and open sediment in decaying vegetation throughout the lake. During the summer months these larvae choose inlet areas, open sediment and vegetation around the lake margin. During the recolonization of the lake margin by the caddisfly larvae in the summer hundreds of larvae drift on the lake's surface.

Situations such as this can lead to some exciting angling if you have a good general understanding of the lake ecosystem and the water to be fished.

EMERGENCE

Caddisfly larvae remain in the larval stage for up to a year gradually growing until they are ready to pupate. Some species, however, grow only until early summer when they enter a period of no growth and no activity for three months. They then undergo a regular pupation period. Eventually, after pupation, the caddisflies emerge into winged adults. During this period the cased larva will outgrow its larval case several times each time having to form a new one to accommodate its larger size. A few weeks prior to emergence larvae begin a migration into water one to three feet deep to an emergence point of their liking, then they seal their cases and stop feeding. This stage of the larva lasts about two weeks during which time the larva transforms into the pupal — and then adult — stage. When ready to emerge the now fully-formed adult begins gathering gas bubbles about its skin and beating its hairy legs while slowly rising toward the surface.

A cased caddisfly larva adrift on the water's surface. John Goddard photo.

Upon reaching the surface the adult pushes against the surface film, eventually hopping out upon the surface and waiting for its wings to develop fully and dry. Still others will swim to the shoreline for cover and finish maturing among the relative safety of rocks and vegetation, or wait out the final stage on surface aquatic vegetation if available. At this time of emergence the adults are subject to fierce predation by fish.

Some of the larger species of caddisflies do not swim or fly to shore after emergence. Instead they "run," chugging right across the surface! The back edges of their wings in the folded position press the water like two sleigh runners and leave two streaks on the surface film. This type of activity triggers a very splashy rise form with trout breaking into the air after taking the insect. The fish cruise at a medium depth of five to eight feet, rather than just under the surface, to increase the visible area of the surface, and they intercept the caddisfly in a dramatic rush.

Those species which spend several minutes on the water's surface with wings splayed out slightly and antennae curving backwards over their bodies are constantly making feeble efforts to fly. These actions do indeed attract fish and feeding frenzies frequently develop at this time.

Most emergences take place during the evening hours but some species come out after dark, in the early morning or at midday. Emergence dates vary but the majority of hatches occur from April through July with May and June providing the most activity. Not all caddisfly species emerge at the same time so a lake conceivably can produce many days of emergent fishing.

This secretive insect shuns direct sunlight, spending the bright daylight hours hiding in vegetation, or among stones, under bridges, on buildings, or just about anywhere a cool, damp hiding place can be found. Adult caddis-flies generally live for about a month but when conditions are extremely dry their life span can shorten to a week or less. For this reason adult caddisflies avoid the midday heat and venture out only when humidity is at its peak which is generally during the hours of darkness.

After the newly-emerged adults have taken to the air they are of little importance until they have mated and begun egg laying. At this time the female caddisfly will either drop her eggs directly into the water, fasten them onto some aquatic vegetation above the water or actually swim below the surface and attach the eggs to some underwater object. Of importance to the fisherman are those females which deposit eggs under or over the surface of the water. These returning adults are the ones most likely to be found spent on the water's surface, thereby setting the stage for surface feeding activity by fish. Look for egg laying to occur late in the evenings and sometimes on cool, cloudy mornings.

AVAILABILITY

Caddisflies are most visibly available to fish just prior to and during emergence. Fish may easily take advantage of the shoreward migration of caddisfly larvae and of the emerging pupae in addition to the newly-emerged adults which linger on the water's surface while drying their wings prior to flight. Airborne adults are taken only occasionally except when the females return to the water to deposit their eggs. At this time the spent adult caddisfly is freely consumed by fish.

In Marion Lake, B.C., fish rely heavily on the larval form during the winter, but then there is a lull in the intake of caddisflies while feeding attention is focused on dragonfly nymphs, damselfly nymphs and midge larvae and pupae. Fish do not actively begin feeding on caddisflies again until the emergence begins to peak in June after which there is another lull in the intake of caddisflies until the larvae have begun to grow and the number of other insects available begins to dwindle. Hence the large intake of caddisfly larvae in November, which continues throughout the winter when many alternative prey species are not available.

From such information you can see the importance of presenting the right imitation at the right place and time. Such selective feeding habits help explain the reasons why one particular fly pattern will produce extremely well for a certain period of time and then suddenly stop being effective. A little foresight and investigation into the approximate times of emergence will allow you to successfully fish hours *before* surface activity is visible. Gary LaFontaine, writing in *Caddisflies*, has some valuable insights into caddisfly availability, presentation techniques and fly representation. We urge everyone to obtain a copy.

FISHING TECHNIQUES

The larvae, pupae, adult and ovipositing stage of the adult female each present a unique set of circumstances, previously discussed, which you must fully understand in order to present your imitation in a manner acceptable to fish. To imitate and present the four stages of the caddisfly, as well as any other aquatic food source, it will help to review the following considerations:

1. Where in the lake are caddisflies most likely to be found?
2. When will they become available to fish?
3. How do they become available to fish?
4. What color and size should the caddisfly imitation be?

CADDISFLY LARVAE TECHNIQUES

There are certain key areas in the lake where you should present your larval imitations. These include aquatic weed beds, along the lake bottom itself and in the case of "free swimming" caddisfly larvae along the entire shoreline of the lake. Since caddisfly larvae in general prefer shallow areas of lakes and ultimately migrate into such areas prior to emergence this is where you should concentrate your efforts. The presence of empty caddisfly cases on the water's surface and along the shoreline itself often will betray areas of current larval activity. It is imperative that you do not disturb shallow areas that you intend to fish by walking directly up to the shoreline or by wading into the water. Such careless actions often will spook feeding fish for a considerable distance.

When stalking fish along the shoreline keep a low profile, making certain your shadow does not project out onto the water where it might frighten the fish. A cast along the shoreline, particularly one lined with shore vegetation, often will produce a fish sometimes within a few feet of shore if the water is sufficiently deep.

To best imitate an insect crawling up an ascending slope the imitation should be cast into deep water and retrieved toward shallow water, thereby keeping the imitation in the feeding or concentration zone for the entire retrieve.

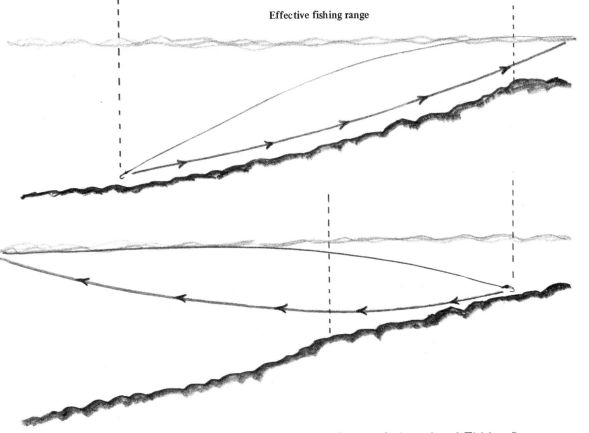

Effective fishing range

The nature of the area to be fished including the depth and the presence or absence of weeds will determine what type of fly line should be used and what length leader will provide best results in presenting a larval imitation. The depth at which the fly is to be presented also may dictate whether or not the fly should be weighted depending upon how buoyant the pattern is.

When fishing over slightly subsurface weed beds it generally is best to employ a floating line and an unweighted fly. The unweighted fly will settle gently into the weedy area and "swim" naturally with any slight underwater currents causing the imitation to rise, fall and sway. Under such conditions an extremely slow and short retrieve would be appropriate. You need only keep the line tight enough so that the take of the fish can be detected. Watch the end of the fly line for any slight movement which might indicate such a strike.

Weeds or snags, of course, will be encountered with this method. When the fly appears to hang up tighten your line gently. If the resistance is not caused by a fish pull the fly clear, let it settle once again and resume the retrieve. Avoid disturbing the water by either stripping or quickly reeling in your line. It is far better to fish out a fly covered with weeds or debris than to create a commotion and spook fish in the area. Upon fishing out a snagged cast, or any other cast, check to be certain the fly is free of weeds and other debris.

The sink and draw method is useful when presenting a caddis larva imitation along the lake bottom. You should usually cast from shallow water toward deep water for this approach allows the fly to appear as though it were creeping up the ascending slope into shallow water in preparation for emergence. An imitation presented in this manner will stay along the bottom the entire length of the retrieve whereas an imitation cast into shallow water and retrieved toward deep water will not remain along the bottom nearly as long depending on the steepness of the slope. See page 113.

Fishing deeper water will require a sinking line with a leader of short to moderate length and tippet size. A leader length of four to six feet generally is sufficient. Under these deep water circumstances the larval imitation should be slightly weighted, the extra weight allowing the fly to reach the intended depth quickly, and, once there, allowing it to remain on the bottom in the prime fishing zone. Remember, caddisfly larvae are not built for speed. Instead, they move along the bottom very slowly usually at a speed hardly perceptible to the casual observer. For this reason it is imperative that the angler simply keep the line tight — no actual retrieve is necessary.

The "free swimming" caddisfly larvae roam throughout the entire shoreline area of lakes either drifting with the currents or swimming in a vertical position, rising and falling in the water while moving in erratic circles. Both the rise and settle and wind drift methods are effective. Wind drifting is often deadly on cruising trout ready to ingest a variety of organisms.

During calm days you should present your imitation with a floating line and retrieve the free-swimming caddisfly pattern very slowly allowing the fly to sink and swim in a natural fashion. Leader length will be determined by current conditions and the depth to be fished but a nine to 12-foot leader generally will prove appropriate. If a shallow area is to be fished an unweighted fly will be best whereas a deeper presentation frequently will require a slightly weighted fly.

CADDISFLY PUPA TECHNIQUES

Because of its frequent and pronounced availability the caddisfly pupa is the most important stage of this insect to imitate, much more so than the larval stage. During periods of caddisfly emergence fish often will concentrate on this particular stage to the exclusion of all other food sources ingesting great quantities in short periods of time.

The actual ascent of the pupa to the surface or its subsequent emergence is seldom observed by the angler but the characteristic movements of the pupa as it rises to the surface and swims beneath the surface film indicate the manner in which the pupa imitations should be presented. The tip-off to such activity, however, is the sudden appearance of adult caddisflies on the surface where none were previously observed or the sudden appearance of empty caddisfly "sheaths." At such times a slight but widening ring will be visible in the vicinity of the recently-emerged adult.

There are two fishing techniques in particular which will prove highly effective during an emergence of caddisfly pupae. One method is referred to as the sink and draw technique where a weighted fly is allowed to sink to the lake bottom and then is retrieved steadily toward the surface in a long, ascending angle to simulate the emerging pupa embarking upon its perilous journey.

The second technique, dead drifting, is perfect for imitating a caddisfly pupa swimming slowly toward the water surface or its behavior just under the surface prior to emergence.

The pupa imitation should resemble the actual insect as closely as possible with color, size and lifelikeness being of utmost importance. Special attention must be given to the fact that the pupal "sheath" contains an air bubble that produces a shimmer of reflected light that may well be the most important trait of the natural. Trout tend to refuse patterns that lack this

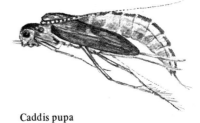

Caddis pupa

Caddis pupae breaking through surface film

trait. In upper New England trout ponds frequently contain the comparatively small caddisfly *Leptocerus americanus* which emerges during the morning in the early summer with activity usually peaking at 6:00 a.m. but continuing until 10:00 a.m. on overcast days. Trout will cruise over the weedbeds picking emergent forms from the surface film. Such fish are very selective and a Sparkle Pupa (size 18, green) works consistently. If there is any doubt as to the color of the emerging pupa capture an adult and inspect it closely for the newly-hatched adult will usually be the same color as the pupa.

A method for determining the color preference and the depth at which fish are feeding on emerging pupae is to fish two or even three different flies at once — the dropper technique.

ADULT CADDISFLY TECHNIQUES

Fishing an imitation of the adult caddisfly is classic dry fly fishing and can be extremely exciting. Fish often rush from unseen depths to savagely attack a caddisfly skipping along a riffled lake surface during its attempt to become airborne. Under such circumstances a floating line always will be required. The key to fishing an adult caddisfly, except for those which are "spent" on the surface or the females of the species that deposit their eggs below the surface, is *movement* or *animation*.

When a newly-emerged adult caddisfly is on the surface it can create a great deal of commotion. It spreads its wings and skitters over the surface of the water in an erratic pattern leaving behind a tiny wake. Often caddisflies in an effort to become airborne will leave the water briefly and fly a short distance only to return to the water's surface and continue their daring dance. Such agitation attracts nearby cruising fish and numerous caddisflies fall prey to fish in this manner.

Both the classic dry fly and skating methods will prove successful. When utilizing the classic dry fly method an occasional twitch of the rod tip and slight hand twist retrieve will represent the surface actions of less violent adults.

During emergence some fresh adults become trapped and often struggle just under the surface in an effort to become airborne. An adult imitation tied sparsely and retrieved very slowly just beneath the surface will prove effective. Another technique for fishing under this condition is simply to allow the imitation to drift motionless just under the surface imparting an occasional "twitch" to imitate the struggling adult.

If you are "fishing the water" and not presenting your fly to any particular fish you should make as long a cast as possible and retrieve the fly the entire length of the cast. By doing so the imitation is on the water and available to fish for greater periods of time.

Adult caddis imitation. Impart occasional twitch.

During those exciting moments when fish are cruising and rising to adult caddisflies the cast should be made accurately within the center of the rise ring or ahead and in front of the cruising fish. Often you will need to coax the fish into taking the imitation by imparting a slight amount of animation just as the fly enters the "window" of the fish and if at first it is refused try again just before the fish turns away from the artificial. Unfortunately, cruising fish have at best a very small window due to the blur created by motion. Thus, anything on a fly or natural "above" the surface is not important. Selection is based on light patterns (pressure points on the meniscus), or on subsurface characteristics.

At times a fish may be induced into taking an adult caddisfly imitation even though the trout are feeding almost exclusively on emerging pupae. Because of the often quick emerging characteristics of some caddisfly species or poor timing on the trout's behalf trout often will miss their quarry. The observant angler will notice a splashy rise followed immediately by an erratic flying caddisfly which just has emerged from the same spot untouched by the trout. When this happens the fish often will linger in the same spot looking for the escaped prey. A properly presented adult imitation cast in the center of the widening rings often will result in an immediate take from the fish. Obviously, well-placed, delicate casts will be required if you are to succeed under such circumstances.

Spent Caddis

Some lakes have shallow or boggy bays containing heavy aquatic vegetation along with dense shoreline vegetation which often extends out into the water. These shallow, brushy areas of lakes usually are ignored by anglers yet fish often will lie in close to such vegetation even during midday. You should employ a stealthy approach to these areas being careful not to alarm the fish. A float tube is a valuable asset in such a situation. Once in casting position the imitation must be presented to the fish delicately and placed among or right up against or even inside the vegetation since fish will be found under, in and alongside it. If you can cast the imitation onto weeds and gently pull the fly off onto the water's surface so much the better. Such a presentation will convince fish that the imitation just fell upon the water. Most strikes will occur within a few feet of the vegetation with fish rushing out from their protective cover to grab the offering. Do not retrieve the fly too fast, allow several seconds between "twitches." The rate of retrieve should be determined by the action of the natural. There is little reason to present your fly to the same spot more than twice. Move a few feet after each cast being careful to cover all the shoreline water. One of the most deadly techniques to employ whether trout are feeding on the ascending pupa, the hatching pupa or the adult on the surface is to use a hatching caddis pattern on a floating line just under the surface film. You should use a long (15-foot) ungreased leader and retrieve with a long, steady pull.

Elk Hair Caddis

ADULT FEMALE CADDISFLY TECHNIQUES

Adult female caddisflies which deposit their eggs on or in the water also are of great value to fishermen. Those species of females which simply return to the water and deposit their eggs *on* the water's surface can be imitated exactly like recently emerged adult caddisflies. Such females will rise and fall in the air and alight at various points on the water creating a slight disturbance as they deposit their eggs.

Some female species actually swim *below* the water's surface to deposit their eggs, swim back to the surface, fly away and return one or two more times to deposit still more eggs! The sink and draw technique is best suited to imitating the diving females and a long-winged, slightly weighted imitation will be necessary.

Occasionally a pupae emergence will coincide with the return of egg-laden females. During times of extreme selectivity fish often will take the

Randall's Caddis

Randall's Caddis Pupa

Emergent Sparkle Pupa

swimming female over the pupa. Fishermen can become extremely frustrated during such periods but a little experimenting with a dropper setup using two different flies should reveal their preference. You should attach a standard emerging pupa at the end of the leader and a long-winged female adult with swept-back wings as a dropper.

The sink and draw technique should be used simulating the sinking and rising of the female while at the same time simulating the emerging pupa.

"SPENT" AND DROWNED CADDISFLY TECHNIQUES

In the early morning you may be able to take advantage of some fine caddis angling if there was a good emergence or a good return of females the night before. Many dead or spent insects may be drifting across the surface available to fish at first light and this opportunity should not be overlooked.

When imitating dying or spent caddisflies, sparsely dressed, low-profile imitations should be fished *on* the water's surface. Flies should rest nearly flush with the surface film and be tied with splayed-out wings, projecting a life-like silhouette. A floating line is used and the sporadic struggling actions of the natural are occasionally imparted to the imitation by a slight twitch of the rod tip.

When fish are feeding actively on dead or drowned adult caddisflies the imitation should be constructed in such a way that it can be fished either on or slightly below the surface of the water. A floating line again must be used and the imitation should be allowed to drift naturally with any breeze. If the imitation sinks from time to time so much the better as fish often will attack a slowly sinking, dead caddisfly. The key factor here is not to impart any motion to the imitation.

FLY SELECTION

As with all insect imitations, size, color and lifelikeness are of primary importance. The color of a newly-hatched adult, particularly the wings, usually is slightly paler than that of older specimens. During times of selective feeding you should be certain your imitation is the proper color. If in doubt capture one of the naturals and inspect it closely.

Recall that adult caddisflies are available to fish as a food source under the following circumstances, each of which will require a specialized imitation:

1. Emerging adults trapped in surface film.
2. Adults on the surface attempting to become airborne or returning females depositing eggs over the water's surface.
3. Returning females depositing eggs below the surface.
4. Spent or drowned adult caddisflies.

Caddisfly larva should be tied in sizes 8 to 20, in assorted colors. Two suggested patterns are Randall's Caddis Larva and LaFontaine's Caddis Larva.

Caddisfly pupa should be tied in assorted colors, sizes 6 to 20. Try Randall's Caddis Pupa, Deep Sparkle Pupa or Emergent Sparkle Pupa.

Adult caddisflies may be imitated with Goddard Caddis, King's River Caddis, Bucktail Caddis, Dancing Caddis, Henryville Caddis, Stimulator, Elk Hair Caddis or Fluttering Caddis, sizes 6 to 20, assorted colors.

Caddisfly adults (drowned) may be imitated by the above patterns plus Diving Caddis in sizes 6 to 20.

Swimming caddisfly females may be imitated by Diving Caddis in sizes 6 to 20.

Spent caddisfly adults may be imitated with the above patterns in sizes 6 to 20.

TERRESTRIALS

Terrestrial insects originate outside of water. The most common and important include ants, beetles and grasshoppers. Terrestrial insects are either washed into lakes with run-off after rain, blown onto the surface by winds, fall off lakeside rocks and vegetation or inadvertently land there during their flights.

When air masses stabilize and cooled air sinks, insects are forced down onto whatever lies below them. This generally occurs at night over areas that are cooler than their surroundings such as cold water lakes. Once terrestrial insects come into contact with the surface of the water various factors come into play to determine their distribution around the lake — surface winds, waves and water currents. Drifting insects are not distributed uniformly across the lake's surface. In very exposed lakes the breaking waves will create foam which has a tendency to form streaks. Drifting insects are then caught in the streaks and move with these foam lines. Eventually the insects will be swept to the windward shore where they may be washed onto land if the shoreline is flat and shallow. If the shore is steep they will accumulate until they sink. Some insects can stay afloat in the surface film for several days.

Along steep shorelines a phenomenon occurs that is helpful to fishermen. The drifting insects in this case do not actually become pressed against the bank but instead remain in the drift line some distance from shore. When incoming waves strike the shore, echo waves are formed which are propelled back out toward the center of the lake. A point of equilibrium is established where the drifting insects are being pushed equally by wave action from both directions so there they remain. Fish in search of food find this situation highly attractive. Some of these insects being buffeted from both sides sink beneath the surface thus enabling trout to feed upon them without actually rising all the way to the surface.

Pine forests of the West periodically suffer infestations of the spruce moth. Trees around lakes literally become thick with these moths and each gust of wind sends these clumsy fliers tumbling onto the water. On the leeward side of one small mid-elevation lake the wind touched the water in a line parallel to and about 12 feet out from shore. There the moths were unceremoniously dumped and trout capitalized upon the easy meal. It seemed every cutthroat in the lake was there. In autumn especially on western lakes large numbers of terrestrial flies often may be found in trout stomachs. Terrestrials may be of particular importance to trout whose other food supplies may be dwindling as the season progresses. Research gathered at two high mountain lakes in Wyoming's Wind River Range provides interesting data. Although seasonal variations are not known information does reveal that in two lakes sampled the percentage by numbers of terrestrial insects consumed varied from 19 to 33 percent and 81 percent of the stomachs sampled from one lake and 82 percent from the other lake contained terrestrial insects.

Research at Castle Lake in Northern California determined that rainbow trout consumed three times as much terrestrial food as brook trout. Furthermore, in terms of the amount of total energy consumed by trout terrestrial insects supplied more than 48 percent. In some lakes this does not happen perhaps because of the abundance of permanent organisms. The interlocking pieces of the lake fishing puzzle are limitless and you must persevere in your attempt to recognize and decipher them.

ANTS (Hymenoptera)

Besides ants this order of insects includes such common winged insects as bees and wasps. Ants are the most important. There are several varieties of ants, both winged and land dwellers, each occurring in a variety of colors. Flying ants are of greatest importance to lake fishermen and swarms of these mating insects often descend upon a lake.

One early June morning we were breaking camp along a lake reputed to contain some very large rainbow but which we had been unable to interest in two days of fishing. Our camp was in a secluded grove of firs about 200 feet from the water's edge but the sudden unmistakable slurping sounds of surface-feeding trout still reached our ears. We headed for the lake to see what all the fuss was about and to our amazement saw a tremendous swarm of large, black, flying ants which had descended onto the lake. The heretofore elusive trout were absolutely gorging themselves!

Racing back to camp we rigged up our rods and searched futilely through a couple of thousand flies for a black fly of the proper size — 8 or 10 — not really being too concerned about the actual pattern. No such luck so we merely used the largest black fly we could find, a meager size 12. The first few casts confirmed our worst suspicions: the trout were extremely selective and apparently would not accept anything but the proper size and color imitation. Frustrated we stretched out under a shady bough and watched the feeding spectacle which went on for about an hour. The rainbows slashed at just about every oversized ant that hit the water and two trout cruising the drop-off in front of us must have risen to the surface at least 75 times in the hour we watched. After this enlightening experience we always have kept a selection of ant patterns in various sizes and colors in our fly boxes and they see plenty of duty.

Such flights of ants usually occur in spring and fall when they are mating. After mating the female sheds her wings and finds a suitable place on land to lay her eggs while the male dies. On waters where ants fall in such great abundance that trout cannot consume them all thousands are collected by the wind and swept onto a windward shore or gathered into wind-formed foam lines. When this occurs trout often will assemble to ingest hundreds of the drowned ants.

Other ants constantly crawl along rocks and vegetation adjacent to waterways and from time to time they are blown off or fall onto the surface of lakes. While such ants provide very little food for trout, under certain conditions you may encounter trout ingesting such terrestrials along some grassy bank or cliff.

Fur Ant

Flying Ant

GRASSHOPPERS (Orthoptera)

In areas where hoppers are abundant trout feed upon them heavily from mid-summer until autumn frost curtails their meadow-hopping antics. Sagebrush and grassy fringed lakes offer the best hopper fishing. Occasional hoppers may be encountered drifting into inlet areas having fallen onto the water upstream. Imitations should be fished with a twitching action on the surface or with a dead drift. If hoppers are falling off overhanging vegetation it is best to cast onto shore, pulling the hoppers off with a resounding splat. While most lakes will see few if any hoppers one can never tell and you should have a few in your fly box.

Hopper

BEETLES (Coleoptera)

Beetles can provide some exciting surface action. To better illustrate this point let us explain an interesting afternoon in New Zealand along the shores of Lake Taupo. A slight breeze was blowing from our backs dancing over the native bush and intermittently riffling the deep blue surface of the lake. Steam vents fumed on the massive shoulder of snow-splashed Mt. Tongariro and distant vistas made it difficult to concentrate on fishing. We had been walking the quiet eastern shore prospecting for a pod of "smelting" rainbow but for unknown reasons the expected run of spawning smelt had not materialized. Jack Moore, Randall's stepfather, spotted a couple of tiny surface disturbances toward the lake drop-off and while most anglers would have casually dismissed these as not worth investigating we did not. Behind us just a few feet from the water line were thousands of green beetles clinging to branches, apparently the front runners of swarms to come. The wind was blowing dozens onto the water and as the wind currents carried them to the drop-off a couple of arm-long rainbow were sipping them under ever so gently. When the wind wasn't blowing we could see them cruising over the light-colored gravel bottom like freshwater sharks.

A size 14 beetle was carefully cast and line paid out as it drifted toward the skittish rainbow. Soon, a near indistinguishable shadow appeared under the bogus beetle and it disappeared from view. The rainbow upon feeling the resistance apparently panicked and became disoriented. Its back rose part way out of the water and it planed non-stop to the most distant part of the drop-off 75 yards away. The reel screamed as loudly as we were and while maximum pressure was applied to the exposed reel frame there was absolutely no slowing this spectacular rainbow down. When it reached the distant drop-off it dived over the edge and the hook pulled free. We all watched in disbelief, shook our heads and agreed we had never seen a trout act like that in any lake.

The December Taupo beetle hatch attracts little local attention with most anglers preferring to fish smelt imitations. Our point is that any number of food sources can excite fish at any time and anything can happen. Being observant, prepared with a great variety of imitations and able to understand such occurrences means more pleasure and fishing excitement.

Some species of beetles are aquatic but these are of only minor importance. Aquatic beetles inhabit weedy areas and are also found among bottom stones. They have many of the same traits as water boatmen and your fishing techniques and imitations should be patterned after them.

Adult beetles at rest on lily pad. R.K.

Beetle

FISH EGGS

There are certain, although limited, circumstances when the imitation of fish eggs can be of vital importance to the lake fly angler. In the coastal regions of Chile, Argentina, British Columbia and especially Alaska, incredible numbers of anadromous fish, such as sockeye, chum and pink salmon, ascend freshwater streams to spawn. Frequently spawning will take place at inlet and outlet areas of lakes. In Alaska we have seen literally hundreds of rainbow, grayling and charr fan out among the redds of sockeye salmon specifically to steal eggs that inevitably fail to settle into the protective matrix of the gravel.

It is not uncommon to see huge rainbows competing with far smaller fish. During years of heavy spawning activity there can be such a saturation of eggs in the gravel that fish will continue feeding for several days after the completion of spawning, ingesting the tasty calorie rich eggs that inlet currents continually serve up. During such feeding opportunities a very significant number of the total fish population of a lake will be concentrated in such areas.

In other less exotic waters, spring spawning trout will lose eggs to fall spawners and vice versa. The logic is inescapable. When fish spawn not all eggs come to rest in the nest. Those that don't become an easy trout food source. And when large numbers of eggs are available they quickly become the major food preference.

At time fish will attack anything that happens along; we have hooked many big rainbow and charr by quickly stripping a bright oversize fly *across* redds. This technique and imitation probably appeals to a fish's greed or aggressiveness. However, the most consistent technique and imitation is that which closely duplicates the food source in relation to size, color and natural presentation. If you present a reasonable egg imitation *above* the gravel bottom and in an unnatural manner, it could be rejected. But let it settle and swirl about the rocky bottom like a natural egg and fish will fight for right of first refusal. The technique is the same as dead drifting a nymph in moving inlet water or wind-drifting or creeping a nymph along the bottom in still water.

Because spawning often takes place in shallow water, egg fishing is usually visual. By stalking and casting to specific fish it is possible to follow your bright imitation right into the fish's mouth. Such visual experiences allow every angler to better understand standard nymphing principles.

Because all fish are released, we usually fish without a hook. During late fall charr in particular will move into shallow water and it is quite possible to entice them into attacking a piece of yarn drifting on the surface. Many are so voracious that they temporarily refuse to let go or the yarn catches in their teeth!

We have found the best flies to be the Babine, Egg and Bright Roe patterns, which should usually be weighted. A wide variety of colors should be carried as eggs will vary in color but the best colors are fluorescent red, orange and pink.

Jack Moore fooled this Alaskan rainbow with an egg imitation at an outlet area. Fish are best revived by holding them by the tail and supporting them underneath, gently moving them back and forth. R.K.

Bright Roe

Egg

Babine

WATER BOATMEN (Order Hemiptera, Family Corixidae)

The order Hemiptera includes many insects similar in appearance to the boatmen the best-known being the backswimmer (notonectidae). The most notable difference between the two families is that the backswimmer swims on its back. The boatmen (or corixa as it is referred to in Great Britain) does not. The habits and habitat of the backswimmer and the boatmen parallel one another so closely that you need focus only on the boatmen.

Trout inhabiting waters containing large concentrations of boatmen often exclude them from their diet completely while trout in other waters rely heavily on them as a food source, particularly at times when they are the predominant aquatic organism available.

In waters where trout do feed on water boatmen they seem to do so only for short periods in the spring and perhaps again in the fall virtually ignoring them during the midsummer months. Such a seasonal feeding pattern may be explained in part by the fact that some species of water boatmen reproduce in the fall. During this time water boatmen are readily available in large numbers so it would seem plausible that trout conceivably accept them as a last resort or as a welcomed alternative to some other food source.

CHARACTERISTICS

Water boatmen have been likened to the shape of a flattened football, or, as their name implies, to a small boat complete with oars. To other observers water boatmen are beetle-like in appearance with large eyes and a hard, shiny back which is well imitated with a piece of lacquered, mottled brown turkey feather. The back of a mature water boatmen is actually formed by its folded wings. An interesting phenomenon of the adult is that it can take flight at any time but seems to utilize its flying capabilities only during times of migration or mating.

Two pair of inconspicuous legs are present at the front of the insect but the third pair of legs protrudes visibly from the body at right angles when at rest. The water boatmen uses this third pair of legs much like a pair of oars, propelling itself with amazing speed and agility. Another obvious visible trait is the opalescent, silvery stream of rising bubbles which trail behind it as it dives toward the lake bottom. Water boatmen lack tracheal gills relying instead on frequent trips to the surface to obtain oxygen in the form of an air bubble which they trap between their hind legs.

The water boatmen goes through a development cycle which includes the egg, five nymphal molts and finally the winged adult stage. The adults hibernate along the lake bottom during the winter months or continue their quest for food under the ice obtaining oxygen from trapped air pockets. A British Columbia angling expert reports that he has successfully thawed frozen water boatmen out of the ice in the spring, reviving them immediately without any visible side effects!

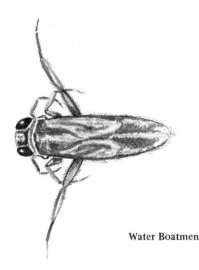

Water Boatmen

Most species attain a length of about one-third inch but other species reach lengths of up to one-half inch. When seen from a distance water boatmen appear to be a drab brownish-black color but closer inspection usually reveals a subtle barring of dirty yellow, brown olive, grayish brown or shades of light to dark brown. The underside of the body is predominately dirty white to dull yellow in color. In the water their underside is usually partly covered with the life-sustaining air bubble, giving a silvery effect to its color.

HABITAT

Water boatmen are widely distributed being found in many types of still waters. Because frequent trips to the surface are required to replenish their oxygen supply they prefer water less than five feet deep. They do not require dense weed beds like other aquatic insects and often are found in lakes containing only a scattering of vegetation along the bottom. We have observed them in many waters where no more than a few wisps of grass were present.

AVAILABILITY

Depending upon the species water boatmen mate and reproduce during early spring or early fall. Their mating flight is very interesting and while it is a fairly common occurrence few anglers are familiar with it. Water boatmen leave the water to mate, the females returning to deposit their eggs on underwater objects, preferably aquatic vegetation. Returning adults hit or splat the water quite forcefully in an effort to penetrate the surface film. During times of heavy surface tension adults sometimes chug over the surface before they are able to break through and dive toward the lake bottom. Needless to say such activity does not go unnoticed by hungry trout foraging for an easy meal.

Remember, while water boatmen make their way to and from the water's surface constantly and are available to trout throughout the entire season trout seldom ingest more than an occasional individual during the summer months, feeding on them only during particular times of the year and only in certain waters.

FISHING TECHNIQUES

When presenting an imitation of the water boatman it is important that you keep in mind the erratic movements and behavior of these insects, remembering their life style is a precarious balance between finding food along the bottom and obtaining oxygen at the surface. In the process of obtaining air they are extremely obvious to patrolling trout and it is during trips to and from the surface that most are taken. Imitations should be presented in this manner, fished fairly rapidly in ascent.

This type of presentation requires a highly specialized fly. There are two styles which you should consider. The first is a realistic imitation which is weighted toward the front of the hook allowing the fly to sink quickly head first. Such a pattern can be fished with either a floating, sink-tip or full sinking line depending on the depth of the water to be covered. After the fly has reached the bottom you retrieve it as an air-seeking water boatmen thus imitating both the rising and the sinking characteristics of the insect.

The other style of imitation reacts in exactly the opposite way. A sponge body and rubber legs may be used to create a floating pattern. This imitation is presented with a fast-sinking or sinking-head line, the leader being slightly longer than the depth of the water to be fished. The fly is cast and the line is allowed to sink to the bottom but the fly remains on the surface much like a resting or returning egg-laden adult. When you want the fly to dive quickly below the surface you simply retrieve the line with quick, steady pulls or incorporate the hand-twist retrieve. When your imitation has reached the bottom you simply stop the retrieve allowing the fly to drift upwards in a natural manner toward the surface. When fishing a fairly long line in shallow water several retrieves can be executed effectively with the same cast. During mating a floating imitation fished to represent the scurrying motion and surface fuss of the natural might be preferred to a diving or rising imitation.

It is very important to keep in mind that for an imitation to be consistently effective it must not only look like the natural but must act like it as well.

John Goddard, noted British lake-fishing authority, has told us that during late July and August in English lakes and reservoirs trout feed heavily on water boatmen in the evening and after dark. At that time even the largest trout abandon all caution as they forage in very shallow water where the largest concentrations of water boatmen are found. John has caught big trout under such circumstances in water so shallow that their dorsal fins could be seen above the surface!

PATTERNS

Two suggestions are Floating Water Boatmen and Backswimmer Boatmen, sizes 8 to 14.

SNAILS (Gastropoda)

Most fishermen are aware of the presence of snails in slow-water environments but few anglers realize that trout often ingest hundreds of these slow aquatic creatures particularly during times of peak availability.

Many snails prefer quiet waters which contain sufficient quantities of lime and calcium in order to build strong shells but other species are found in running water. Silt bottoms, muddy areas, reed and dense aquatic vegetation all are conducive to snail populations with *Chara* weed being particularly attractive. In such weed beds snails often may be counted by the hundreds clinging to stems and leaves. Water depths of 15 feet can harbor good snail populations and even depths of 30 feet are to their liking if suitable habitat is at hand.

Snails generally are fairly small but specimens over an inch in diameter are reasonably common. Their shells usually appear brownish-black in color but several species are mottled tan, black, olive and dirty yellow.

In waters where snails are found in sufficient numbers to be of interest to trout these armored organisms are usually no more than a supplement to their diet but in some lakes trout rely on them for up to 80 percent of their

food. If a shoreline is littered with broken shells or if piles of empty casings are observed under and around bird perches chances are there is an abundance of snails in the lake and the trout no doubt will take advantage of them.

Trout occasionally cruise through underwater vegetation and pick snails from the stems of weeds or suck them off the bottom. When snails commence a mass migration to the surface they become of special interest to trout. This phenomenon still is largely unexplained but it seems likely that such migrations are related either to mating, population disbursement or to the need for additional oxygen. Migrations usually occur during the summer months when the oxygen level may be low. We have observed snails in aquariums behave rather randomly in this manner with all snails suddenly bobbing to the top, each resting with its foot in the surface film.

Snails in lakes often remain at the surface for several days adhering to the underside of the surface film with their shells hanging toward the lake bottom. It is during this time they become most vulnerable to trout.

When trout are feeding on surface-drifting snails the rise from them is much like that of the rise to a midge pupa, referred to as a "head-and-tail" rise. Many anglers probably have been faced with this occurrence in the past without recognizing it. From a distance such floating snails are mostly invisible since they are under the surface and can only be seen readily when you look directly down into the water.

Some innovative techniques and imitations are required to deal with this phenomenon. Keep in mind that the snails will be drifting with any prevailing winds so any imitation should be allowed to drift naturally, just subsurface, using a floating line.

Chapter Ten

Reading the Rise Form

When you see a fish rise, throw your fly beyond him, and draw it gently over the place where he rose; and if it is a proper fly for the season, and you cast it with a nicety, the fish is your own.   T. Best, *A Concise Treatise On the Art of Angling* (1804)

Lakes have two feeding seasons: one when fish mainly feed on the bottom and another when they feed on the bottom *and* on the top. Surface foods attract fish for relatively short periods of time but make up an important percentage of the total food consumed by fish.

A trout's willingness to rise involves more than just a change of diet. Possible factors responsible for a trout's willingness to rise include an abundance of flies on the surface (availability), favorable temperature, atmospheric pressure and wind, preferred oxygen concentrations and probably several other reasons not yet understood. If driven by hunger, however, fish may endure unpleasant conditions for short periods of time.

While the above factors help determine *if* fish will rise it is quite likely that light is a strong factor controlling *when* fish will rise. The regularity of the evening rise is very striking. It starts almost the same time each evening after sundown becoming progressively later as days lengthen and earlier as days shorten. It should be noted that true twilight as we know it does not exist underwater. As the sun sinks below a certain angle, light is totally reflected leaving only incidental light to enter the water thus the onset of darkness is comparatively sudden underwater.

The surface disturbance caused by a feeding fish is known as a "rise" or "rise form," and the ability to read the rise form can mean the difference between angling success and failure.

While fishing an extremely prolific dun hatch some years ago we could not help but notice an angler anchored about 50 yards away from us. He was hooking about four hefty rainbows to every one of ours. We decided to take some photos and simultaneously observe our neighbor through a telephoto lens with the hope of picking up the reason for his success. A half hour and two lunker trout later the riddle was solved.

During that time he made only four casts but each cast covered a trout. Never did he cast his fly into the "ring of the rise," or blindly onto the water. He was "reading" the rise forms very accurately, observing each trout for a couple of minutes before casting, estimating the time and place of the next rise and exercising patience. By so doing he also was selecting only the largest trout as revealed by their rise form. That day's hatch soon ended but the following morning we put the same technique into practice and doubled our success.

An amazing amount of information can be gained by observing rise forms. They not only reveal that a trout is feeding but its size, location, the size and type of food upon which fish are feeding, whether fish are feeding on or below the surface, from which side of the mouth the fish is feeding and the direction in which it is feeding. Furthermore, successive rise forms substantiate the direction and reveal its feeding rhythm which tells you *where* it is likely to feed next.

TIMING THE RISE

Fish which are traveling but not feeding consistently should be cast to immediately with your fly placed slightly ahead of the fish. But in which direction is the fish moving?

After a fish betrays its location and settles subsurface it has a 360 degree choice of direction. By paying close attention to a rise you can often foretell which direction the fish is moving. If the fish does not settle too deeply before moving you will see a very subtle, upside-down "V" exiting the surface ring. From this you will be able to note both the direction and speed the fish is traveling.

When food is plentiful in lakes trout settle into a definite, predictable feeding rhythm. A specific amount of time will pass between rises and a fish may or may not travel far between rises. In smaller lakes and ponds which offer the cover of snags, dense weedbeds or sheltered, submerged boulders fish sometimes take up a stationary feeding position close to their "home." When this occurs you need only calculate the approximate time of the next rise and have the proper imitation waiting. When fish are not traveling it is best to cast the instant the fish turns down with its prey thereby lessening the chance your offering and cast will be observed. Then, when the trout turns its attention toward feeding your imitation will be waiting.

In larger or less structured waters or when food is not so plentiful trout will cruise some distance between rises, the distance often being quite predictable. Such cruisers even settle into a definite cruise pattern, repeating the pattern several times. A fish might cruise the perimeter of a weedbed or perhaps a particularly productive shelf, cliff or drop-off.

With understanding and patience you often will be able to predict not only precisely *where*, but precisely *when* the fish is likely to surface again. Obviously this is a tremendous advantage allowing you to be reasonably certain of covering a fish with each cast instead of covering water that might be empty. Reading the rise is especially important when a multitude of insects are available. When such is the case fish need not veer even a couple of inches off their predetermined "beat" or feeding path. They probably are not even "looking" for food, knowing it will be everywhere once they are ready to feed again.

There is no particular reason why a fish must accept your offering, after all there are a great many naturals going uneaten also. However, if your fly is always in the right place at the right time it is only a matter of percentages until your fly disappears in a swirling surface disturbance, hooked solidly to a real prize. Sometimes a slight variation in size or color or a slight twitch executed just *before* the fly is *clearly* in view of fish will entice a strike.

Keep in mind that when wind riffles the surface trout tend to feed in a more or less straight line headed upwind. When the surface is calm they usually cruise a curving or circular path.

When a fish is rising at spaced intervals the timing of the cast is critical. It is a good idea to cast several feet ahead of cruising fish presenting your imitation well in advance of the fish's arrival at the point the next rise is expected to occur. If you are fishing an emerging nymph whereby you are swimming it from a submerged position toward the surface be certain to allow enough time to sink your fly to the desired depth. Also, with this strategy you will avoid spooking the fish and you will have time to correct an imperfect cast and gather your thoughts.

When trout are cruising and feeding in a definite circle or short "beat," you should cast to the closest point on the beat while the fish is at the most distant point and wait for the trout to complete its circle. If more than one fish is following the same circular path and you hook one, apply immediate pressure to draw the fish away from the others to keep from spooking them.

In Alaska we came across two "pods" of grayling feeding very close to one another. One pod contained half a dozen smaller fish while the other more distant pod contained three fish in excess of 20 inches. We had to carefully hook all the smaller fish, pulling them away from the others, before we could cast to the big ones. By the time we got the small ones out of the way the larger grayling had wandered close to a school of salmon and our first cast was quickly ravaged by a ten-pound silver, scattering the grayling!

"Gulpers" will often feed in a tight circle and if you hope to hook more than one fish from the same pod you will have to be very careful not to spook them.

Its a good idea to cast several feet ahead of rising fish.

TYPES OF RISES

During periods of late evening calm trout often may be observed "dimpling" the surface. Occasionally the nose or head of a trout is seen just before it slowly disappears under the surface. At other times no part of the trout is observed. In either case a "rain-drop" type of ring is left to fade quickly into the surface. This type of rise often denotes trout feeding on

"Raindrop ring"

tiny midge pupae or emerging midge adults. It could also denote a trout feeding below the surface and perhaps its fin or tail created a slight disturbance as it turned to capture some sort of prey.

Trout rising in a slow, deliberate manner usually are feeding on smaller insects which are unlikely to escape such as mayfly spinners or nymphs preparing to hatch into duns.

A small "sip" rise leaving behind a residual bubble is a tipoff that trout are feeding on some helpless insect trapped or resting in the surface film. A

"Sip rise"

close inspection will reveal exactly what it is, with terrestrials, spinners and perhaps cripples being prime possibilities.

Frenzied, hurried rises usually indicate the trout are feeding on a fairly large insect which is more likely to escape from the surface such as mayfly duns, caddisflies and some species of midges.

SURFACE OR SUBSURFACE FEEDING?

Perhaps the most puzzling question is whether trout are feeding on the surface at all despite obvious surface disturbances. At one time or another all of us have wasted time casting dry flies over trout we thought were feeding on the surface but which turned out not to be. Frequently trout disturb the surface after taking something immediately below, even two or three feet deep. Fish could be feeding on bottom organisms in two feet of water and disturb the surface as they feed. Such activity can sometimes be compared to "tailing" bonefish whereby their tail is exposed as they feed along the bottom. During such times surface imitations will provide you only with casting practice. The best clue to subsurface film feeding is the "fin," "tail," or "curving back" rise. When feeding in this manner trout often take the prey on their way down. Such a rise also is referred to as a "nymphing" rise but this can be misleading since trout also take leeches, scuds, minnows and a host of other underwater food forms in the same fashion.

The foregoing observations are only general guidelines and do not always hold true but once you have developed an understanding and familiarity with different types of rises you should be able to figure out with fair consistency what is taking place.

If two or more insects begin hatching simultaneously the rise form should make it possible to determine which one the trout are after. Suppose, for example, there is a coincidental hatch of tiny midges about equal to a size 18 hook and larger caddisflies about size 14, along with a sprinkling of mayfly spinners. The trout are "dimpling" and exposing their noses. You can almost certainly rule out the caddisflies since they frequently provoke a splashy rise. And, since trout seldom feed on adult midges when emerging midge pupae are present chances are trout are feeding on the spinners.

Even the absence of rises can offer clues to what, or where, fish might be feeding. We had heard that a south central Oregon lake was providing some excellent surface fishing for large rainbow. It was three weeks before we could break away. When we arrived we found its mirror-like waters littered with millions of mayfly duns but not a surface feeder was to be seen. Close to dark we realized nothing was going to happen — not tonight, not tomorrow night. A quick check with the thermometer revealed the lake surface to be a warm 74 degrees, also indicating the shallows were probably low in oxygen. This information was enough to inform us that we would have to search out cooler, deeper water and probably fish imitations of permanent organisms (leeches, minnows, scuds).

In nature there is a logical reason for nearly every event. While we might have stumbled onto a few *reasons* for trout not feeding at this particular time and place we do not know *why* nature did not allow trout to be there. Observation and brain power are our best tools for uncovering the answers and creating a basic understanding.

The interpretation of rise forms unquestionably is one of the most important but perhaps neglected aspects of lake fly fishing. Such knowledge will save you a lot of frustration on the water. Close observation of rise forms and the general habits of trout certainly will improve your angling techniques and allow you more success.

"Splash rise"

Chapter Eleven

Lake Fishing Tackle

So much of the charm of fly fishing is in the way it leads one on to more ambitious techniques and more intricate understanding of fish and their ways. R. Haig-Brown, *A Primer of Fly Fishing* (1964)

Remember that fishing trip when the mosquitoes outnumbered trout ten thousand to one and you didn't have any repellant or head net? How about the time your very last terrestrial pattern wouldn't float because you didn't bother to buy some fly floatant? Or that cold evening you spent shivering in wet waders because a patch kit wasn't available? Remember when you spooked all those rising trout because your leader wouldn't straighten out? And the night you spent the last ten minutes before darkness trying vainly to attach a fly to your leader? A pocket light would have been helpful then and again when you stumbled through the boggy meadow on your way back to camp.

Such experiences are frustrating but easily avoided with a little foresight. The purpose of this chapter is to assist you in selecting proper equipment for fly fishing lakes and prevent unpleasant events such as those described above. Needless to say, you want to experience the most enjoyment from your lake fishing adventures so you should obtain all the items on the tackle list at the end of the chapter. Leaving out one seemingly insignificant item could cost you both trout and physical comfort at some future time.

FLY RODS

During the long and fascinating history of fly fishing, fly rods have evolved out of many materials and have been produced in many varying lengths with varying dynamics. Such specifications have been dictated by the demands of fishermen which themselves vary according to fishing conditions.

A quality graphite rod nine to nine-and-a-half feet in length which handles a 5, 6 or 7 weight line is an excellent choice for most lake fishing conditions. There are no disadvantages to fishing a graphite rod. Be advised, however, that just because the label reads "graphite" does not mean the rod is a highly refined, current state-of-the-art casting tool. There is a great deal of junk on the market in every price range. A good fiberglass rod is better than a bad graphite rod. If you are unsure which rod is best for your needs, talk to an expert.

Rod length is critical when fishing lakes. A longer rod will allow for higher backcasts (avoiding obstructions behind you and keeping your line off the water) and allow you to lift more line off the water's surface. When a hooked fish heads for weeds or a snag you are able to hold a more vertical line and keep the fish under control. When a fish is running out line you want to lift all the line possible off the water. This will alleviate much line drag, or tension, taking pressure off your leader.

A long rod also permits better line control, allowing you to manipulate your fly to much greater advantage. Roll casting, which is a valuable tool to the lake angler, is improved with the longer "lever arm" created by such a rod. Change of direction casts also are easier and more accuracy is obtained.

When wading deep, sitting in a boat or fishing from a float tube casting an eight-foot rod is comparable to casting a six-foot rod on shore. Some anglers under these circumstances often prefer a 9½' to 10½' rod. Finally, a longer rod means you can cast a longer line when necessary.

You should have one rod to handle a 5 or 6 weight line and another to handle a 7 or 8 weight line. As a general rule the lighter the line weight the more delicate the presentation but the less powerful the rod. A heavier-lined rod allows longer casts with heavier, more bulky flies and has more backbone or power needed for larger fish. The same rod will not allow you to present a small, delicate fly over selective fish and drive a 1/0 minnow imitation into the wind without sacrificing something rather significant on both ends.

REELS

We believe *fishermen break off fish*, not that fish break off fishermen. Once a fish is hooked it usually should be landed unless *you* make a mistake. One of the biggest reasons fish are lost is because of ineffective reels. When fish take line from a reel the reel suddenly becomes your most important piece of tackle. Imagine, if you will, a three-pound fish hooked on two-pound test leader screaming out a hundred feet of line. If your reel has the least hesitation or a rough spot chances are very good that your leader and fly will go in different directions.

Weight is also an important factor. An extra ounce or two can really drag you down during a long fishing day.

It makes little sense to purchase a lightweight graphite rod and put a cheap, ineffective, heavy reel on it. You certainly aren't doing yourself any favors. Buy the best reel you can. A good reel will pay for itself many times over. With proper care a quality reel should last a lifetime.

LINES

During the course of a single day fish may be feeding at different levels ranging anywhere from the surface to depths of 25 feet or more. You could be in the best place at the best time with the perfect fly but if fish do not *see* your offering there is no chance of a hook up. It is the fly line which ultimately allows you to *show* your fly to fish.

Anglers are advised to take advantage of current fly line technology. Manufacturers offer over 275 possible line combinations! Eventually (the sooner the better) you will want about six line types of a particular weight. Fly lines just like flies must be matched to fishing conditions.

For example fish may be feeding on migrating dragonfly nymphs in eight feet of water. If like many unsuccessful fishermen you were to use a floating line, long leader and weighted fly the fly would *eventually* reach the bottom, but as you retrieve the fly will come *up* and *off* the bottom leaving the feeding zone. A medium or fast sinking line or 20-foot sink tip will carry your fly to the bottom quickly and, as you retrieve, the fly will stay along the bottom *in* the prime feeding zone for the entire retrieve. There is no question as to which technique will produce the most fish. (See page 137.)

Suppose fish are feeding a foot below the surface on migrating damselfly nymphs and there is a fair breeze blowing. A floating line will be caught and blown by the breeze creating a belly and unwanted and unnatural pull or additional speed on your fly. If an intermediate line were employed it would sink slightly subsurface thereby eliminating any wind problems and allowing a controlled retrieve without any belly in the line to thwart strikes.

Lake anglers are confronted with nearly every conceivable fishing situation. Anglers should match their tackle to current situations. Jack Moore in Alaska. R.K.

Select a color of line *you* can see best. Any color of line is visible to fish. A fly line is generally viewed by fish from below and therefore backlighted by a lighter sky making all colors appear as a dark silhouette. Being able to see your fly is a great advantage and we fish the brightest lines we can find. Pick a color you feel comfortable with but one that affords good visibility.

Your fly line is more than just something you tie a fly and leader to. Since the flies are nearly weightless the fly line must provide the casting weight. Your rod's performance will be greatly hindered if the wrong size of fly line is used. Line weights are determined by the manufacturer by weighing the first 30 feet of the line in grains. A single number from 1 to 15 is assigned to each range of grain weights to simplify line designation. The most commonly used weights are from 4 to 12. The smaller the number the lighter the line.

There are two basic fly line designs: weight forward (WF) and double taper (DT). Weight forward lines, sometimes called torpedo or rocket tapers, make longer casts much easier than a double taper because they carry most of their weight in the forward section of the line. The weight forward line quickly tapers down to a fine running line which shoots through the guides with less resistance for added distance. Double taper lines have a level center section which tapers down to a fine point at each end. Because of their design double taper lines are the easiest to roll cast. A weight forward line requires less reel space which means you will have more space for backing — or you can use a smaller, lighter reel.

Backing, made of long-lasting braided dacron, goes onto the fly reel spool before the fly line. The fly line is attached to the backing and the latter acts as a reserve store of line. Generally, 75 yards is adequate for most lake fishing.

LEADERS

The leader is the most important part of your terminal tackle. The leader will determine how the fly will land, how it will react on, or in, the water, and, finally, whether you will be able to land your fish.

All leader knots and terminal tackle connections must be smooth. A rough, weakened area or a wind knot in your leader will reduce its breaking strength causing it to break very easily.

A leader should be thought of as an extension of the fly line. Many anglers fear they cannot handle or cast a long leader so they don't use one. This feeling is without merit. Any problem associated with a long leader is eliminated when the leader is properly tapered and balanced with the fly. If you can cast the fly line you can cast the long leader.

The butt section of the leader which is attached to the fly line should be slightly smaller in diameter than the fly line itself. This is necessary to continue the taper and the transition from fly line to leader tippet. Each succeeding section of the leader should be smaller in diameter and slightly shorter in length than the preceding section until the desired length and tippet size are reached. The tippet is the last section of the leader the one to which the fly is attached. Generally you will want this final section to be 18 to 30 inches in length. If the leader is not properly tapered your fly will not "turn over" and the fly and leader will land in a tangled mess on the water.

Matching the leader tippet to the fly also is very important. The size, weight and wind resistance of the fly all must be considered. The tippet must be heavy enough to carry the weight of the fly but light enough to allow the fly freedom of movement on the water. You cannot, for example, cast a large, heavy fly with a 7X tippet because the weight of the fly will collapse the leader and the tippet. Similarly, you would not want to present a size 20 spinner imitation with a 3X leader because such a heavy tippet would not allow any freedom of movement to such a small fly and would certainly be visible to fish under conditions which would allow such fishing.

The angler should select a fly line-leader combination which keeps the fly in the optimum feeding zone as long as possible

Incorrect: Fly is being pulled away from trout

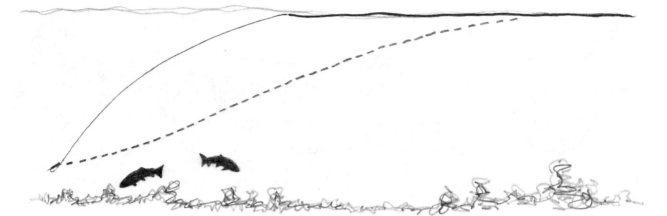

Correct: Fly stays in prime feeding zone for longest possible time

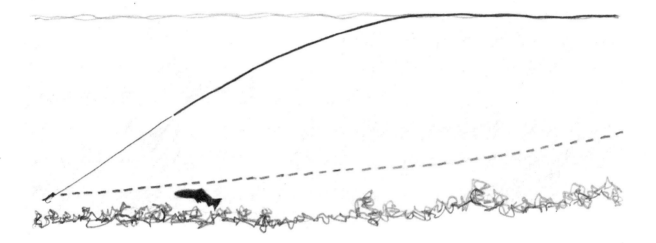

If your leader is properly balanced to your fly and fly line the tippet section will carry the fly out the entire length of the leader, depositing it delicately and accurately on the water. Once on or in the water the fly should drift, float, sink or swim in a natural, lifelike manner essentially unimpeded by the leader.

A good rule is to use the smallest possible diameter and the longest leader in relation to the fishing conditions and the size of fly you are using. Besides fly size other variables to consider when choosing a leader are water depth and clarity, light, wind, and of course, the size of trout expected. Periods of dim sunlight, wind rippling the water and off-colored water all allow the use of a leader that is slightly shorter and of slightly larger diameter than you would use normally.

Small, shallow lakes and ponds often pose the greatest leader demands. Such waters frequently are crystal clear and if the day is windless and bright you could be faced with some of the toughest fishing conditions conceivable. Such a situation may demand a 20-foot leader tapered to 7X or even 8X to prevent spooking the fish.

Another very important consideration during highly refined dry fly fishing conditions is to be absolutely certain your leader is not lying on the surface. A sunken leader is necessary to prevent shadow or any skipping action which might disturb the surface of the water, possibly spooking any trout in the area. We prefer to hold our leaders under the water a few moments or wipe some lakeside mud on them. Leader sink compounds contain agents such as lead and do not help the fishing or the environment.

When leaders become twisted or coiled run them through a leader conditioner. This will straighten them out quickly making them pliable and easier to cast but be careful, for such treatment also can weaken the leader. Use a simple, steady pull.

There are several brand-name leaders available on the market both knotted and unknotted. Commercial leaders easily satisfy the casual fisherman but the serious angler will find it difficult to obtain the exact length and tippet size demanded by various conditions. For this reason you should consider tying (knotting) your own leaders, a task which requires only a few minutes and which will save a substantial amount of money.

Keep in mind that diameter is the standard by which leader tippets are characterized. The strain under which various tippet sizes will break varies from one manufacturer to the next; check the leader packet carefully. Both diameter and breaking strength should be listed. The "X" designation reveals the diameter. Subtract the "X" number from the number 11. For example, 3X subtracted from 11 is 8; hence the diameter is .008, or eight thousandths. Do not use standard spinning line for leaders. It is not refined and consistent enough.

Alpine anglers must anticipate their every need, or go without. Wyoming Rockies. R.K.

VESTS

A fishing vest is your "tool box." Inside should be everything you will need while on the water. There are several considerations to keep in mind when shopping for a vest. Look for a well-constructed vest with lots of pockets. Look for large inside pockets and a good-sized outer back pocket that closes tightly. Some models have velcro pockets (which offer one-hand access), while others have snaps or zippers. If you intend to do any deep wading pick a shorty vest. The regular-length vest will get soaked under such conditions.

The color of a vest should blend with the surroundings. Good choices include olive or tan. A bright or light-colored vest reflects sunlight making you highly visible to fish.

When considering size remember you often will be wearing a heavy coat underneath so allow for the extra bulk.

When selecting and organizing a vest keep in mind that much of the best lake angling occurs from dusk to dark. All tackle and accessories should be arranged so that you are able to easily locate any item in the dark. For this reason a leader tippet dispenser, organized fly boxes, accessories attached to "retrieve-it" chains and a flex light are essential. We like to attach all hanging tools to the inside of the vest thereby eliminating unnecessary tangling with your fly line.

WADERS

Today, you have a choice between bootfoot or stockingfoot style waders. We recommend the more comfortable stockingfoot waders which are available in several fabrics. Our current favorite is made of neoprene with built-in velcro suspenders. These are like a mini-survival suit, are perfect for all seasons and a must for float tubers. Wading shoes must be worn over the outside of stockingfoot waders. The most comfortable and best-fitting wading shoes possible should be purchased. You may want to add a pair of gravel guards to this system to keep out sand and rocks. An inexpensive patching kit or neoprene sealer also is a necessity.

FLY BOXES

Fly boxes are available in many sizes and designs. Dry flies should be stored loosely and never put in clip or spring-type boxes. Clip or spring-style boxes smash hackles and the springs also can dull hook points. When stored loose several hundred flies can be kept in a small box. When buying boxes keep in mind the size of your vest pockets since many vests will not hold some of the larger fly boxes now available.

Fly boxes may be made of many materials. Aluminum boxes are available in a wide range of sizes; some models have flip-up, transparent spring-loaded lids over individual compartments. They are extremely durable. Some anglers prefer colored plastic boxes with styrofoam liners. The soft plastic compartmented boxes are durable and crush-proof and available in several sizes and designs. These are our personal favorites.

Do not put your flies away wet — they will become matted and rusty. Dry them out thoroughly by allowing them to dry on the sheepskin patch on your vest.

FLY FLOATANT

Fly floatant is available in several forms and marketed under several brand names. We prefer paste floatant which becomes liquid when rubbed between your fingers. Paste that turns liquid does not stick hackles together, it is easy to use and keeps the fly floating longer. A drying agent (available currently as Dry-Ur-Fly) cleans and dries your flies almost instantly, allowing you to retreat them with floatant.

ACCESSORIES

Fly floatant, leader conditioner, hook hones and angler's clips are extremely easy to lose. A retractable chain is ideal for holding these often-used items on your vest where they will be available immediately without fumbling through pockets.

While some anglers like forceps for a wide variety of chores we prefer a pair of smooth, flat-nosed pliers. These come in handy for repairs, debarbing hooks and removal of flies from deeply-hooked trout.

A flex light, lens light, or waterproof flashlight will prove invaluable for tying on flies during late evening and in finding your way back in darkness.

A waterproof match case takes up little space and can prove extremely valuable in wild or isolated areas.

A nail knot tool will help you tie nail knots quickly and easily.

A mosquito net may attract some smiles but the comfort it will provide in the midst of a swarm of hungry mosquitos is unbelievable. These nets take up very little space yet they can certainly save the day. Be sure to include insect repellant as well.

Pick up a small diary and begin keeping pertinent fishing records. You will be surprised at all you can forget from one season to the next — information which can spell the difference between future success or failure.

BUYING CAREFULLY

Tackle, especially rods, reels, lines and waders can be confusing to buy. It is easy to purchase the wrong tackle for your intended purpose or to spend "top dollar" and still not get the best. Buy from a reputable dealer, preferably one who has a broad knowledge of fish and conditions you intend to encounter.

A knowledgeable, well equipped angler has the best chance of releasing oversize trout. R.K.

TACKLE AND EQUIPMENT LIST

Rod	Tippet Material, OX-7X	Pocket Nymph Net
Reel	Tippet Dispenser	Mosquito Net
Lines	Nail Knot Tier	Waterproof Matches
Waders	Pliers or Forceps	Hook Hone
Wader Suspenders	Light	Clippers
Wading Belt	Split Shot	Diary - Pen
Wading Shoes	Leader Wallet	Goretex Jacket
Socks	Pocket Nymph Net	Hat
Gravel Guard	Dip Net	Pocket Knife
Repair Kit	Float Tube	Toilet Paper in
Vest	Fins	Plastic Bag
Flies	Hard-Sole Booties	Fingerless Mitts
Fly Floatant	Tube Suspenders	Sunglasses
Drying Agent	Fly Line Dressing	Sunglasses Strap
Leaders	Thermometer	Binoculars
Leader Conditioner	Mosquito Repellant	Water Bottle
		Flask

HOW TO BECOME A GOOD FLY FISHERMAN

We are often asked, "How can I become a good fly fisherman and how long will it take?" Fly fishing rewards participants with great amounts of pleasure regardless of their level of expertise. The hooking of fish is not necessary for enjoyment, but you could, on a scale of 0-10, reach 6-8 in two or three seasons. To achieve such levels of sophistication you would have to seriously delve into the sport. We suggest that all aspiring fly fishermen read, question others and fish.

READ EVERYTHING

There have been over 1,500 books published on the sport! A dozen anglers could fish for 50 years, pool all their knowledge and still not necessarily know what is common knowledge to the dedicated, ardent readers. Subscribe to fly fishing magazines. It is these magazines which keep you informed about new innovations.

QUESTION EVERYONE

Fly fishermen are usually happy to share some of their knowledge and it is a rare angler who will not talk fishing along the water, in the camp or campground. Get into the habit of casually observing fishermen. If you have a fishing partner the two of you will glean many insights into the sport by comparing notes and ideas. If you have a fly fishing establishment nearby get into the habit of "hanging around." Bits of knowledge are constantly drifting across the counter. Consider joining a local club.

FISH, FISH, FISH

Once you have an idea of the fundamentals there is no substitute for spending time on the water but such time should be spent constructively. You can read all the books, see all the films and listen to all the stories but there is no substitute for having a well-rounded professional *show* you first hand. Attend a fishing school which offers lectures, casting and actual fishing. Such a school will save beginners as much as ten years of struggling and experienced anglers will become aware of their habitual mistakes and pick up many new pieces of the puzzle.

NO KILL AND YOU

An angler was walking back to his car after spending a very productive day fishing a famous lake. The lake is not very large as lakes go and while it is reasonably isolated a great many anglers take advantage of the fine fishing it offers. Its waters are not stocked and its wild fish are protected with a no-kill, barbless hook regulation.

As the angler walked through the check gate he asked why he could not keep just *one* fish to eat. The gate attendant related some facts most anglers fail to consider. The lake supports about 4,000 fish which seems to be a healthy number as the fish are in excellent condition and food sources do not seem to be declining. This season over 2,000 angler days will be tallied. If each angler kept just one fish what would the fishing be like next year or the year after?

Lack of fishing pressure in conjunction with suitable habitat is what allows any water to provide outstanding angling. In waters where a "kill" is allowed, wild fish cannot populate to their maximum density and size. You cannot eat them today and expect to catch them tomorrow — certainly not the larger, more exciting and challenging fish.

There are many waters throughout the country which could provide unbelievable angling if they had less *harvest management* and more *protection*. Nearly every water in the country is open to the catch and kill, factory fish philosophy. Perhaps a few more waters which are able to sustain populations of fish without the hatchery truck should be protected. Many such waters come to mind where, instead of catching hatchery fish, we could be releasing three- to six-pound trout on a consistent basis. Why plant expensive and inferior hatchery trout when nature will provide them at no cost?

Wild trout provide such immeasurable pleasure, thrills and enjoyment that it is impossible to equate them with dollars or to be so selfish as to justify eating one. It simply does not make sense to kill wild trout, or *any* big fish.

There are no disadvantages to protecting self-sustaining fisheries. Catch and release fisheries ultimately provide what all anglers dream about — large numbers of healthy trout of all age groups. Such waters provide the utmost enjoyment for the maximum number of anglers.

With the expertise of today's huge population of fishermen and diminishing habitat for fish the future is bleak for wild fish and quality angling unless there is a turnaround in state management policy toward those waters capable of natural reproduction. If you enjoy fishing over maximum numbers of big trout without spending $4,000 and traveling 3,000 to 7,000 miles, there is only one solution: *no kill and you.*

State fish and game departments need to hear your views on a consistent basis. Write, call and drop into their offices from time to time and support organizations which actively support such views. We support the following organizations and urge you to do the same. While some of these organizations are not directly related to fisheries, they are greatly concerned with protecting the environment, or habitat — and without habitat there are no fish.

Trout Unlimited, Box 1944, Washington, D.C. 20013. 202-281-1100.
Federation of Fly Fishermen, Box 1088, West Yellowstone, MT 59758. 406-646-9541.
Cal-Trout, Box 2046, San Francisco, CA 94126. 415-392-8887.
Oregon Trout, Box 19540, Portland, OR 97219. 503-246-5890.
Sierra Club, 530 Bush St., San Francisco, CA 94108. 415-981-8634.
National Wildlife Federation, 8925 Leesburg Pike, Vienna, VA 22180. 703-790-4000.
Nature Conservancy, 1800 North Kent St., Arlington, VA 22209. 703-841-5300.

HOW TO LAND AND RELEASE FISH

Try to land fish in a reasonable amount of time. The longer some fish are played the more lactic acid builds up in the bloodstream and the more difficult it becomes to revive such fish. Most fatal damage occurs to fish through improper handling, not during the actual hooking and playing of fish.

It is best not to handle or remove fish from the water. When a fish is removed from the water it begins to suffocate immediately and the risk is great that the fish will flop about on the bank, slip from your grasp or that you may squeeze it to death. If you must handle fish be certain your hands are wet for wet hands will not destroy the protective mucous film on fish (especially trout).

To remove the hook gently grip the fish by the tail or jaw with one hand, removing the hook with the other. If you are wading both hands can be freed by slipping the rod into your waders. If a fish is hooked really deeply the hook can often be removed with the aid of a long-nose pliers or forceps. If the hook is barbless (it should be), push back and turn it sideways. If the hook cannot be removed cut the leader leaving the fly in the fish. Nature supplies a built-in mechanism which will dissolve the hook in a matter of days. Often a friend can lend a hand in unhooking and reviving tired fish.

A barbless hook will help insure safe handling and facilitate a quick release. You seldom have to touch the fish because barbless hooks can usually be backed out very quickly using only one hand.

We have mixed emotions about using a net. When fish become entangled in the mesh and struggle there is a negative impact upon them. A net can

Twilight, when visions of slurping trout occupy the minds of all anglers. R.C.

alleviate fish flopping and thrashing over rocks in shallow water and can greatly aid you in landing a fish when you are waist deep in water or fishing from a float tube. Don't allow fish to become entangled in the mesh.

Do not release a tired fish until it has completely recovered. Hold a played fish firmly by the tail with one hand and gently support the fish from underneath just behind the head with your other hand. Face the fish upstream (when current is available) in an upright position in fairly calm water where there is enough oxygen to allow the fish to breathe easily. Move the fish back and forth in this position. The gills will begin pumping life-giving oxygen into its system, thus the fish is allowed to rest and regain strength lost during the battle. In lakes it will be mandatory to move fish back and forth to ensure the flow of oxygen-rich water through their gills.

Fish being revived will often attempt to escape before they are completely recovered. Do not let the fish swim away the *first* time it attempts to. When fish are released prematurely they will often swim out of sight, lose their equilibrium, turn onto their side and die. It doesn't hurt to revive fish a bit longer than you feel is necessary. This will insure a complete recovery without complications. This process usually takes a minute or two but fish that are extremely tired can require several minutes. We have revived bleeding and exceptionally tired fish for 30 minutes or longer. Fish tire easily preceding, during and after spawning periods and should be left alone.

When you release a fish do so in calm water allowing the fish to swim away at its leisure. Never toss fish back into the water! After releasing a fish, move slowly, for sudden movement may spook the fish prematurely.

If you wish to take a photo set up everything before you remove the fish from the water. Cradle the fish and lift it just inches above the water so that if it should happen to fall it will not crash onto the hard shoreline. Do not lay fish on their sides. Do not put undo strain on fish by lifting them by the tail or in an unnatural position. Never put your fingers in their gills for this is like puncturing a lung. Never squeeze fish; vital organs are easily damaged. Fish will seldom struggle when handled gently or turned upside down.

A quick, harmless way to measure fish is to tape off measurements on your rod or buy a tape which adheres to your rod. Simply slide the rod alongside the fish in the water and you get an accurate measurement. Spring scales are deadly for fish and should only be used for hoisting a net with the fish inside. It is easy to estimate the weight by the length and condition of the fish. The important consideration is to release fish quickly and unharmed. A fish which is bleeding slightly will probably survive. Even a fish that is bleeding profusely can usually be revived if *you* are patient enough.

BARBLESS HOOKS

There are only positive reasons for fishing a barbless hook. There are no disadvantages. More fish (especially big fish) are hooked on barbless hooks because they have tough, bony mouths and barbed hooks have difficulty penetrating or sinking in. A barb forms a resistant wedge.

How many good fish have you missed on the strike? How many of those would you have hooked if the hook point was sharp and the barb smashed flat? Remember the last time you had a good fish on and the line suddenly went slack? Chances are the hook never penetrated and just fell out of the fish's mouth. The fish was never hooked — you were!

We have tested barbless hooks on all varieties and sizes of fish. We hook twice the number of fish on barbless hooks. Pull a barbed and barbless hook into a piece of cardboard. You'll see and feel the difference.

When a hook sinks to the bend of the hook (instead of only part way) you have the fish until you back out the hook exactly the way it went in or until it breaks through the skin.

Barbs are easily smashed with smooth nose pliers

Do you remember the last time you hooked your clothing or yourself? Smash the barbs and avoid the pain and frustration of being hooked.

The best way to debarb a hook is to smash it flat using a flat-nose pliers. Be careful not to damage the hook point.

In Alaska we tested the fishing speed of barbed vs. barbless hooks. The angler fishing barbless hooks was able to release nearly twice as many fish as the angler fishing a barbed hook. The time consumed in handling fish, working out barbed hooks with pliers or forceps, plus the time required to properly revive fish handled in such a manner, drastically reduced actual fishing time and catch rate.

We are confident you will find barbless hooks a pleasure to fish.

Epilogue

Nearly thirty years have flashed by since my father rigged me up for my first fishing trip. We went to one of the many irrigation reservoirs near our Colorado home. Our tackle consisted of split bamboo rods, uncontrollable automatic reels and inferior salt and pepper level C fly lines. We fished for bullheads, crappie, perch . . . just about anything, and were occasionally surprised with the flashing brilliance of a rainbow which probably found its way into these waters during high spring flows.

Today, anglers choose from a multitude of refined rods and reels designed especially for almost every fishing situation. We choose from a selection of trouble free fly lines which allow us to quickly and effectively present our imitations at any depth. Float tubes allow stealthy access to fish which as a kid were only splashy dreams far beyond reach. Flies have undergone a complete metamorphosis and many foods of trout are realistically represented. Techniques which used to be little more than chuck and chance are now balancing on the scientific scale. The sport of fly fishing has probably advanced more in the past 15 years than it had in the previous 200.

As with any field of endeavor there are always those few who devote their fullest talent and attention and progress quickly and far beyond the comprehension of the casual devotee. Randall Kaufmann and Ron Cordes are two such anglers and in *Lake Fishing With a Fly* they have shared their slow-earned knowledge with everyone. Had *Lake Fishing With a Fly* been in print at any point in time during my long lake fishing career it would have, almost instantly, propelled me beyond my current level of expertise. This book has not answered all my questions or solved all my problems, but I would not want it to. Glancing into the past the fish I remember best are those I was unable to deceive. In that respect little has changed today, for I seldom forget the uncatchables . . . they teach me the most.

There are several lifetimes of lake fishing information assembled within these pages and while these will not be the last words on the subject, *Lake Fishing With a Fly* will be the foundation upon which all other lake fishing literature will be built.

Jack Moore
June 1, 1984
Tigard, Oregon

Bibliography

Aass, P. Crustacea, especially Lepidurus arcticus pallas, as brown trout food in Norwegian mountain reservoirs. Ins. Freshwater Res. Drottningholm.

Ahren, T. and Grimas, U. The composition of the bottom fauna in two basins of Lake Malaren. Inst. Freshwater Res. Drottningholm.

Allen, G. H., and Claussen, L. G. Selectivity of food by brook trout in a Wyoming Beaver Pond.

Andrusak, H., and Northcote, T. G. 1971. Segregation between adult cutthroat trout (Salmo clarkii) and dolly varden (Salvelinus malma) in small coastal British Columbia lakes. J. Fish. Res. Bd. Can. 28(9)

Arbona, Fred L. Jr. 1980. Mayflies the Angler and the Trout. Tulsa: Winchester Press.

Bates, J. D. 1966. Streamer Fly Tying and Fishing. Harrisburg: The Stackpole Company.

Bay, E. C. 1974. Predator-prey relationships among aquatic insects. Ann. Rev. of Ent. 19.

Benson, N. G. Limnology of Yellowstone Lake in relation to the cut-throat trout. U. S. Dept. Int., F. & W. Serv. Res. Rpt. No. 56.

Bergman, R. 1973. Trout. New York: Alfred A. Knopf.

Brooks, C. E. 1976. Nymph Fishing for Larger Trout. New York: Crown Publishers, Inc.

Brooks, C. E. 1974. The Trout and the Stream. New York: Crown Publishers, Inc.

Bryan, J. E., and Larkin, P. A. 1972. Food specialization by individual trout. J. Fish. Res. Bd. Can. 29(11).

Calhoun, A. J. The bottom fauna of Blue Lake, California. Calif. F & G.

Chu, H. F. 1949. The Immature Insects. Dubuque: Wm. C. Brown Company Publishers.

Clarke, B. 1975. The Pursuit of Stillwater Trout. London: Adams & Charles Black.

Crossman, E. J. 1959. A predator-prey interaction in freshwater fish. J. Fish. Res. Bd. Can. 16(3).

Crossman, E. J. 1959. Distribution and movements of a predator, the rainbow trout, and its prey, the redside shiner, in Paul Lake, British Columbia. J. Fish. Res. Bd. Can. 16(3).

Doudoroff, P. Food of trout from lakes in the Klamath River water-shed. Trans. Amer. Fish Soc.

Efford, I. E., and Tsumura, K. 1973. A comparison of the food of salamanders and fish in Marion Lake, British Columbia. Trans. Amer. Fish. Soc. No. 1.

Eggleton, F. E. 1939. Problems of lake biology: role of the bottom fauna in the productivity of lakes. Amer. Assoc. Advmt. Sci. No. 10. F. R. Moulton, Ed.

Frost, W. E., and Macan, T. T. 1948. Corixidae (Hemiptera) as food of fish. J. of Animal Ecol. 19:174.

Ginetz, R. M., and Larkin, P. A. 1973. Choice of colors of food items by rainbow trout (Salmo gairdneri). J. Fish. Res. Bd. Can. 30(2).

Goddard, J. 1977. The Super Flies of Still Water. London: Ernest Benn.

Goddard, J. 1969. Trout Flies of Stillwater. London: Adam & Charles Black.

Goddard, J., and Clarke, B. 1980. The Trout and the Fly. London: Ernest Benn.

Hafele, R., and Hughes, D. 1981. The Complete Book of Western Hatches. Portland: Frank Amato Publications.

Harris, J. R. 1970. An Angler's Entomology. London: Collins.

Irving, R. B. 1956. Ecology of the cutthroat trout in Henry's Lake, Idaho. Amer. Fish. Soc. Trans. 84.

Johnson, L. 1975. Distribution of fish species in Great Bear Lake, Northwest Territories, with reference to zooplankton, benthic invertebrates, and environmental conditions. J. Fish Res. Bd. Can. 32(11).

Kaufmann, R. 1975. American Nymph Fly Tying Manual. Portland: Frank Amato Publications.

Krecker, F. H. A comparative study of the animal population of certain submerged aquatic plants. Ecology 20(4).

LaFontaine, G. 1981. Caddisflies. New York: Nick Lyons Books.

LaFontaine, G. 1976. Challenge of the Trout. Missoula: Mountain Press Publishing Company.

Lantz, R. L. Influence of water temperature on fish survival, growth, and behavior.

Larkin, P. A., and Smith, S. B. 1953. Some effects of introduction of the redside shiner on the kamloops trout in Paul Lake, British Columbia. Trans. Amer. Fish. Soc. 83.

Larkin, P. A., Terpenning, J. G., and Parker, R. R. 1956. Size as a determinant of growth rate in rainbow trout Salmo gairdneri. Trans. Amer. Fish. Soc. 86.

Leonard, J. W. 1947. Differences in the occurrence of nymphs of two species of burrowing mayflies in fish stomachs. Annals Entom. Soc. Amer. XL.

Leonard, J. W., and Leonard, F. A. An analysis of the feeding habits of rainbow trout and lake trout in Birch Lake, Cass County, Michigan. Trans. Amer. Fish. Soc.

Linn, J. D., and Frantz, T. C. 1965. Introduction of the opossum shrimp (Mysis relicta loven) into California and Nevada. Calif. F. & G. 51(1).

Macan, T. T. 1962. Ecology of aquatic insects. Ann. Rev. Entom. 7.

Marinaro, V. C. 1976. In the Ring of the Rise. New York: Crown Publishers.

McCormack, J. C. 1962. The food of young trout (Salmo trutta) in two different becks. J. Anim. Ecol. 31(2).

McGaha, Y. J. 1952. The limnological relations of insects to certain aquatic flowering plants. Trans. Amer. Microscopical Soc. 71(4).

Moodie, G. E. E. 1972. Predation, natural selection and adaptation in an unusual threespine stickleback. Heredity 28 (part 2).

Moon, H. P. 1940. An investigation of the movements of freshwater invertebrate faunas. J. Anim. Ecol. 9(1).

Morgan, N. C. 1958. Insect emergence from a small Scottish loch. Inter. Assoc. Theoretical and Appl. Limn. XIII: 823-825.

Morgan, N. C. 1956. The biology of Leptocerus aterrimus steph. with reference to its availability as a food for trout. J. Anim. Ecol. 25:349.

Morgan, N. C., and Waddell, A. B. 1961. Diurnal variation in the emergence of some aquatic insects. Royal Entom. Soc. Lon., Trans. 113.

Needham, P. R. 1969. Trout Streams. San Francisco: Holden-Day.

Nielsen, L. A., and Reynolds, J. B. 1975. Freshwater shrimp. Farm Pond Harvest (spring).

Nilsson, N. Seasonal fluctuations in the food segregation of trout, char, and whitefish in 14 north Swedish lakes. Inst. Freshwater Res. Drottningholm.

Norlin, A. The occurrence of terrestrial insects on the surface of two lakes in northern Sweden (Ankarvattnet and Blasjon). Inst. Fresh-water Res. Drottningholm 45:196.

Norlin, A. Terrestrial insects in lake surfaces. Their availability and importance as fish food. Inst. Freshwater Res. Drottningholm.

Northcote, T. G., and Lorz, H. W. 1966. Seasonal and diet changes in food of adult kokanee (Oncorhynchus nerka) in Nicola Lake, British Columbia. J. Fish. Res. Bd. Can. 23(8).

Oliver, D. R. 1960. The macroscopic bottom fauna of Lac La Ronge, Saskatchewan. J. Fish. Res. Bd. Can. 17(5).

Oliver, D. R. 1971. Life-history of the chironomidae. Ann. Rev. Entom. 16.

Palmisano, J. J., and Helm, W. T. 1971. Freshwater food habits of Salvelinus malma (Walbaum) on Amchitka Island, Alaska. Bio-science 21(12).

Pearsall, W. H. 1920. The aquatic vegetation of the English lakes. J. of Ecol. 8(3).

Pentland, E. S. 1930. Controlling factors in the distribution of Gammarus. Trans. Amer. Fish. Soc. 60:89.

Pieczynska, E. Ecological interactions between land and the littoral zones of lakes (Masurian Lakeland, Poland). Coupling of Land and Water Systems, A. D. Hasler, Ed.

Platts, W. S. 1959. Food habits of the cutthroat trout in Strawberry Reservoir. Utah Acad. Proc. 366.

Rabe, F. W. 1967. Age and growth of rainbow trout in four alpine lakes. Northwest Sci. 41(1).

Schwiebert, E. 1973. Nymphs. New York: Winchester Press.

Schwiebert, E. 1978. Trout. New York: Dutton.

Sparrow, R. A. 1966. Comparative limnology of lakes in the southern Rocky Mountain Trench, British Columbia. J. Fish. Res. Bd. Can. 23(12).

Speirs, G. D. 1974. Food habits of landlocked salmon and brook trout in a Maine lake after introduction of landlocked alewives. Trans. Amer. Fish. Soc., No. 2.

Swift, M. C. 1970. A qualitative and quantitative study of trout food in Castle Lake, California. Calif. F. & G. 56(2).

Swisher, D., and Richards, C. 1971. Selective Trout. New York: Crown Publishers.

Usinger, R. L. 1974. Aquatic Insects of California. Berkeley: Univ. of California Press.

van Someren, V. D. 1940. The factors conditioning the rising of trout (Salmo trutta) in a small freshwater lake. J. Anim. Ecol. 9:89.

Veniard, J. 1970. Reservoir and Lake Flies. London: Adams & Charles Black.

Ware, D. M. 1971. Predation by rainbow trout (Salmo gairdneri): the effect of experience. J. Fish. Res. Bd. Can. 28(12).

Waterman, C. F. 1972. Modern Fresh and Salt Water Fly Fishing. New York: Winchester Press.

Webb, D. W. 1965. Limnological features of Cedar Lake, Manitoba. J. Fish. Res. Bd. Can. 22(5).

Wilson, L. D. 1978. Tying and Fishing the Terrestrials. New York: A. S. Barnes and Company.

Winterbourn, M. J. 1971. The life histories and trophic relationships of the trichoptera of Marion Lake, British Columbia. Can. J. Zool. 49.

Wissing, T. E., and Hasler, A. D. 1968. Calorific values of some invertebrates in Lake Mendota, Wisconsin. J. Fish. Res. Bd. Can. 25(11).

Index